Organizational Behaviour and Change in Europe

Case Studies

EUROPEAN MANAGEMENT SERIES

The European Management Series derives from a unique collaboration, the Community of European Management Schools (CEMS), which was formed in 1988 and integrates both academic and corporate members. Together they develop and disseminate a shared body of European knowledge in the field of management and award the CEMS Master's degree.

With particular emphasis upon meeting the needs of management students for high-quality European-based material, the series aims to bring to international management education a strongly European perspective. Prepared by CEMS faculty, it includes textbooks, case studies and other volumes that examine key European and international management issues.

Organizational Behaviour and Change in Europe

Case Studies

edited by
Françoise Chevalier and Michaël Segalla

SAGE Publications
London · Thousand Oaks · New Delhi

First published 1996

SAGE Publications Ltd
6 Bonhill Street
London EC2A 4PU

SAGE Publications Inc
2455 Teller Road
Thousand Oaks, California 91320

SAGE Publications India Pvt Ltd
32, M-Block Market
Greater Kailash -I
New Delhi 110 048

British Library Cataloguing in Publication data

A catalogue record for this book is available from the British Library

ISBN 0 8039 7909 6
ISBN 0 8039 7910 X (pbk)

Library of Congress catalog record available

Typeset by Photoprint, Torquay, Devon
Printed at the University Press, Cambridge

Contents

Preface

This book has been a truly collective effort by all the case authors. Over the past three years we have met on numerous occasions to forge a working relationship and collaborative framework. We have read, critiqued and used each other's cases in our own courses, and have all learnt a lot from this. The process of writing the cases has been a long, happy, troublesome, painful and rich one. We strived for complex rather than simple, open-ended rather than finished, and multi-cultural rather than multi-national cases.

Our basic structural framework is the Community of European Management Schools (CEMS) which provided us with the opportunity to work together to create the book. We want to thank our other colleagues in the Inter-Faculty Group: Finn Borum (Denmark), Peter Dachler (Switzerland), Lorenz Fischer (Germany), Marja Floris (Netherlands), Anna Grandori (Italy), Steven Hill (UK), Ces Lescure (Netherlands), Raul Nacamulli (Italy) and Ricard Serlavos (Spain) for their discussions and comments. Also colleagues at our institutions have offered helpful comments and students have made useful suggestions when we have taught the cases. The authors also want to thank Françoise Chevalier and Michaël Segalla for accepting the responsibility of co-ordinating the project so that our cases would be as uniform as possible in style, language and content. It goes without saying that we all share the responsibility for the book.

The case authors are willing to provide editorial commentaries on request. You can contact the authors through the editors, at Ecoles des Hautes Etudes Commerciales (HEC), 1 rue de la Libération, 78351 Jouy-en-Josas, Cedex, France.

Notes on the Contributors

Françoise Chevalier is Associate Professor of Management at Groupe HEC (Ecole des Hautes Etudes Commerciales) in France. Her research and publications include work on new forms of organizations, quality management, and human resource management. In addition to her academic work, she acts as a consultant.

Søren Christensen is Professor of Organizational Sociology at the Copenhagen Business School. He received his training at the Copenhagen Business School and at the University of California, Irvine.

Martin Gjelsvik is Director of the Social Sciences Department at the Rogaland Research Institute in Norway, and former Lecturer at the Norwegian College of Hotel Administration and a doctoral student at the Department of Organization Sciences, Norwegian School of Economics and Business Administration. Before entering academia, he worked for a long time in different managerial positions in banking, the last five years as a Managing Director in a bank and later in an insurance company.

Evelyne Leonard is Assistant at Institut d'Administration et de Gestion (IAG), Université Catholique de Louvain (UCL), Belgium. She holds a doctorate in 'Sciences du travail' from UCL. Her research interests and publications include human resource management, from a sociological perspective, and organizational behaviour.

Hugo Letiche is Associate Professor of Qualitative Research Methodology at Rotterdam School of Management, Erasmus University, Rotterdam, Netherlands and (part-time) Professor of International Management and Research Methodology at Keele University, UK. His writing centres on postmodern managerial research issues, focusing on the epistemology of interactive research and organizational experimentation.

Jan Löwstedt is Associate Professor in Organization Theory at the Stockholm School of Economics, having obtained his PhD in business administration there. His main areas of publication are organization and technological change, managerial and organizational cognition, and work organization change.

Jan Molin is Associate Professor of Organizational Psychology at the Copenhagen Business School. He received his training at the University of Copenhagen and at the Copenhagen Business School.

Odd Nordhaug is Professor of Administrative Science, Chairman of the Department of Organization Sciences, Norwegian School of Economics and

Business Administration, and Research Director at the Norwegian Foundation for Research in Economics and Business Administration. He has authored and co-authored 17 books and published numerous articles in international research journals.

Carlos Obeso is Professor of Management in the Human Relations Department at ESADE, Barcelona, Spain. He earned an MBA at ESADE, a Licenciatura in Economics at the University of Cordoba, and an MSc in industrial relations at the London School of Economics. For 10 years he directed the Health Care Management Programme at ESADE.

Karl Sandner is Professor of Management at the Vienna University of Economics and Business Administration. His research interests include processes of power and control, order and conflicting rationalities, and changes in the normative context of management.

Michaël Segalla is Associate Professor of Management at Groupe HEC (Ecole des Hautes Etudes Commerciales) in France. He has taught in New York City, Atlanta and Montreal in the areas of management, human resource management, organizational behaviour and industrial relations. His research interests include international strike behaviour, comparative human resource management, cultural influences on managerial decision making, and the process of organizational internationalization.

Armand Spineux is Professor at Institut d'Administration et de Gestion (IAG), Université Catholique de Louvain (UCL), Belgium. He holds a doctorate in sociology from the Université Catholique de Louvain. His research and publications include work on industrial relations and human resource management, organizational culture, interactions between work and family life. Besides his academic work, he also acts as a consultant for national and international firms, in the areas of human resource management and organizational culture.

Carlo Turati is Professor of Organization Theory and Design at the Luigi Bocconi University, Milan. He received his PhD from Bocconi University. His research interests include inter-organizational alliances and international management.

Introduction

While it is clear that the European economic landscape is changing, it is not clear what exactly is happening. The easier flow of capital, goods, services and staff across borders increases competitive pressures on European firms, leading to a need for improvements in organizational efficiency and effectiveness. These competitive pressures take several distinctive forms. On the one hand, we observe firms struggling to build economies of scale in both financial markets and production facilities, mergers and acquisitions being examples of this. On the other hand, we observe corporate restructuring and re-engineering which aim to create flexible organizations and regional cultural strengths.

The varying organizational responses to these changing conditions have several implications for organizational behaviour and change, as well as for the relationship between firms and their employees. But so far they have been defined mostly in terms of universal theories and standard responses.

Theories of psychology, sociology, organization and human resource management offer a rich and multi-faceted contribution regarding the impact of national, regional and organizational differences. Styles of communication, negotiation, decision making and problem solving may be culturally embedded. As people from diverse cultural origins come into more frequent and closer contact, particularly as partners rather than merely as customers and competitors, managers and professionals must be educated to appreciate and deal with these cultural differences.

The implications of psychology, sociology, organization and human resource management theory for cultural diversity include:

- an even stronger push into the area broadly labelled multi-cultural (rather than cross-cultural) management;
- more emphasis on understanding the role of national and regional 'business recipes' and their impact on organizational structure, change, leadership and decision making;
- discussions of the social role of organizations in the preservation of a country's or region's cultural identity and integrity.

As borders become more permeable, European companies will no longer limit their recruitment activities to their country of origin. Students from European countries will now be competing directly with each other for jobs. This increases the need for educators to offer much more diversified and culturally rich course material. This is what this book aims to provide.

More specifically, the authors agree that too many cases used in teaching *organizational behaviour and change* fail to do justice to this immensely

	Basic profile	Internationalization management	Organizational control governance	Organizational culture	Organizational structure design	Industrial relations	Leadership	Power	Organizational change	Management of professionals (knowledge workers)	Human resources development/ organizational development	Strategic HRM	Organizational learning	Environmental adaptation	Decision making
Crédit Lyonnais	A large French commercial bank	●		●					●		●	●			
Glaverbel	A large Belgian glass company			●	●	●						●			
Humanitarian Foundation	A large Danish voluntary organization with international activities		●	●	●										●
Italdata Italiana	A small–medium-sized Italian company				●			●	●						
Joaquin Candel	A medium-sized Spanish hardware wholesaler				●		●							●	
Kogen Österreich	A large Austrian consumer co-operative			●				●	●					●	
Rhine and Rhone Transport	A major Dutch internationally operating transport company		●	●				●	●					●	
SR-Bank	A medium-sized Norwegian savings bank								●			●	●	●	
Rodeby School	A Swedish municipal school				●					●				●	

Figure A *Matrix showing the coverage of each case*

complicated topic. They tend to take a fairly simplistic approach to a subject that is, by its very nature, inherently complex. They also tend to assume that there is some preferred solution to the case that is appropriate for all domains, although all of us who teach international material are very much aware that such definitive solutions are not very likely.

Cases in this genre are generally short, focused on narrow issues, and intentionally universalistic. In this volume, we adopt a more realistic approach using cases that are longer and richer, and that consider more explicitly the contextual effects of different cultures. The typical case in our field also seems to assume that students are short of experience, imagination and access to multiple perspectives for analysing the case. The presumption seems to be that the case and its analytical approach must be more or less specified by the case-writer to make it 'go'. Metaphorically speaking, 'BATTERIES ARE INCLUDED': all you need to do is to install them and the case will run as intended. That approach, while convenient, is not very appropriate for the contemporary business world.

Our approach is different. We have written cases that can be taught in a variety of ways using a variety of theoretical frameworks. Here the batteries are *not* included: instructors and students need to bring their own! This volume has an underlying general theme in that it recognizes that different cultures imply different problems, different approaches and different solutions. It encourages a strong sensitivity to cultural issues as they apply to the management of organizations and organizational change. This focus allows students to develop analytical skills by using richer, more complicated cases situated in the cultural context of Europe. There are no easy solutions nor well-defined problems.

Therefore, all the cases have been written explicitly for this book and follow the same format. The cases are embedded in very different cultural settings: Austria, Belgium, Denmark, France, Italy, the Netherlands, Norway, Spain and Sweden (see Figure A). They include a public (state) school, a consumer co-operative and a private not-for-profit organization. Most of the cases, however, are drawn from private or state-owned for-profit organizations in wholesale, manufacturing, banking and transport. Each case opens with an abstract followed by a presentation of the cultural context, which summarizes the history and values of the national culture(s) in which the organization is embedded. These are followed by the main text of the case, some of the major theoretical themes or practical issues which arise, recommended assignments, and suggested reading.

This volume is the collaborative effort of the Inter-Faculty Group in Organizational Behaviour of the Community of European Management Schools (CEMS) and therefore benefits from the inter-European and international perspectives of the authors and other group members. The volume was designed to bring an explicit European multi-cultural perspective to the teaching of organizational behaviour, change and management.

Søren Christensen

1

Crédit Lyonnais

The internationalization of a French bank

Françoise Chevalier and Michaël Segalla

This study of Crédit Lyonnais, one of the world's largest banks, examines the organization and human resource management strategies thought necessary to survive the rapid market changes in European banking. Crédit Lyonnais provides a particularly good example of a large bank which is determined to succeed through growth in products and extensions into new markets. Realizing early that its product and market strategies required an equally strong and defined human resource strategy, it set out to define the changes it needed and to develop programmes and policies to achieve its goals. The Crédit Lyonnais Group grew very rapidly during the late 1980s and early 1990s, principally by the acquisition of foreign banks throughout Europe. To benefit from its acquisitions many Crédit Lyonnais managers believe they must integrate their European banking network in terms of common product offerings and client management.

This case study chronicles the successes and difficulties of Crédit Lyonnais. The case touches on a number of theoretical and practical issues regarding international human resource management and organizational change. Perhaps foremost among these is the extreme difficulty of actually internationalizing the HRM policies of a company that already thinks of itself as international simply because it has a tradition of foreign operations and more recently has doubled its size through the acquisition of foreign banks.

Cultural context

To have a good understanding of the cultural environment of this case one needs to consider the culture of France, particularly its political/economic history and the style of management and organization often associated with French companies.

Political/economic history

In France the state plays a key role in the economy and in society. The establishment of a strong central power, first royal, then republican, has been the French government's traditional response to reducing the diversity of the regional and provincial cultures and promoting economic development. The first great architect of state-centred economics was the French statesman and financier, Jean Baptiste Colbert (1619–83), who established state control of the economy, regulated commerce and industry, developed national companies and actively searched for foreign markets for French products. Although he died over 300 years ago, his beliefs of strong centralized political control and the combination of interventionist and market-based economic policies have been largely followed by the intervening governments of Louis XIV, Napoleon and the current Fifth Republic. The latter regulates economic development through fiscal and budgetary measures and economic planning, directed by the *Commissariat Général du Plan*, a government department-cum-forum which draws up blueprints and voluntary targets for growth, in different sectors, over a five-year period.

Therefore the nineteenth-century development of French banking in general, and Crédit Lyonnais in particular, was closely linked to France's economic position in international financial markets. Crédit Lyonnais continues to have strong links in the political arena; some of its past presidents have been members of parliament. As one of the last large nationalized banks, Crédit Lyonnais still enjoys strong governmental interest.

The French banking sector experienced tremendous expansion in its branch network between 1967 and 1975. But the industry also became more concentrated and many banks disappeared as a result of mergers (288 in 1945 and 80 in 1975). The period was dominated by the deposit banks Banque Nationale de Paris, Crédit Lyonnais, Société Générale and the two merchant banks Paribas and Indosuez, but the savings banks (equivalent to building societies) also expanded rapidly to compete both on interest rates and number of branches.

By the 1980s, there was a growing crisis in the financial system stemming from the rising number of clients using cheques (for which there is no charge in France) which was rapidly increasing overhead costs. This also resulted in a still growing surplus of labour (sometimes dismissed, often retained) in banks because of new technology and products. The final chapter in French banking was the privatization of Société Générale, Paribas and Indosuez. Crédit Lyonnais and BNP, the two *vieilles dames* (old ladies), were left in state hands for the time being.

Although the rapid expansion of new bank branches in the 1970s had caused many experts to believe that France was 'overbanked', foreign banks have remained interested in buying small but rich regional deposit banks. With a savings rate of 12.2% of disposable income, the French market is still attractive to medium-sized banks capable of offering sophisticated customer services.

During the 1980s the general business culture of France had to come to terms with the realization that the *Trente Glorieuses*, 30 years of constant growth since 1945, were finished. Profits and investment rapidly declined, but the government managed to maintain the workers' expected standard of living through wage indexing and increased social charges (taxes charged to employers for various types of social insurance). An ill-timed reflation of the economy by a Socialist government in 1981 brought yet more grief, and it was only in the mid-1980s that French business slowly began to recover from the changed circumstances of the previous 10 to 15 years and to adapt to the competitive challenge of a wider European market. In the 1990s there is a general awareness that some considerable catching up has been achieved and France has rapidly closed the gap on its major industrial competitors.

Certain workforce demographic trends also strongly influence the French political economy:

- The French government is the direct employer of more than 2 million people who work in the government and government-owned companies. The state's salary budget represents more than a quarter of gross national product (GNP).
- About 90,000 more people enter the labour force than leave it each year.
- Between 1982 and 1988 the rate of female participation in the labour market went from 64 to 72%.
- Owing to early retirement only 25% of men over 64 years old work. In 1982 the figure was 40%.

Most of France's important labour legislation was adopted during moments of global or local socio-political crisis, particularly in the years 1936, 1945 and 1968. The French government plays a primary role in establishing the basic relationship between employers and employees. French industrial relations is based on a tradition of conflict between autocratic managers and reactionary labour unions, both of which seem to prefer 'war' to negotiation. French labour unions are highly ideological, very fragmented, and directly represent less then 10% of the workforce. Where they can, labour unions have tried to improve on these basic conditions of work. Their power comes from the fact that the collective agreements they negotiate generally apply to all employees in the industry. Therefore labour unions maintain a level of power greater than their direct membership implies.

One of the industries where labour unions are relatively strong is the banking sector, where a collective agreement (*convention collectif*) between the principal trade unions and the French Banking Association (Association Française des Banques), which represents the directors of the major banks, governs working conditions. This agreement was made during the period of economic growth after the Second World War (1952) and its provisions for recruitment, remuneration, working hours, career advancement, training, dismissal and social benefits are relatively generous. Today, however, the banking sector is faced with new needs and the collective agreement is considered by many bank managers as an impediment to competitiveness.

Despite the constraints embedded in the French political economy, the Hudson Institute, an American think-tank, issued a report predicting that France was likely to become the Japan of Europe. Some of the country's underlying strengths are:

- a nationwide consensus on the importance of education and training;
- a concerted effort by many companies to become more internationally oriented. Overseas investment increased by a factor of five over the late 1980s as companies increased market share with foreign acquisitions;
- a new type of self-made business leader is emerging to challenge the élitist structure of French management.

Considerable concern and question marks remain, however, in a number of areas:

- Although it stabilized in 1992 at 10% of the working population, unemployment will still prove difficult to contain without sustained growth over the coming years.
- The élitist management education system has been criticized by some for not providing the right calibre of flexible, international managers, capable of responding quickly enough to shorter product life cycles.
- This same system, which rigidly links hierarchical status with graduation from the 'right' schools, suppresses the aspirations of supervisory and lower-grade personnel who find it difficult to be promoted into managerial positions.
- In spite of increased overseas investment, often managers lack the international vision and experience of their counterparts in Germany, the Netherlands, the UK and the USA.

We now turn our attention to France's management and organizational culture.

Management/organizational culture

The French approach to management is often characterized as élitist. In fact the managerial class, *cadre*, is officially recognized by tradition and law. This status gives managers special pension, social insurance and representation privileges in employee committees governing certain employee/employer matters. As in some other Latin countries and Japan, there exists an educational pyramid with the *grandes écoles* at the top. These schools select an élite corps of students through very difficult entrance examinations. The exams test for analytical and reasoning capacity rather than interpersonal skills or professional aptitude. The diploma of a *grande école* is sometimes considered an 'entrance ticket' into the fast-track of a public or privately owned company. In effect the task of the *grande école* is to select France's future business leaders.

Research by Bauer and Bertin-Mourot (1993), who examined the career histories of top managers in large French and German companies, identifies three distinct managerial career paths. These are: the 'entrepreneur' managers who are 'spotted', recruited and trained and who may have capital resources to contribute; the 'institutionalists' with valuable political or state connections; and the 'career' managers who spend their careers in the same firm. Of French top management 45% are 'institutionalists', as compared with only 8% of top German managers. Germans are generally 'career' managers (65.5%), whereas only 21.8% of French managers fit this category. Only 16% of senior French management can be described as 'self-made' men or women.

According to Bauer and Bertin-Mourot the importance of the *grande école* is evident in that among top managers, 27% graduated from the *polytechniques*, 19% are former students of the ENA (Ecole Nationale d'Administration), and 7% of HEC (*hautes études commerciales*). These three schools, which produce only about 500 graduates a year, provide over 50% of the top managers in French companies. Thus in France, an individual's self-education or entrepreneurial attitudes are less likely to contribute to success than his or her diploma and capacity to develop social/political relationships. Because they are destined to rise rapidly up the career hierarchy, *grande école* graduates often rotate very quickly through a wide variety of company positions gaining scope, sometimes at the expense of depth.

The traditional French model of organization described by Michel Crozier (1963) is a combination of bureaucratic and aristocratic behaviour. Organizations generally have many hierarchical levels which, of necessity, restrict managers at each level to a narrow range of responsibilities and areas of action. Managers (as well as non-managerial workers) aggressively guard their areas of prerogative from encroachment. Philippe d'Iribarne (1989) has characterized French organizations as societies of castes, where each group tries to preserve its profession and independence. Even though this implies that organizational structures and hierarchical relationships are likely to remain relatively rigid, formalized work rules are frequently vague or absent.

French workers influence organizational and managerial styles through their attitudes toward work and family life. Perhaps because of their Catholic heritage, French employees have traditionally considered work a simple necessity, rather than a focus for personal and collective fulfilment. During the 1970s the role of human resource managers consisted principally of negotiating the transfer of firm profits to its employees by way of improved remuneration, benefits and working conditions. Employees had little concern for the future well-being of the company. During the 1980s, however, this separatism between individual long-term job security and the organization's long-term ability to generate profits began to erode. Human resource managers refocused on creating a linkage between the individual's and the firm's future. This linkage appears to be well established in France in the 1990s as companies actively discuss the social contract and how individuals should interact with business.

Crédit Lyonnais

As the Crédit Lyonnais case is organized as an 'in-basket exercise', it comprises three documents representing the type of material which would normally be available, such as external and internal reports. The documents used in the case come from a variety of published and unpublished sources. The case authors have created fictitious departmental managers to annotate or pass on documents to represent the variety of data sources which often offer input into complex organizational issues.

Note from the Economic and Financial Research Division This is an extract from an article by Michaël Segalla that appeared in an international banking journal. We believe that it is relevant to some of the issues related to integrating market strategies and human resource policies.

Changing requirements and needs: banks adjust to the European market

Environmental change equals organizational adaptation

Much has been written over the past few years about the changing capital, legal, and technical challenges facing financial institutions operating in Europe's new marketplace. There have also been several summaries and speculations about the market strategies banks are, or should be, adopting. Surprisingly little, however, has been written about the organizational and human resource management strategies needed to turn planned market strategies and profit projections into reality. This is unfortunate since common wisdom usually suggests that highly regulated, protected markets often result in over-staffed, over-bureaucratic organizations. These are the types of organization which are and will be finding the massive market changes in the European community difficult to survive, and constitute exactly the type of organizations many European banks have become. Because the products of the industry are remarkably undifferentiated and almost instantaneously copied by competitors, the quality and effectiveness of a bank's employees is probably the most critical factor to its success. Banks cannot build quality into their product design and then turn on an automated assembly line. Quality must be delivered by people who, as experience has taught us, can be inconsistent, unco-operative, unmotivated, and sometimes work actively against the changes required to become a dynamic, profitable organization.

Opportunities, competition, and changing regulations The European Union has created extraordinary new opportunities, new competition, and a new regulatory environment – all at the same time. Banks have seen regulatory, national, and international trade barriers fall. For example in 1986 London's Big Bang permitted banks to become more involved in international securities trading, in 1988 new bank capital-adequacy ratios were agreed upon by Western central banks, and in 1993 the EU's Second Banking Directive came into force allowing European banks to freely move into any other EU state. This has encouraged many bank directors to expand their company product offerings into other, more lucrative, services and sectors such as insurance, brokerage operations, and underwriting corporate debt, to mention just a few. Indeed one of the dominant competitive strategies of the largest European banks in the late 1980s was to develop a wide range of products offered in all the major European markets. This strategy, called the 'universal bank', usually involves the merger of banks both domestically and internationally.

One result of these changes has been the adoption of a new product mix at banks which has not corresponded particularly well to the industry's human capital. Bankers have often been characterized as conservative, reserved individuals who are very attentive to detail. As banks move increasingly into other product lines, such as life insurance sales (Figure 1) their employees must emulate the gregarious, enthusiastic personality profile of a salesperson.

This transformation is particularly important as banks are finding that new sales-oriented products and services are providing an increasingly greater share of income for banks (Table 1.1). These new opportunities come at a particularly propitious moment for banks because their traditional role as an intermediary between lenders and borrowers has been generating less and less profit.

Profits from lending money have fallen as lending capacity has increased, customers have found alternative sources of money, and the banks' traditional role of assessing risk has been taken over by the securitization[1] of debt. But taking advantage of the new opportunities has been neither risk-free nor particularly easy. Nor has the process of internationalization been particularly

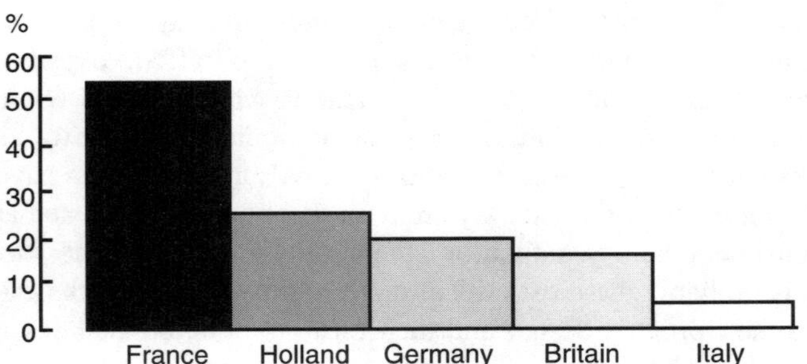

Figure 1.1 *Percentage of new life insurance sold through banks in 1990*
Source: Tillingast; 'Europe's bancassurance beasts', *The Economist*, 17 October 1992, p. 82

1 Securitization refers to the practice of collecting a large number of individual loans (e.g. mortgages or car loans) and selling them as a package to investors. The default rate, or risk, of each package can be calculated and is reflected in the selling price of the package. This decreases the importance of assessing the risk associated with each individual borrower.

Table 1.1 *Percentage of net income coming from new product sales at banks*

	1986	1987	1988	1989	1990
France	14.4	17.01	17.01	21.2	20.1
Germany	29.5	29.8	30.4	36.0	35.7
Japan	19.7	25.1	25.8	23.8	24.1
Switzerland	49.4	51.6	47.1	50.9	49.1
United Kingdom	36.3	38.1	37.6	39.2	40.1
United States	29.8	30.2	30.1	31.8	32.8

France commercial banks and credit co-operatives, Switzerland all banks, other countries commercial banks.

Source: OECD; 'World Banking', *The Economist*, 2 May 1992, p. 49.

easy. Having the opportunity to expand into other markets and countries is a double-edged sword – others can expand into your market!

The previous oligopolistic competition provided European banks with large quantities of asset-based muscle, but becoming large bureaucracies calcified their competitive spirit (Figure 1.2). Further concentration is unlikely to create a competitive spirit. It has been so common for European governments to protect their banking markets that some bankers differentiate between destructive and non-destructive competition when arguing for further protection.

This differentiation reveals bankers' and governments' fears that some of Europe's banks are destined to fail or be acquired by stronger competitors. Such distinctions, however, clearly ignore consumers' need for high-quality, low-priced banking services. In France, where chequing accounts do not receive interest, a recent offering by Barclays of an interest-bearing, chequing-type

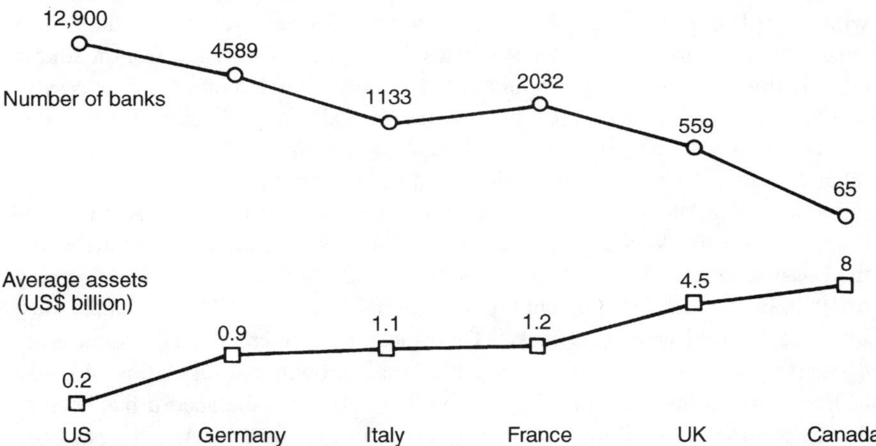

Figure 1.2 *Number of banks with more than average assets (US$ billion), 1990*
Source: Bank of America; 'World banking', *The Economist*, 2 May, 1992, p. 5

account was so threatening that French banks were able to lobby their government into outlawing the Barclays offering. Although other similar accounts by American Express, La Caixa and Cortal were available to French consumers, the Barclays offering triggered the ban because of the bank's aggressive expansion plans in France. While accepting government help, most banks are also concentrating on guarding their markets by improving service to their existing customers. More convenient hours, larger numbers of automatic teller machines, improved training for bank staff and improved customer relations are common prescriptions.

In countries with ageing populations, savings patterns are changing. Often independent investment advisers (sometimes a euphemism for high-priced insurance salespeople) have flourished by providing advice to those contemplating retirement in a decade or so and to those who inherit the savings of their parents. In Germany it is estimated that nearly 100 billion ECU will be inherited each year by the younger generation. Banks must often choose whether to compete using their own independent investment units or integrate the service into their existing branch bank services. Either choice requires a change in the selection, training, appraisal, and remuneration of employees.

Bank employee attitudes toward customers is another area especially targeted for change. As the traditional services offered by banks are increasingly duplicated by other competitors, bank directors are devoting more attention to improving service quality. This cannot be accomplished without asking bank employees to fundamentally change their attitudes toward the bank's clients. Clients must be viewed as customers and not supplicants. As in all service-oriented businesses, the development and maintenance of strong interpersonal relationships is critical to the long-term success of the bank.

Finally, many regional banks are developing international relationships not with the idea of serving the entire European market, but rather their own customers who operate in other countries. This model can range from a simple cross-national agreement providing ATM (automatic teller machine) access to another bank's customers, to buying part or all of a foreign bank. Such arrangements can be used to guard against the loss of clients who might otherwise find the network of a 'universal bank' attractive.

Banking regulators in Europe have given banks more freedom. At the same time, however, banks must meet certain capital ratio requirements established by the Basel Accord of 1988. These ratios, which were effective from the beginning of 1993, refer to the amount and types of capital (Tier 1 and Tier 2)[2] banks must set aside for each loan they make. The ratio for commercial loans is currently 8% and its imposition has discouraged the asset growth and regulation of banks in favour of profitability and supervision. One effect of the accord has been to decrease competition of loan volume in favour of loan quality. Another has been an increased push to move from low-profit, capital-intensive loans to higher-

2 Tier 1 capital is equity or near equity while Tier 2 is subordinated (i.e. riskier) debt and provisions against bad debts.

profit services such as brokering bond or stock issues. Again the impact on human resource management policies is clear.

This brief summary of the opportunities and challenges in European banking will be used below to illustrate the organizational and human resource issues banks must address to ensure that their strategic choices can be effectively implemented.

Problem in adaptation: efficiently utilizing human capital

New markets, worrisome competitors, and capital requirements receive the lion's share of bank directors' attention. Though understandable, it is dangerous to focus exclusively on the external environment. Internally, most banks have less publicized, but equally vexing problems with another important type of capital – human capital. Whether a bank's strategic plan is growth oriented or entrenchment oriented, in almost every case it depends upon an effective redeployment of human capital. Human capital is the sum of the skills, training, and experience of employees. It might be considered the 'Tier 3' capital of a bank. Without it an organization simply cannot survive. As the Basel Accord establishes new demands for different mixes of Tiers 1 and 2 capital, the new marketplace has created its own demands for new mixes of 'Tier 3' capital.

Banks have essentially three types of human capital problems: over-capitalization or having too much of the same type of capital; under-capitalization or having too little of the type of capital needed; and mis-capitalization or having the wrong type of capital for the firm's current job requirements. Examples and implications of each are discussed below.

Over-capitalization: the wrong employees with the wrong skills Many European banks simply have too many of the wrong kind of employees. They are over-capitalized with 'old-style' managers who are under-educated generalists in an increasingly specialized industry. Over-capitalization is defined as having too many managers who essentially have identical training and skills. The human capital of this type of manager is almost a commodity good and therefore more or less interchangeable. Human resource directors of banking and other financial institutions often estimate a 10 to 20% excess of these managers in the industry. They are the skilled workers of the type of banking that is no longer profitable. They started their careers when banks were less automated, more profitable, and depended upon detailed risk analysis rather than securitization to assess the risk of their loan portfolios. They are, by self-description or careful training, risk-averse, serious professionals in an industry which needs fewer and fewer of them each financial quarter as securitization, computerization and commercialization increase. They are therefore under-utilized, costly assets.

Under-capitalization: not enough of the right employees with the right skills Many banks are under-capitalized with the young, multi-lingual technically-oriented Euromanagers. Under-capitalization is defined as having too few of the right type of assets, in this case risk neutral, multi-lingual, service-oriented, technically trained managers. As Europe's banks intensify competition, either through foreign expansion or aggressive defence of their domestic markets, banking's equivalent of the Euromanager, the 'Eurobanker', will be in short supply. Europe's *grandes écoles* and top business schools will find strong demand for their finance majors, especially those with multi-cultural training and strong computer information skills.

Mis-capitalization: the right employees with the wrong attitudes Other banks are mis-capitalized with employees who, except for their inappropriate attitudes, have the necessary training and skills to contribute to the bank's success. Mis-capitalization can be found in those organizations where the traditional attitudes of employees toward work, rewards, risk and corporate mission no longer match the environment in which the firm operates. Examples in France include employees who equate using a computer with secretarial work, employees in Norway who believe that selling something is below their dignity, or managers in Spain who insist on making all decisions themselves.

Some earlier large-scale examples of such mis-capitalization can be found in the United States. The telecommunications and airline industries saw the closely regulated, cartel-like competition change dramatically. Firms reacted to the intensified competition and lower or negative profit margins by demanding more co-operation from their employees who had become accustomed to high-salaried, secure jobs. More recent examples can be found in the automobile and consumer electronics industries where product development cycles must be cut in half for a company to remain competitive. Such industries need to find methods to modify the corporate culture with the active participation of the firm's workforce. In Europe's highly unionized banking industry the sobering US history in this area must be given careful consideration.

Strategies for adjustment

Strategies for adapting a firm's human capital come from the field of human resource management. A number of choices that can be adopted by bank directors are outlined in Figure 1.3.

The new needs Success in the new banking environment in Europe is essentially based on four strategies:

1. Growth through acquisitions with the goal of dominating niche markets such as personal banking, investment, or small business banking.
2. Becoming a universal bank which offers all types of financial services in all major markets.
3. Defending domestic markets by creating or enhancing personal client relationships.
4. Selling more services and/or new products such as financial advice or insurance.

These strategies are not exclusive and are often mixed to some degree. Each requires a re-organization of current human capital in order to be effective. Banks realize that old-style employee attitudes such as disdain for selling

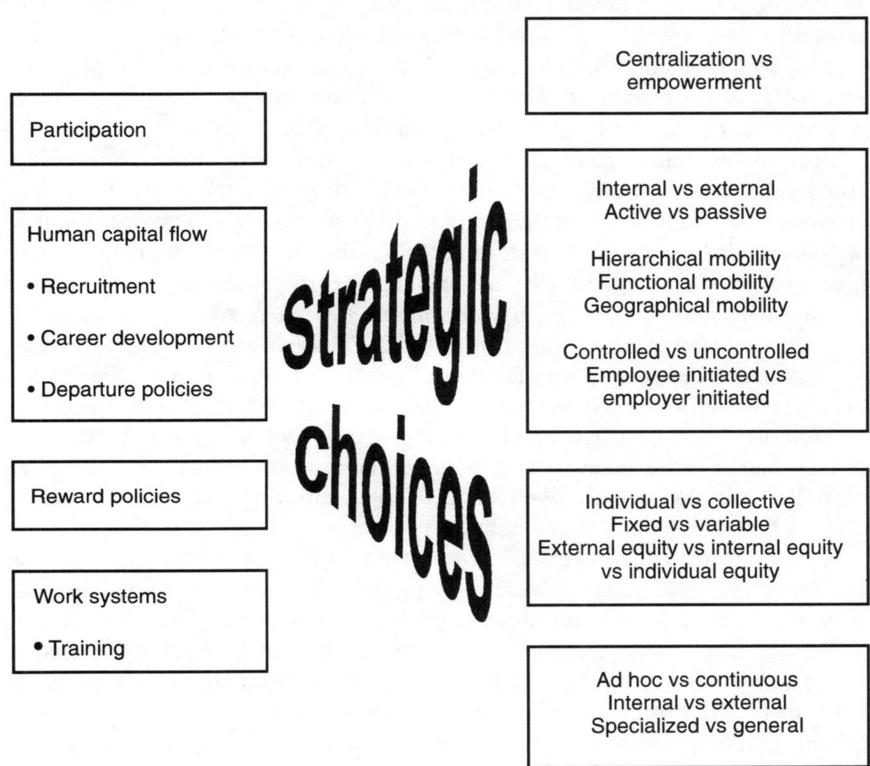

Figure 1.3 *Strategies for adjusting human resource policies*

services, demand for guaranteed income independent of personal or corporate results, and the perception that depositors are supplicants rather than customers, must change. How to change these attitudes is an important problem banks are facing.

The new policies Most of Europe's banks have already started addressing some of these problems. Three dominant, but not mutually exclusive, strategies prevail. One is to transfer excess capital to other sectors of society, another focuses on organizational restructuring and the final on the development of new human resource management systems. The last is often the first strategy attempted since it is generally considered less disruptive to the social contract between the banks and their employees. It is often accompanied or followed by organizational restructuring. In emergencies, however, when immediate action is necessary, banks reluctantly turn to the first strategy.

The over-capitalization problem is often addressed with the first strategy. Essentially this strategy reduces employment opportunities for generalists in the banking industry. This can be achieved through reduced hiring rates, early retirement programmes and forced departures. The first method is dysfunctional as it reduces the recruitment and training of the banks' future labour pool. The second method, forced departures, is often thought to be dysfunctional because it demoralizes remaining employees and is therefore avoided as long as possible, especially on the Continent. The last is expensive but more palatable to bank managers and politicians, so is often the most popular method.

Over the past few years early retirement programmes aimed at the least competent workers have been widely used. Sometimes the most competent employees took advantage of these programmes and went on to prosper in other organizations. The North American term for this is 'double dipping'. Some industry observers suggest that at best these early retirement programmes, coupled with normal turnover, have been able to reduce over-capitalization by only 10%. Transferring the remaining excess human assets will be a more difficult and disheartening task for those firms which need quicker adjustments than a 10-year long, 1% per year reduction schedule. The gentle prodding characteristic of many early retirement programmes will be replaced by stronger signals and will be addressed to a larger portion of a firm's human asset portfolio. In doing so executive managers will be making increasingly difficult choices between equally capable, but surplus assets.

New structures and systems are often used to manage the other two 'capitalization' problems. New structures are particularly important to solving the under-capitalization problem which requires banks to attract and retain young, well-trained managers. Turnover among this group can be high, especially in banks with top-heavy bureaucracies or 'nationals only' promotion policies. Such structures do not offer the rapid career development the best young managers expect. Therefore the reduction of highly centralized bureaucracies and loosening of tightly cloistered, ethno-centric staffing and promotion policies are important imperatives. Citibank, an American bank with offices worldwide, found that its European Management Associate Program (a two year training programme for high-potential recruits) had nearly a 90% turnover rate. Turnover rates like these are likely to put pressure on banks to abandon their traditional internal promotion policies and hire at all levels directly from the external marketplace, or to adopt performance appraisal systems designed to allow 'high potentials' a shortcut to the top. Crédit Lyonnais, a French bank with offices in over 60 countries, has made serious efforts towards solving this problem by promoting non-French employees to very high levels of the bank and by special programmes designed to identify and train high-potential managers on an international level.

Another reason that the restructuring area is ready for change is that the highly centralized structure of many banks hides problems in service quality. Reducing layers of hierarchy not only makes good economic sense for recruiting and career advancement, it helps the bank monitor its customer needs more directly. The days when loan applications took weeks to be approved must be left behind if customer service is to receive greater attention. Linked to this need to refocus the organization on the needs of the customer is the existence of modifications in the relationship between the four different cultures found in universal banks: corporate/investment banking (often further divided into large corporate accounts and small/medium enterprises), retail/private banking (often divided into high-wealth and average customers), market traders (currency and bond traders) and the back-office services needed by all.

Managers in these four areas do not always work together as a team, often because the needs of each are not always aligned with the needs of the ultimate consumers. Corporate/investment banking usually requires large amounts of back office support in terms of risk and/or credit analysis, processing trading activities, and issuing letters of credit among other services. The retail network also requires credit analysis, but in addition it needs to have cheques processed and new retail marketing strategies identified. Traders require special remuneration and career management systems as their work is directly linked to market movements and they tend to burn out (i.e. become too stressed to continue working) in their forties. They also require substantial back-office support in the area of economic forecasting as well as motivated sales people from the corporate/investment area. Some banks have decentralized these operations in an attempt to make them more responsive to their respective internal clientele, but this duplicates services. Others try to link reward policies to productivity increases in back-office services but have to decide how to measure productivity. Furthermore they face the problem of rewarding inappropriate behaviour should their policies by design or accident favour one bank activity at the expense of another.

The development or improvement of human resource management systems is often the most effective choice for solving the mis-capitalization problem. Increased training, better performance appraisal, development of new remuneration systems, and attempts to modify the corporate culture are the most common strategies. Retraining is often the most viable method for adjusting mis-capitalized human resources. It offers the advantage of keeping employees who are already familiar with the bank and it reduces employee hostility concerning personnel reductions.

Some firms are developing performance appraisal systems and linking them to salary increases. The hope here is to use the traditional corporate reward system to modify outdated employee attitudes. This approach, however, is less often used in those countries, such as Germany, where merit pay systems are avoided. The most aggressive banks are also instituting salary cost containment and total compensation management programmes to limit further upward salary growth. These can help executive managers aim salary increases at smaller targets, presumably those whose workplace behaviour is most profitable for the organization.

Bringing in new employees in an attempt to create an élite cadre of 'new-style' managers is also being used to readjust human capital needs. This strategy is even being pursued at over-capitalized banks who have stepped up termination pressure in a effort to shrink both their capitalization of old-style bankers and their overall capitalization of employees, while simultaneously investing aggressively in new managerial talent. Sometimes banks couple this search for 'new blood' with a strategy of increasing the number of cultural outsiders who are given important roles at all levels of the bank's hierarchy. The earlier examples of Crédit Lyonnais and Citibank fit this strategy.

Perhaps the best method of matching current human resource capital with new needs should:

- accept that a bank's human capital is its most important asset and therefore should rest at the centre of its strategic plans;
- communicate to employees the serious challenges of the new environment;
- invest heavily in employee development and attitude restructuring to achieve the critical mass necessary to propel the organization forward;
- involve employees by giving them increased authority and responsibility.

Note from the Director of Communications This document is a short introduction to Crédit Lyonnais, prepared by the Communications Department. It introduces the bank not only to new bank members but also to people from outside the organization. It contains a short history of Crédit Lyonnais, presents its organization, and its human resources in France, and gives a brief description of the Crédit Lyonnais Group.

Introduction to Crédit Lyonnais: from a regional deposit bank to a global universal bank

Rapid growth of a regional bank

Crédit Lyonnais was created in Lyon in 1863. The primary goal of Henri Germain, the bank's founder, was to collect savings from individuals and lend them to small developing companies situated in Lyon, then a major trade centre. This was a period of growth in the textile, metallurgy and chemicals industries, and of extension of France's railway network. From Lyon, Crédit Lyonnais soon branched out to Marseilles, Paris and London. Later it opened branches in south-eastern France, then abroad in Algeria, Alexandria, Constantinople, Cairo, Madrid, Geneva and St Petersburg. On the eve of the First World War, Crédit Lyonnais was the world's largest bank in terms of assets.

The First and Second World Wars were damaging to bank operating conditions, although Crédit Lyonnais succeeded in being the only French bank to make profits continuously during this period. After the Second World War it was nationalized. It remained France's largest bank until 1966; it fell to second place with the creation of Banque Nationale de Paris (BNP), then to third place following the spectacular growth of Crédit Agricole.

Development in a competitive climate

The world economy was profoundly altered by the 1973 oil price shock. It gradually expanded once again in the 1980s, after years of recession, although the environment had changed. The emphases were now on increasing globalization of business, open competition, and widespread use of information technology. For instance, Crédit Lyonnais has modernized its domestic network by diversifying its customer services (such as installing automated teller machines and offering home banking) without appreciably increasing the number of branches.

Today, Crédit Lyonnais's goal is to remain both a universal and a global bank. As a universal bank, it serves all customer categories – from individuals and the self-employed to small businesses, corporations and institutions – providing them with a broader range of services. Crédit Lyonnais is active in all lines of the banking business. It collects demand, savings and time deposits.[3] It grants loans and provides services to a large number of private and corporate clients, as well as to French and foreign financial institutions with which it maintains close relationships. In 1989, Crédit Lyonnais was ranked 12th out of 500 international banks by *American Banker* magazine (according to total deposits).

Crédit Lyonnais's organization

In accordance with French law concerning the democratization of the public sector, the Board of Directors of Crédit Lyonnais is composed of 18 members:

- six representatives of the French government;
- six individuals selected for their expertise, their knowledge of the different sectors of the banking business, or their position as representatives of consumers or users;
- six employee representatives who are elected by the entire staff.

Decisions concerning the company's major economic, financial and technological policies are made only after deliberation by the Board of Directors. The French government appoints the Chairman (Figure 1.4) who is nominated by the Board of Directors. He has the broadest powers to act in all circumstances in the name of Crédit Lyonnais, with the exception of powers expressly reserved for the Board of Directors or the Annual Shareholders' Meetings, as well as applicable laws and regulations. He fulfils the functions of Chief Executive Officer, makes all appointments, especially to management positions, and may designate one or two General Managers who participate directly in the general management of Crédit Lyonnais.

The French Branch Network Division has responsibility for the entire domestic network. The operating network is now organized into specialized units according to customer category (corporate and individual/self-employed/small business). It establishes the administrative processing organization and

3 A demand deposit, like a checking account, is instantly accessible; a savings deposit may have restrictive rules for access such as a 48-hour withdrawal notice; a time deposit, such as a certificate of deposit, generally requires one to wait until the end of a fixed 1–5-year period before withdrawing the money.

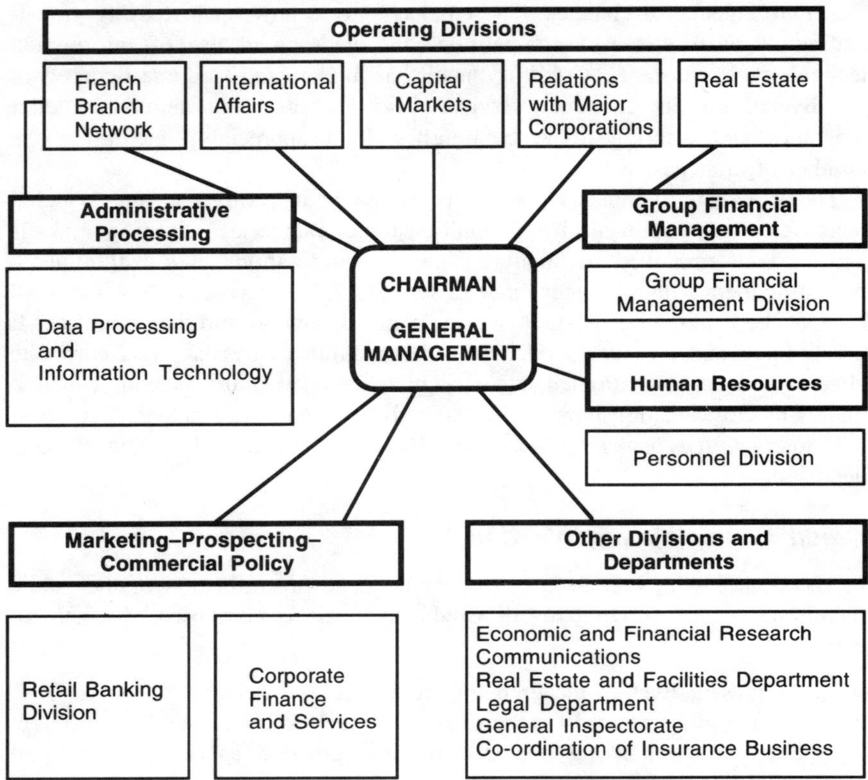

Figure 1.4 *Simplified organization chart of Crédit Lyonnais*

sales support for the commercial units. Decision-making authority held by the General Management is partly delegated and sub-delegated to staff members at various levels, from the director of the core division to customer service representatives.

The International Affairs Division defines, implements and co-ordinates activities that are part of Crédit Lyonnais's international strategy.

The Capital Markets Division runs and co-ordinates all activities of the Crédit Lyonnais Group dealing with market operations, including corporate finance. It offers customers a vast range of financial products and services, based on an organization designed to operate in all the capital markets. It also has a strong presence not only in Paris, but in all the world's financial centres, via the branch network and International Affairs Division, and via its own units in Hong Kong, London, Madrid, New York, Tokyo and Zurich.

The Relations with Major Corporations Division is responsible for Crédit Lyonnais's policy regarding major international, French and foreign corporations, which it handles directly. It monitors the business of some 5000 companies in over 220 French and foreign corporate groups. It has its own Commitments Division, which analyses risks, either alone or in conjunction with the commitments divisions of the various units that initiate or submit credit applications, although it makes the final decision.

Through its Real Estate Financing and Development Department, the Real Estate Division studies all real estate proposals it receives, and after analysing the risk involved, it issues a technical opinion and authorizes credit within the limits of its authority. It also maintains direct relations with most major real estate corporations nationwide.

The Retail Banking Division prepares the marketing strategies to be used in the domestic retail banking markets. It conducts market surveys among existing and potential customers, as well as among operators prior to new product and service launches. It helps the units of Crédit Lyonnais's European network to define their strategy for individual customer markets. The division also designs new products and updates existing products to satisfy changing customer needs, and to enhance the profitability of current products.

The Corporate Finance and Services Division handles marketing and promotes advisory services, corporate finance, and specialized financial products. Amid strong competition, it stresses the sale of high-value-added products, backed by the strength of the Crédit Lyonnais network and its expertise in financial markets.

Created on 1 June 1989, the Group Financial Management Division has several tasks, principal among which are the preparation of the accounts and corporate finance for the Group (i.e. optimization of its organization and monitoring of subsidiaries).

The Administrative Processing Department's purpose is to maintain high levels of competitiveness for Crédit Lyonnais's production and information systems teams, to enable them to provide products and services adapted to market needs at the lowest cost as well as managing the Administrative and Information Processing Centres. Its current goals include supplying operators with powerful computerized sales and commercial management aids and satisfying customer demands, and consequently those of partners in the commercial network through the implementation of a 'total quality' approach, training and adaptation of organization.

Human resources at Crédit Lyonnais, France

In accordance with guidelines established by the General Management, the Personnel Division is responsible for designing and implementing human resource policies (including remuneration policy, staff management, and individual management) and handling the human relations of the Crédit Lyonnais Group.

As one of the institutions belonging to the French Association of Banks (*Association Française des Banques*), Crédit Lyonnais is subject to the collective agreement (*convention collectif*) in this sector of activity. This agreement was concluded in 1952 between the French Association of Banks and the representatives of the major labour unions, and it has since been modified by

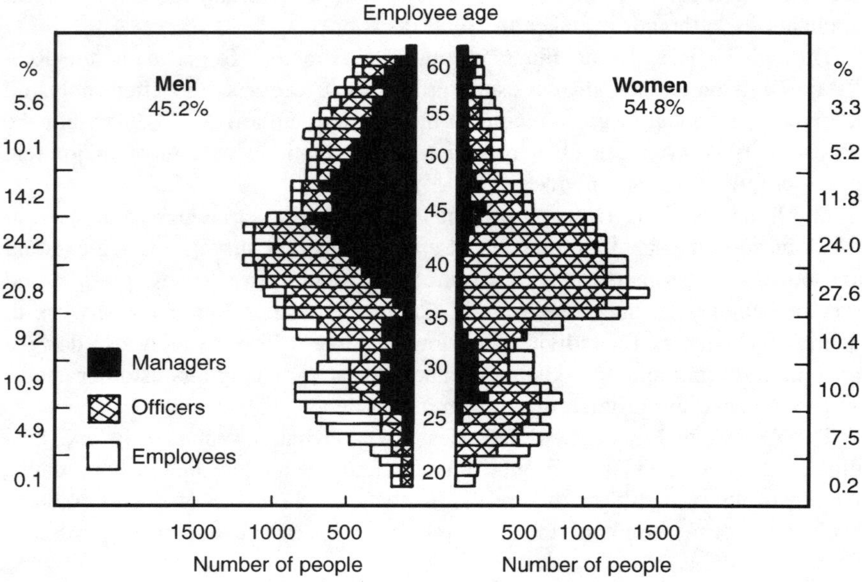

Figure 1.5 *Age distribution pyramid at year-end 1990 (figures for France only)*

numerous agreements. It handles all of the employment conditions and the social guarantees applicable to the salaried staff in its field of application.

Employment At the beginning of the 1990s Credit Lyonnais's French Division had 2460 offices and about 42,000 employees. Crédit Lyonnais experienced a short burst of rapid employment growth during the early 1970s, which is evidenced by its age pyramid (Figure 1.5). This period has left Crédit Lyonnais with a staff that is too concentrated in the 40- to 50-year age group, thus creating a strong bias in the age pyramid. There is also a bias against female managers – 55% of the employees are women but they very seldom have managerial positions. This lack of equilibrium in age and gender has serious consequences for the development of careers.

As has the entire banking sector, Crédit Lyonnais profited during this period from important computer-based productivity improvements. In order to adjust the number of staff to actual needs, the bank has been constantly reducing its personnel by an average of 1% a year since 1976. To reduce social hardship this reduction has been realized through early retirements, financial aid for employees volunteering to leave, and the increased use of part-time workers. Overall growth, however, has increased recently due to acquisition of foreign banks by the Group.

Recruitment Trends in recruitment have been closely related to staff turnover, volume of business and increasing productivity. Since its peak recruiting years between 1970 and 1975 (yearly average 5175) Crédit Lyonnais has significantly decreased its net intake of new domestic employees (1989–90 average 1701). Since the sharp reduction of new recruitment after 1975, the average age of the domestic workforce has steadily risen and stood in 1990 at 39 years of age. New recruits increasingly have more academic training than their predecessors. Currently most new recruits have remained in school until about the age of 20 (in France this is called a BAC + 2), and a third have degrees from a university or *grande école*, (specialized business training school), which most students finish at 22 or 23 years of age.

Remuneration The remuneration of salaried staff is regulated by the Collective Agreement. Jobs are classified by hierarchical coefficients expressed in points. The monetary value of a point is determined annually in negotiations with the union representatives. The classification of jobs is thus the basis of the remuneration system that determines pay according to the position held rather than the individual employee. All of the employees receive a seniority bonus and in the past seniority was an important element in promotion decisions. Although Crédit Lyonnais still uses position and seniority, it is making greater efforts to reward individual performance. This is being hampered somewhat by what one high-ranking manager called the 'lack of courage by many managers to give a poor performance appraisal report in favour of promoting someone out of their unit so another manager has to deal with a problem employee'.

The growth of personnel costs, salaries and other expenses such as bonuses, payroll taxes, and retirement and other miscellaneous benefits, doubled (2.4% to 4.8%) between 1986 and 1990. The nearly 11 billion francs paid spent on employees in 1990 for remuneration costs was divided between remuneration (salaries, bonuses, and other remuneration paid to all employees), 63.5%; payroll taxes, 30%; other contributions (taxes to promote transportation, housing, training, and employing the handicapped), 6.5%.

Training The amount and cost of training which has taken place over the four years 1987–91 is presented in Figure 1.6. Both the time spent in training and cost are rising. In 1987 training costs were 4.4% of salary while in 1991 they were estimated to be 8.1% of salaries, which is well above the government's required training budget of 1.9% of salary costs. Traditionally, training has been oriented toward practical banking techniques.

The Crédit Lyonnais Group

In Europe the network has been expanded in recent years with the opening of new branches (Stockholm in 1986, Copenhagen in 1989), and especially with the takeover of, or acquisition of shareholding interests in, networks of foreign banks (Spain in 1991, Germany in 1993). The Crédit Lyonnais Group's various commercial banking units have been reorganized in two stages. The first consisted of transforming groups of branches into subsidiaries, as in the case of Crédit Lyonnais Suisse SA and Crédit Lyonnais Belgium. The second involved grouping the various European subsidiaries into specific entities in each country

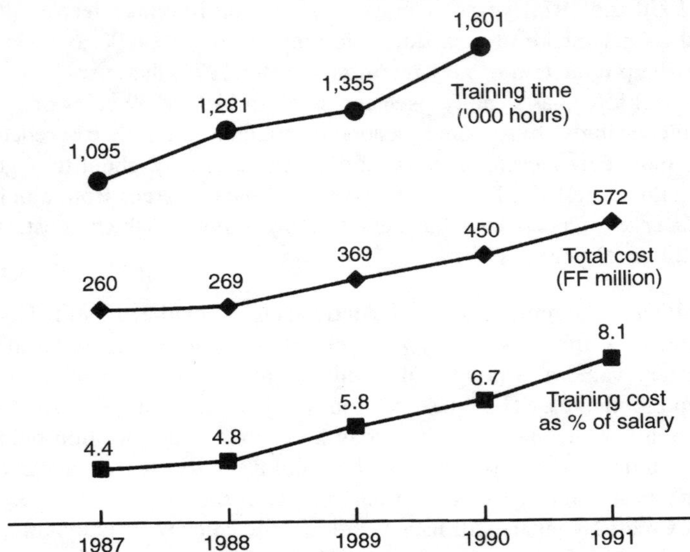

Figure 1.6 *Training hours, costs and percentage of salaries (figures for France only)*

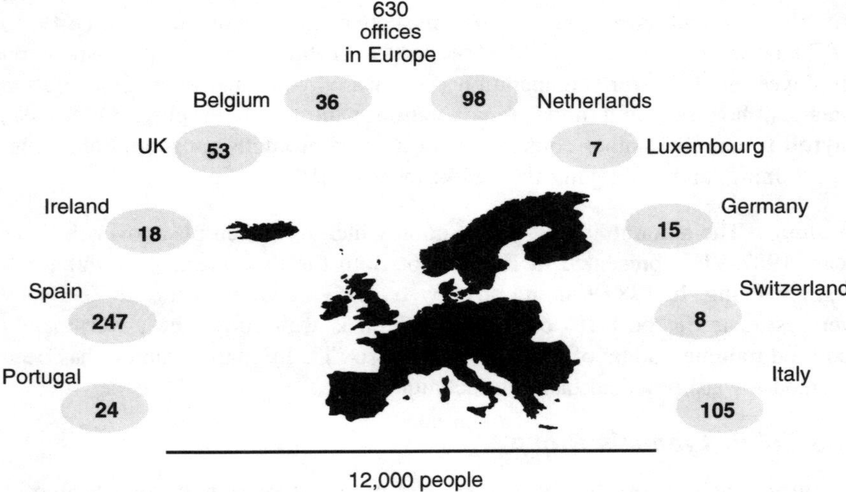

Figure 1.7 *Crédit Lyonnais worldwide*

and then placing them under Crédit Lyonnais Europe SA. There are over 630 Crédit Lyonnais offices in Europe (Figure 1.7).

The Crédit Lyonnais Group had 72,500 salaried staff in 1991, compared to 53,800 in 1986, which represents an increase of nearly 35% in six years. The breakdown of its global workforce is as follows:

- Europe: 54,300, of which 39,700 are in France and 14,600 in the other countries.
- America: 5500, of which 800 are in North America and 4700 in South America.
- Asia/Africa: 1100.
- Africa: nearly 3000

Since 1986 the staff of the parent company has decreased by approximately 7%, reaching 39,700 in France. Thus within the group as a whole, the percentage of French employees has significantly decreased (78% to 57%).

The Group's banking activity elsewhere in the world has grown, and is conducted through its 610 offices outside Europe: foreign branches, subsidiaries (majority shareholdings), associated companies (minority shareholdings). Crédit Lyonnais has offices on all continents, and in the countries where it has operations, it applies one of two growth strategies: organic growth (increasing the activity of its branches and subsidiaries, or opening units – branches, representative offices) or acquisitions/mergers involving either takeovers or purchase of minority interests in local banks. In the UK Crédit Lyonnais is expanding its retail banking operations by opening new agencies and expanding its corporate and commercial operations through acquisitions and joint ventures. In Spain it purchased two banks and merged them with its own longstanding Spanish operations.

While intensifying its banking activity through a growing commercial network, Crédit Lyonnais has also expanded its capital market activities in Europe's leading financial centres (Paris, London, Madrid, Amsterdam, Milan), North America (New York) and Asia (Tokyo, Hong Kong, Singapore). It is for this reason that the Capital Markets Division was created, enabling Crédit Lyonnais to operate in all markets. It is present in Paris and all other international financial centres through the network of foreign branches of the International Affairs Division and via its own offices.

Note from the HRM Director This document is an abstract of a report drawn up by the consultancy TEMS (TransEuropean Management Specialists) for Crédit Lyonnais, based on interviews with bank staff. It presents a short diagnosis of Crédit Lyonnais's corporate culture and discusses the bank's international human resources policies.

The internationalization of management: facts and problems

Background to the problem

The Crédit Lyonnais Group has grown very rapidly over the past few years and will continue to grow with planned expansions into Germany, Italy, and Spain (see Table 1.2). To benefit from its acquisitions, many Crédit Lyonnais managers

Table 1.2 *Crédit Lyonnais European expansion since 1987*

Belgium	1989: takeover of Chase Banque de Commerce 1990: creation of Crédit Lyonnais Belgium SA/NV 1991: acquisition of Security Pacific Eurofactors
Denmark	1989: opening of the Crédit Lyonnais Denmark branch in Copenhagen 1990: opening of a branch in Aarhus
France	1990: creation of Crédit Lyonnais Europe SA 1991: creation of Crédit Lyonnais Leasing International SA
Germany	1988: creation of a German company, Crédit Lyonnais SA & Co (OHG) 1990: acquisition of an 85% stake in CL PK Leasing GmbH 1991: attachment of Bankhaus Wolbern (100% owned by CLBN) to Crédit Lyonnais SA & Co. (Deutschland) acquisition of CL Factoring GmbH
Greece	1990: creation of a leasing subsidiary: Leasing Ethniki Lyonnais SA
Ireland	1991: stake in Woodchester Investments plc increased to 45.4% acquisition of Mercantile Credit Company of Ireland creation of Credit Lyonnais Financial Services (Ireland) Ltd 1992: corporate banking started at Woodchester Investment Bank take-over of UDT (Dublin) by Woodchester Investments plc
Italy	1988: acquisition of a 20% stake in Banca Lombarda (Milan) 1989: acquisition of a 48% stake in Credito Bergamasco 1991: stake in Banca Lombarda increased to 30% stake in Credito Bergamasco increased to 56.4% acquisition of a 57% stake in the Leasimpresa leasing company creation with Gemina of an SIM (securities dealing firm)
Netherlands	1988: acquisition of Nederlands Credietbank (NCB) and merger with CLBN 1989: creation of Notolion BV and Crédit Lyonnais Bénélux BV 1991: creation of Foncier Lyonnais Hypotheken VOF 1992: creation of Crédit Lyonnais Leasing Nederland NV 1992: creation of CL Eurofactors Nederland NV
Portugal	1988: creation of Leasimo 1989: transfer of Crédit Franco Portuguais branches to CL Portugal SA 1989: stock exchange flotation of Crédit Lyonnais Portugal SA 1992: creation of Slibail Portuguesa
Spain	1987: creation of Crédit Lyonnais Sociedad de Credito Hipotecario 1990: creation of Crédit Lyonnais Ibérica de Factoring acquisition of Banco Comercial Español acquisition of a 40% stake in the financial group Iberagentes

Table 1.2 *continued*

Spain	1991: takeover of Banca Jover stake in Iberagentes increased to 50% 1992: creation of CL España SA via the merger of CL branches in Spain with Banco Comercial Español
UK	1987: acquisition of Alexanders Laing & Cruickshank, renamed CL Capital Markets Ltd (1989) 1989: opening of the Birmingham branch 1990: acquisition of stakes in the Woodchester Group in London and Dublin opening of branches in Bristol, Leeds and Manchester 1991: opening of branches in Newcastle, Ashford, Southampton and Cambridge acquisition of a 70% stake in Woodchester Trade Finance (factoring) 1992: opening of the Nottingham branch

believe that they need to integrate the network in terms of common product offerings and management of their clients. For example, they would like to be able to contact one of their Italian branches, such as Credito Bergamasco, and arrange for a Crédit Lyonnais UK client, who want to establish a business operation in Northern Italy, to be favourably received. The trouble is that in banking trust is something that is not gained quickly. There is little incentive for the Italian loan officer to do any favours for an English one: they do not know each other. If the English loan officer gives good clients to an Italian branch of Crédit Lyonnais he receives no specific reward. If the Italian loan officer arranges for the loan, and the client later defaults, the English loan officer bears no responsibility.

Presentation and methodology

Recent developments in the banking sector in general, and in that of Crédit Lyonnais in particular, have contributed to a disturbance in the equilibrium of a system that for a long time has relied on the dominance of French management in its pure form and the foreign operations of which have been centralized around an international division. Taking into account the demands imposed by a new, very competitive environment, the directors of Crédit Lyonnais have started to focus their efforts on understanding and improving the bank's international management of human resource policies. As a start it has decided to identify the critical elements of the situation by means of a qualitative diagnosis.

As suggested by our position as consultants, our methodology is qualitative. It is principally based on interviews with French and foreign higher-level employees who hold very diversified positions in different countries, namely in the USA, the Netherlands, Belgium, the UK and Spain. It allows us a better focus on their personal concerns and sensitivities such as the feeling of belonging to the group, the views that non-French employees have of the Group, and resistance to certain changes. The report that follows presents in summary form both the major characteristics of the culture of Crédit Lyonnais and important consequences of current human resource management policies. The diagnosis on the whole leads us to consider new orientations in the international management of human resources.

Results and diagnosis

The history of Crédit Lyonnais has generated a specific corporate culture, characterized by pragmatic career management, independent systems of career management for French and non-French managers, and expatriation as the main link between headquarters and foreign countries.

Crédit Lyonnais's historical influences We have found during interviews, especially with the main directors, and in the documents provided to us that Crédit Lyonnais's history appears to be marked by four essential influences: its tradition of being a deposit bank; a belief in the value of internationalization for nearly a century; its use of 'feudal-like kingdoms' for managing its worldwide affairs; and its rapid adoption of new technology to enhance its competitiveness. These are explained below.

Crédit Lyonnais has traditionally been a deposit bank. The development of its commercial banking operations was made possible by recent changes in government legislation and began only 15 years ago. This strategic evolution has transformed the organization of the bank. Its classic administrative organization was for a long time characterized by stability in work procedures. These favour the gradual accumulation of competencies and a slow progression to expert status. This development has been supported by promotion rules based on seniority, resulting in managers who are almost always older then their subordinates. The increasing focus on commercial (i.e. selling) activity turns the hierarchy of professional values upside down. Thus the bank has broken its rules of 'promotion by seniority' by recruiting and promoting university graduates in order to compensate for the lack of commercial competencies.

Furthermore, the increasing technological sophistication of banking interferes with the previous division of promotion resources between younger and older employees. The computerization of administrative procedures and the appearance of expert systems have rendered the technical competencies of the older generations progressively obsolete. Recent surveys have found that clerical, support and operational positions will decrease in favour of new positions for business specialists in the areas of investment securities, information systems, economics, corporate and retail lending, insurance underwriting and other technical fields. The younger generation with more technical training realize that their status as experts provides them with a strategic resource for obtaining promotion within the bank's hierarchy. Therefore the evolution of an administrative culture towards a commercial and technical one contributes to a reduction in the expert power on which the 'old' generation has based its competencies; which, in turn, explains the present resistance to change.

Crédit Lyonnais's international expansion began almost at its creation. First it started with branches in the world's major cities, followed by branches in the different countries where France had economic interests, political activity or colonies (especially in African countries). In this sense, the internationalization of Crédit Lyonnais is frequently described as having been a 'colonisation', and has been carried out in the same spirit.

Historically Crédit Lyonnais's organizational structure had been based on the requirements of managing a worldwide organization and therefore local bank directors were delegated large amounts of power. Respect for their personal responsibilities became strongly ingrained throughout the organization. The existence of 'territories', which were geographical in the case of branches abroad, directed by virtually autonomous local managers, led to the creation of 'feudal-like fiefdoms' which have often resulted in internal competition ('One doesn't give a customer to somebody else!') Efforts were made to reduce this isolation by restructuring the organization chart and increasing professional mobility. Co-ordination, however, remains a constant preoccupation.

The development of the bank's activities has always depended on the adoption of technological innovations. This enabled Crédit Lyonnais to adopt, often before its competitors, new techniques and equipment which allowed it to make continual improvements in productivity.

Corporate culture's two main values These four influences have combined to create a corporate culture at Crédit Lyonnais characterized by the particular importance given to:

- fame: the perception of working for a bank considered to be one of the most important in the world is very significant to Crédit Lyonnais managers. This is also true for foreign employees who, at worst, consider their tenure as an enrichment of their curriculum vitae.
- caution: which has an importance far beyond what can be considered a basic condition required by the business. It is perceived as a characteristic well suited to considering innovations or technical improvements. But it is also a barrier, since this carefulness creates a certain distrust, particularly toward what is 'foreign'.

The 'French' career management system Crédit Lyonnais's career management system has been strongly oriented toward its French managers, but is increasingly confused as the bank becomes more internationalized. In general, each country is responsible for its specific human resource management practices and therefore often has markedly different rules and procedures. At the group level the organization maintains two independent systems for managerial career development, one for French managers and another, much less developed, for foreign managers. The recruitment and development of French managers is the responsibility of the HRM department. A few years ago the bank established a policy of recruiting university graduates and experienced professionals for high-ranking managerial positions, and by 1989 it was hiring equal numbers of both groups.

Management training is currently given to about 600 high-ranking French staff per year, and management and quality training accounts for 30% of the training budget. Access to advanced, French-based training for high-ranking foreign staff is expanding but lags behind. French performance evaluation is also divided into two separate systems, one applicable to grades VIII and HC or *hors classification* (literally out of classification, the highest possible ranking) and another for staff below grade VIII. Some type of performance appraisal is usually carried out throughout the worldwide network but can vary considerably from country to country. In the not too distant past, some local nationals were evaluated using French-language performance appraisal forms which they could not read. Because of the bureaucratic culture and seniority-based promotion system, the information obtained through both local and international evaluation procedures is not very useful in career management. The result is that career development depends more on the available vacant jobs and a manager's personal relationships with his or her superiors. This 'management by job vacancy and contacts' discourages strategic development of managerial competency. Strong personal networks and being associated with prestige projects are generally the preferred methods for advancement.

Generally career paths still follow the traditional model and reflect three strategies: internal promotion, professional mobility and geographical mobility. Managers who entered the bank at the beginning of their career still have favoured access to jobs of considerable responsibility, even if they lack the necessary skills for the position. The policy of recruiting university graduates was an attempt to provide better-educated managers for the future. However, little change in actual promotion practices has been noticed. Some of the high-ranking staff entering the bank in mid-career have experienced difficulties of integration and subsequent career advancement as a result of this internal promotion prejudice.

The policy of encouraging professional mobility was introduced in the 1970s in order to reduce internal divisions within the corporate structure. It seems still to be applied, considering the career paths of many of the high-ranking staff. However, managers perceive a possible danger in 'de-specialization' and the 'maturing of generalists', which could hamper the increase of professionalism required by the evolution of product and service activities.

The third career strategy is geographical mobility. This policy arose through Crédit Lyonnais's international activities and structure. The use of expatriates has noticeably increased during the past few years as the bank has expanded internationally. There are about 380 expatriate managers of French nationality and about 80 foreign nationals. Expatriate status is less available now for French nationals but more available to foreign managers. (There has been only a 13% increase in French expatriates but nearly a doubling of foreign ones over the last four years.)

Finally, high-ranking local managers are normally managed locally, without formal co-ordination from Paris. As far as recruitment is concerned, it is carried out according to local needs and labour markets. Career management is the most difficult problem for foreign branches, as the possibility of promotion is limited to the local structure where the majority of high-level jobs are occupied by French expatriates. The opportunity of going to France for training is limited.

Generally it is used as a 'reward' to retain high-performing local managers whose promotion opportunities are limited. When such training is available it normally consists of a one- or two-week seminar which limits the manager's ability to search for vacant posts or develop a personal network of contacts.

Expatriation is the main link between headquarters and foreign countries Although some Paris-based French managers have occasionally worked abroad and some foreign managers have trained or worked in France, it is the French expatriates who supply the link between Paris and the foreign subsidiaries. Paris-based managers rely heavily on these expatriates to help facilitate or implement programmes which must be transferred to foreign units. Because of the important role played by French expatriates, most local employees believe that certain positions in their home countries are, and will always be, reserved for French nationals.

There are essentially three explanations for this 'presumed' policy. First, French managers are familiar with the internal workings of Crédit Lyonnais – its organizational culture. Secondly, they help to preserve the supremacy of corporate interests over local or personal interests. Finally, they believe that 'family members' should be given certain advantages in the course of their careers. This state of mind is reinforced by the belief among top managers in France that it is easier to solve common problems with expatriates of French nationality than with foreigners. While non-French managers disagree with this attitude/policy they are essentially resigned to the *status quo*.

French expatriates often find expatriation can become a career. Employees who have already spent time in foreign countries are considered international people, who together with their families are able to adapt to different environments, to different life and work styles, and who are open to other mentalities and cultures. This phenomenon is confirmed by the fact that about one-third of current expatriates have spent nearly all of their careers abroad, and will probably end them abroad. The ability to develop the international work style captured by the catch phrase 'Think global, act local', without necessarily having worked in a foreign country, is believed to be difficult to accomplish.

Being an expatriate provides financial and professional advantages. Financially expatriates receive a salary supplement and generally better living conditions (primarily a more comfortable residence by Parisian standards). Professionally, aside from work which is often more interesting and challenging, expatriation bestows a privileged way to climb the hierarchy. Working abroad offers increased responsibilities and real autonomy in business and personnel management, reinforced by geographical distance. The prestige of having a 'top job' is a major inducement. Above all there is often a sense of adventure reminiscent of the colonial spirit of conquest. Top foreign postings are sometimes considered as personal empires which has led to a type of *regalien* (king-like) managerial style.

Closed structure Crédit Lyonnais is a French bank with an international dimension. This last characteristic is an important motive for foreign executives to join and remain with the bank. But they perceive the bank as very *cloisonné*, or partitioned. First, on a vertical level, the possibilities of joint work and exchanges between branches are limited, even impossible ('We don't give business to another branch, because the result won't be attributed to us.') Horizontal interactions often fail because of a desire to maintain local practices. There is little sense of being involved in any strategic process of development because information flows very hierarchically ('The meeting reports are transmitted with missing pages!') Foreign executives consider the impossibility of obtaining top local or French jobs as evidence of this closed structure ('There is no example of an international career for a foreigner.') This feeling is reinforced by the limited promotion possibilities in the usually small local branches and the absence of an 'appeal' committee in charge of this matter. Time spent by some foreign managers in the Paris headquarters is perceived as a reward but has often not met their expectations, because they were considered as 'tourists', or because they had the feeling of being confined to activities not suited to their real skills or potential.

Detrimental effects and new initiatives The state of affairs described above, inherited from its history and reinforced by its culture, seems to be detrimental to Crédit Lyonnais's international expansion in several respects. It leads to a lack of multi-national teams that could generate behaviours and mentalities necessary for an international outlook by both French and foreign managers, which could form the basis of a real international network. Furthermore, it does not meet the ambitions of the young graduates recruited by the bank, the majority of which are in favour of international geographical mobility. Equally, the methods used today to manage human resources do not allow foreign employees to have positions of greater responsibilities in the parent company, which in turn makes it difficult to maintain the loyalty of the best of them. The international network is waiting for the nomination of foreign managers to high positions in Paris as proof that Crédit Lyonnais wants to be 'truly' international and can ensure a real career to foreign managers. The possibility that the directors of Crédit Lyonnais will adopt such policies creates unease among French expatriate managers, as they see their personal career goals and way of life threatened.

However, change has been noticed by a majority of French and foreign managers, leading them to think that 'things may be moving'. This applies especially to the decision taken by the Chief Executive Officer to entrust the management of the Belgian branch to a Belgian director, which reinforces management's determination to move in this direction. Being faced with its new environment and the conclusions of this report, Crédit Lyonnais should think about ways of enriching its culture with external ideas and internationalize its management in order to respond to the ambitions of its foreign network.

Issues Crédit Lyonnais must resolve

All the high-ranking staff we met, whether French, foreign or expatriate, have been attentive and sensitive to the messages sent out by the Chief Executive

Officer about the initiatives that have been implemented. They have shared their hopes, anxieties and questions. We leave you with the issues that Crédit Lyonnais must adequately address if it wants its internationalization process to be successful:

- What kind of career possibilities can be offered to foreigners who have responsible jobs in their own countries, particularly the 'top ones'?
- How is it possible to '*Credit Lyonnaise*' foreigners?
- How is it possible to incorporate foreign ideas into Crédit Lyonnais's culture without it losing its identity?
- How is it possible to internationalize teams so they become a real means of development and not a point of fracture?
- What kind of human resource policies (including social and fiscal aspects) provide the necessary incentives to encourage geographical mobility among employees?
- What kind of career development incentives, apart from expatriation, can be offered to expatriates?
- How is it possible to meet the expectations of the young university graduates hired over the past few years?
- What kind of means of assessment and co-ordination should be implemented to permit decentralized development and the creation of synergy?

Themes/issues to consider

Human resource development and organizational development

According to systems theory, organizational structures and the human personalities that help to define and sustain them are so complex that our sometimes simplistic assumptions about human resource development and organizational development are simply inadequate to achieve their intended goals. The interaction between organizations, their members and the underlying social or cultural environment makes designing effective development programmes increasingly difficult – especially in multi-cultural environments. Therefore the more managers know and understand about the environment in which the HRD/OD programmes are destined to operate, the more likely they will be to be able to incorporate this knowledge into the programme's structure.

Organizational change

Crédit Lyonnais faced an extraordinarily difficult organizational change situation. At least three change vectors existed at the same time. First, it had to deal with the changing role of banks in the financial markets. Secondly, it had to cope with the increasing competition fostered by the European Common Market. Finally, it was faced with integrating foreign subsidiaries and joint ventures into its organization. This last problem was made more difficult by the rapid expansion of the bank (it more than doubled its number of European offices outside France between 1988 and 1990 and added an additional 400 new offices outside Europe during the same period).

Strategic international human resource management

Schuler, Dowling and De Cieri (1993) have worked to develop a framework for strategic international human resource management. They argue that the two major strategic components of multinational enterprises (MNEs) most important to HRM are inter-unit linkages and internal operations. Inter-unit linkages are important to efficient operation because MNEs operate in several countries. MNEs must balance the need to be able to differentiate foreign subsidiaries while maintaining enough integration to provide the co-ordination and control necessary to financial success. This integration may be achieved more easily through the use of HRM policies and management development. Evans (1992) believes that management development can be used as a 'glue' to maintain a tightly integrated network of otherwise loosely linked entities. Although each foreign unit does not have to have the same degree of integration with other units, its *internal* operations must reflect local conditions within its national or regional environment. This requires firms to develop HRM policies that absolutely reflect local requirements, while at the same time attempting to respond to the co-ordination needs of the MNE. Crédit Lyonnais's policies were developed to meet its local needs and its rapid foreign expansion required it to consider what types of HRM policies it must have to achieve its aim of being a universal bank with global operations.

Changing organizational culture

Identifying and adapting an organization's internal culture will be one of the major hurdles faced by European firms as they begin the process of becoming Euronational. Anthropologists, sociologists and organizational theorists all write about the difficulty of even identifying existing cultural rules. Thinking about how to change the unknown becomes an extraordinarily difficult problem, but of course it is absolutely vital to the integration of developing Euronational companies. Failure to create some agreed values will create a constant and heavy drain on an organization and is likely to lead to its eventual failure as a competitive actor in European markets.

Managerial staffing policies for internationalizing firms

Perhaps one of the most difficult actions to take is to give up or share power, especially when this will favour a stranger. However, this is a vital act during the internationalization process. When a firm such as Crédit Lyonnais begins expanding outside its home country by buying foreign companies, it is essentially hiring people with expertise in their local markets. These employees also have career aspirations. Cutting off their career paths in favour of the buying firm's nationals would encourage the best to seek careers elsewhere, leaving behind those with lesser ambitions, and perhaps capabilities. Therefore internationalizing firms must quickly create career management systems applicable to all employees, regardless of nationality. At Crédit Lyonnais most foreign employees appear to believe that career advancement for them will always be limited. The question the bank must face is whether it can be a world-class competitor while at the same time restricting the career advancement of some of its most capable employees. If the answer is no (as certainly it must be), then what must the bank do to share power?

Assignment

You have been hired to be the new special assistant for human resource management planning, reporting directly to Crédit Lyonnais's HRM Director. (Alternatively you could be a young consultant assigned to make preliminary policy and implementation proposals.) The HRM Director has assembled and gives to you a dossier with various reports and policy positions which you can use as background information to familiarize yourself with the challenges faced by banks in Europe, and by Crédit Lyonnais in particular, and to make a diagnosis of the situation and then make recommendations. This file includes:

- overview of French business, managerial, banking and work culture;
- article entitled 'Changing markets and changing needs: banks adjust to the European market';
- article entitled 'Introduction to Crédit Lyonnais: from a regional deposit bank to a global universal bank';
- an external consultant's report on the bank's current international human resources policies;
- a reading list of books and articles to help you develop a framework of analysis.

Your team's task is to make policy and implementation proposals to the HRM Director, providing him with options for matching the bank's HRM policies to its market strategies. More precisely, some of the top management are worried that the bank will not be able to capitalize on the purchase of its large, expensive international network without some type of cultural integration or internationalization of management.

What type of actions would you propose based on your diagnosis of the situation?

After your team has prepared its proposals you will be required to deliver a presentation before the executive committee of the bank.

Suggested reading

Bates, Paul (1994) *Strategies for Cultural Change*. Oxford: Butterworth-Heinemann.

Brewster, Chris (1991) *The Management of Expatriates*. London: Kogan Page.

Mendenhall, Mark and Oddou, Gary (1991) *International Human Resource Management*. Boston: PWS-Kent.

Perlmutter, H.V. and Heeman, D.A. (1974) 'How multinational should your organization be?', *Harvard Business Review*, November–December: 121–32.

Randlesome, C., Brierley, W., Bruton, K., Gordon, C. and King, P. (1993) *Business Cultures in Europe* (Second Edition) Oxford: Butterworth-Heinemann.

Tung, Rosalie, L. (1988) *The New Expatriate*. Cambridge, Mass.: Ballinger (Harper and Row).

Zeira, Y. (1975) 'Overlooked personnel problems in multinational companies', *Columbia Journal of World Business*, 10 (2): 96–103.

Note

This case was made possible by the support and efforts of a number of people at Groupe HEC and Crédit Lyonnais. At Groupe HEC we would like to thank Jean-Marc De Leersnyder, Director of HEC and Jean-Louis Scaringella, former Dean, Academic Institutions. At Crédit Lyonnais we extend our thanks to Marie-Therese Boucher, International Co-ordinator, Corporate Human Resource Management; Claude Brassens, Senior Vice President CL USA; Paul Grol, Director of CIMES (the international management training centre); Serge Vandaele, first as Director of Recruitment and later as Director of Training; and the other 100 or so Crédit Lyonnais managers in France, the UK, Spain, Italy, the Netherlands and Turkey who generously gave their time and trust.

Our CEMS Inter-Faculty Group also deserves a note of thanks for its valuable critiques and suggestions. We would specifically like to thank Odd Nordhaug, Professor of Management at the Norwegian School of Economics and Business Administration, and Dr Lorenz Fischer, Professor of Management at University of Köln. Both provided detailed reviews of the case.

In the end, despite the excellent help, good ideas and useful suggestions we received, we accept credit for all faults of execution in assembling the parts.

References

Bauer, M. and Bertin-Mourot, B. (1993) 'Comment les entreprises françaises et allemandes sélectionnet-elles leurs dirigeants?', *Problems Economiques*, N. 23337, 11 August, 14–17.

Crozier, M. (1963) *Le phénomène bureaucratique*. Paris: Seuil.

Evans, P. (1992) 'Management development as glue technology', *Human Resource Planning*, 15 (1): 85–106.

d'Iribarne, P. (1989) *La logique de l'honneur. Gestion des entreprises et traditions nationales*. Paris: Seuil.

Schuler, R.S., Dowling, P.J. and De Cieri, H. (1993) 'An integrative framework of strategic international human resource management', *International Journal of Human Resource Management* 4 (4): 717–64.

Postscript

During the final stages of this book's production Crédit Lyonnais entered a period of extreme financial difficulty, as have many other global banks, due to the collapse of real estate market and other property-related investments. As part of the 'bail-out' agreement for receiving fresh capital from the French government, European Union regulators required the bank to sell some of its extensive international network. Operations in South America and the Netherlands were among the first to be sold. This has put pressure on the bank to increase the profitability of its remaining network either to increase its potential selling price or to simply obtain a profit from its acquisitions. For organizations in competitive international markets nothing is static, except for the continued challenges of adapting to the demands of changing markets.

2

Glaverbel

Success story or realpolitik?

Armand Spineux and Evelyne Leonard

This case concerns a large Belgian company in the glass industry. The company underwent considerable difficulties during the 1970s which almost brought it to bankruptcy. However, it succeeded in achieving a turnaround and even further growth in the 1980s, with the aid of a thorough overhaul of its operating strategy, particularly with regard to its organization, production methods and approach to sales and management.

Today, Glaverbel is the foremost manufacturer of plate glass in the Benelux countries and the biggest plate glass manufacturer in Central Europe. To reach this position it has had to cope with numerous important changes affecting all areas of company activity: markets, products, technology and production methods, management structures and systems, labour policy, qualifications and human resource management.

The case retraces these main developments. In a very difficult situation, within specific environmental constraints, Glaverbel had to implement deep transformations in interconnected areas (strategy, organizational structure and culture, personnel management, etc.). The case aims to help students understand and analyse the complexity of organizational behaviour, human resource management and industrial relations in a change process.

Cultural context

Belgium is a small but complex country with a population of 10 million. Three national languages, two communities, three regions (Flanders, Wallonia and Brussels) and a web of institutional and interwoven powers have made Belgium a remarkable blend where highly convoluted political and institutional constructions in the legislative sector are matched by a striving for pragmatic management in the private sector.

Belgium is a rich country, but it has suffered significantly from the economic effects of the last decade's recession. The traditional and now obsolete industrial sectors have been forced to introduce comprehensive restructuring projects reducing employment, and to encourage vital, creative innovation leading to a new industrial network and completely new services.

The country has always been the centre of new movements, ideas and many kinds of influence. A crossroad of civilizations, scene of cultural shocks (the most obvious example is the confrontation between Latin and Germanic cultures, respectively represented in the French-speaking and Flemish parts of the country, each with its own history and identity), the country remains open to foreign influence and is able to distil from it those elements which are likely to improve its own specific model of existence. Recent 'invasions' have been of a peaceful and technological nature, and Belgium has been strong enough to resist temporary trends and to apply in a pragmatic way only those novelties which promise durable advantages. But another consequence of this attitude is an extremely slow process of change.

Belgians also know that in order to make an enterprise move forward, all its components should be taken into account, radical action should be avoided as much as possible, and negotiation should be the motto, always and everywhere. The phrase 'a compromise in the Belgian way' illustrates this attitude, which although prudent and often slow, is always down to earth.

The forces in place

The Belgian model of human resource management cannot be described without taking into consideration the fact that the rate of unionization is 70% – one of the highest rates worldwide and far above those of the neighbouring countries (for instance, union membership is about 10% in France, 23% in the Netherlands, and 39% in Germany, without former East Germany)[1].

Three consequences immediately emerge from this very strong union basis. The first is that employers and politicians recognize and accept trade unions. As a result of this legitimacy trade union organizations hold a strong position and are officially represented wherever the main lines of economic and social policy are set. The Central Council of the Economy, the National Labour Council, the highest levels of Social Security, the National Employment Office, the National Bank as well as the public credit institutions are only some of the most striking examples. Belgian unions, unlike those of some other European countries, are thus fully integrated into every important institutional policy-making body in the country. There, they not only have a power of recommendation and influence, but also a power of joint decision making with both employers' representatives and the State.[2]

The second consequence stems from the acknowledgement of trade union pluralism in Belgium as well as from the obligation of enterprises employing 50 people or more to establish a committee for safety, health and hygiene in the workplace. Likewise, enterprises with 100 or more employees are required to establish a works council. These two bodies function by the principle of equal representation (50% of the members representing the workforce, 50% representing the employer). This almost automatically entails the presence of one, but more often two and sometimes three major trade union organizations in the majority of Belgian enterprises (there are three major unions: the CSC (Confédération des Syndicats Chrétiens or, literally, Christian Trade Union Confederation); the FGTB (Fédération Générale des Travailleurs de Belgique, or socialist general federation of workers of Belgium); and the CGSLB (Confédération Générale des Syndicats Libéraux de Belgique, or general confederation of liberal trade unions of Belgium).

The third consequence is a direct outcome of the previous two and has a decisive impact on the human resource management model in Belgium. It relates to the establishment and operation of the system of industrial and professional relations. This system is based on collective bargaining between employers and workers' representatives, and the State recognizes that the so-called 'social partners' (that is, employers and unions) have autonomy to define together, through collective bargaining, a large part of the rules concerning the use of labour, at several levels: nation, plant and branch.

In this framework, regardless of the position of an enterprise towards the trade unions or collective bargaining as such, it is impossible for it to deviate from the constraints imposed by the system of industrial relations. Bargaining between representatives of the employers and trade union experts indeed takes place at three levels. The first level is nationwide bargaining. Agreements concluded at this level affect all enterprises and all workers in the country. The second is the branch or industry level (textiles, chemicals, steel, etc.). These agreements concern all companies in the particular industry involved in the negotiations. The third and final level is the individual company. Here, bargaining is a matter between the management and the shop stewards and the outcome only affects the workers at that company.

Typical of the system is that an agreement reached at branch level, or *a fortiori* at local level, must always be more beneficial to the worker than the agreement first concluded at the industry or nationwide level. For instance, if the guaranteed minimum wage is set at 100 for all workers in the nationwide agreement, it will amount to $100+x$ at the branch level and to $100+x+y$ at the company level in that branch.

Whereas a company is compelled to comply with the conditions determined by negotiations at a higher level, it is not obliged to offer conditions beyond those negotiated. Nevertheless, the strength of the trade unions and the competition among branches or companies have resulted in pressure for more, and what workers would call 'acquired rights', often being the rule.

This status of law ascribed to the agreements concluded by the social partners, but also the possibility for enterprises and unions of self-regulation of the system, have coloured human resource management in Belgium in a very particular way. The system is very well codified and for almost 30 years has governed industrial relations between employers and workers in Belgian companies, because of the agreements signed.

A company's autonomy in relation to human resource management is strongly limited by the agreements signed outside the framework of the company by representatives of each party. More often, the task of personnel departments tends to be limited to the mere administration of people and making sure that the company complies with prevailing agreements, labour and social law.

Little autonomy, little innovation and constant adjustment to new regulations emerging from agreements reached nationwide or at branch level have turned the personnel manager into an administration and law specialist. These 'working conditions' have hardly been conducive to the introduction of new human resource management policies, at least not in the theoretical and coherent manner described in many recent publications on personnel management.

It would be an overstatement to claim, however, that in view of the very long tradition of institutionalized collective bargaining, mostly outside the company, Belgium is marked by a bureaucratic form of personnel administration, hardly inclined to innovate. This would neglect the emergence of new ideas and policies for human resource management, supported by modern company managers who thus hope to meet the qualitative needs in the different personnel categories and to take advantage of this strong motivation lever in order to strengthen and improve the general productivity of the enterprise.

The social objectives of the company *vis-à-vis* its personnel are no longer looked on by management as only depending on whether the organization's financial situation is healthy. On the contrary, social and economic targets are now considered to be an integral part of the company's activities. They both have to be met in order to maintain a market position. For instance, management tries to encourage participation, to stimulate individuals' commitment to 'organizational culture', to develop competencies – using communication systems, training, performance appraisal, quality circles, etc. – not with some kind of 'paternalist' attitude, but as a way to generate performance. As in other countries, this modification in attitudes cannot be considered as the rule but, as John Storey and Keith Sisson notice, 'there are at the very least many fragments of evidence of a veritable shift in the approach to employment management'.[3]

The old adage prevailing in the 1960s and the 1970s that 'employers are primarily interested in economic goals – making profit – and trade unions are only interested in social progress as the redistribution of profits' is gradually being replaced by another point of view, notably that the enterprise's viability can only be safeguarded if all its members co-operate in the realization of general objectives, meaning that each party would better understand the other's needs and potential contribution to this joint construction.

Indicators of change

Human resource management has had to face much disruption resulting from major restructuring during the 1970s and 1980s. The economic crisis has hit many companies, leading to massive redundancies, unemployment and deterioration of the relationship between employers and unions.

International competition, technological change and development of new products and services are only some of the main indicators of thorough and irreversible change, and have produced two effects with direct impact on human resource management in Belgium since the early 1970s.

The first relates to changes in the composition of the labour market and in employers' demands for qualifications. In this respect some very contrasting situations have occurred, where on the one hand huge reserves of labour remain unutilized and on the other companies' demands for highly qualified workers remain unsatisfied.

The second is the weakening of the traditional system of bargaining, the exhaustion of the logic of redistribution of quantitative advantages (wages, holidays, social protection, etc.) and crumbling internal consensus among trade unions (blue vs white collar, private vs public sector, employed vs unemployed workers, etc.) as well as among employers (large corporations vs SMEs (small manufacturing enterprises), Belgian vs foreign companies, etc.).

Particularly in the late 1980s, these two important effects – together with the search (linked to new market conditions) for flexibility, decentralization, simpler organizational structures where individuals are performing their jobs more independently – have paved the way for a new issue in the negotiations: more weight is given to quality and the individual; and the negotiations at company level have gained importance while national and branch bargaining has lost some significance and substance.

The situation of Glaverbel in the 1970s and 1980s was representative of the crisis many Belgian firms underwent in those years, particularly in industrial sectors functioning with obsolete equipment and production methods. To survive the recession, the company had to combine revised strategic orientations, intended to answer to new environmental conditions, with deep but progressive transformations on the shopfloor, adapted to the specific situations of a factory in the Belgian context.

The Glaverbel case illustrates this capacity of Belgian management to implement original solutions with pragmatism, and can be extrapolated to many other Belgian firms that try to achieve, in their policies, a difficult reconciliation between environmental challenges and specific national or regional constraints.

Glaverbel: transformations in context and strategies

Created in 1961 from the merger between two large plate-glass manufacturers, Glaverbel became the world's leading producer of blank glass during the 1960s. Those were the 'Golden Sixties', during which the company's various factories made profits by selling mainly glazing glass and cut glass.

At the beginning of the 1970s the company had eight factories in Belgium, employing some 10,000 people, in addition to the many subsidiaries in which it had a controlling interest, in Belgium as well as abroad.

In 1972, Glaverbel was taken over by the French group BSN. At that time production of glazing glass constituted its main activity, but it was evident that glazing glass would disappear, to be replaced by float glass (one float produces twice as much with less than half the labour required for a glazing glass furnace). In 1972, it was hoped that this changeover would be slow and gradual. The oil crisis and rapid inflation in Belgium were to precipitate the disappearance of glazing glass furnaces and placed Glaverbel in serious crisis.

Affecting the plate-glass industry in the 1970s there was, in addition to important technological changes, a drastic drop in consumption of glass products because of the recession in the building and automobile industries. A reduction in sales prices occurred at the same time as increases in production costs owing to the rise in oil prices, pay awards and transportation costs.

As observed in a company document:

> in this context, Glaverbel was particularly vulnerable due to the fact that its activities were mainly centred on basic products with a very considerable proportion of drawn glass, which consumed large amounts of oil and were very labour-intensive. Moreover, with regard to competitors abroad, the company was burdened with heavy commitments to rising salaries because they were automatically linked to the rate of inflation in Belgium, which at that time was galloping.[4]

Five years of consecutive losses brought the company to the brink of bankruptcy in 1979. A profound restructuring along with a sizeable reduction in its workforce between 1975 and 1985 allowed the company to stabilize.

In 1981, BSN sold Glaverbel to the leading Japanese glass manufacturer Asahi Glass. Belonging to the BSN group had given the company a European dimension and financial resources, but it had imposed restraints on Glaverbel, particularly with regard to exports in Europe because of the co-existence within the same group of French and German factories. Becoming part of Asahi Glass not only helped financially, but above all gave the company independence in management matters and complete liberty on the European market.

The takeover of Glaverbel by Asahi Glass was crucial to the survival of the company for many reasons:

- Asahi Glass furnished the company with the financial means to obtain indispensable but very costly production equipment (for float glass).
- Asahi Glass's significant outlay of capital for the restructuring and modernization of equipment demonstrated not only that Glaverbel alone was unable to finance the changes, but also that the need for change was immediate to deal with better equipped competitors.
- Asahi Glass became the main shareholder in the Belgian company, but its policy from the beginning was to leave an entirely autonomous Belgian management team without imposing any 'Japanese management method'. In human resource management matters, particularly, in which the 'Japanese model' might seem superior, Asahi Glass had no influence on Glaverbel and

the latter had to develop its own policies in relation to its specific characteristics and context.

- Moreover, the Japanese group enabled the Belgian company to expand in the European market, something which neither the English, the French, nor the former majority shareholders had been able to accept because of their respective positions in the European market.

This situation of economic crisis and struggle for survival was accompanied by massive layoffs. Even though these dismissals provoked intense conflicts, they were always resolved without driving the company into the ground. This illustrates how crucial the survival of the company was in the eyes of the principal union negotiators.

So in the 1980s Glaverbel became the centre of development activities for the Japanese group with a situation of renewed growth, while the competing companies in Europe had been changed by the break-up of BSN and independent glass processing firms appeared and prospered in the industry. Glaverbel then pursued a strategy of redeploying its activities. In 1987 it was quoted for the first time on the stock exchange in Brussels and at the end of the 1980s it embarked on a phase of growth and globalization.

Today, Glaverbel is the foremost manufacturer of plate glass in the Benelux countries, the third largest producer of plate glass in Europe and the European leader in specific market niches. Through international expansion and its acquisitions, it has also become the largest manufacturer in Central Europe and the second biggest in North America.

Between the middle of the 1970s and the beginning of the 1980s, during the crisis years and those which followed, the Group experienced numerous important changes, affecting all areas of activity: markets, products, technology and production methods, management structures and systems, labour policy, qualifications and human resource management. These changes involved the whole Group, but they were also adapted in the factories according to their individual characteristics.

'To deal with its structural weakness, Glaverbel decided in 1973 to diversify into glass processing by buying up companies specialising in this field . . . In 1977 however, the company's extremely critical situation demanded that radical measures be taken at various levels.'[5] In 1977, a new Managing Director, Jean-Marie Descarpentries, took control of the company with a new management team. Today, although he has now left Glaverbel, Descarpentries is still regarded as the one who conceived the industrial and commercial 'vision' which enabled the company to make its turnaround. That vision was pursued, sustained and adapted by his successor as head of the company, Philippe Bodson. In the words of one the company's executives, the staff thought it was 'the only way out; people were convinced that restructuring was a condition for the company's survival'.

This restructuring had several dimensions:

- Industrially speaking, its activities ceased, new equipment was developed (floats) and processing activities assumed a position of importance.

- Commercially speaking, priority was given to European markets which were nearby and profitable (France, Germany, the Netherlands, etc.), as well as to selling glass products tailormade to more specific needs (insulating glass, security glass, etc.) and with high added value.
- At the corporate level, the objective was to reduce the cost of wages and salaries in relation to the turnover by reducing the number of employees, by training them to use new equipment and by adopting a policy of salary moderation. On matters of labour relations, company management and factory chiefs developed a systematic policy of dialogue with the trade unions.
- Linked to a desire for decentralization, from 1978 a new system of management by business units (BU) was established. Replacing the former management by production units (in which production planning, finance, relations with customers, control systems, etc. were organized plant by plant), the business unit system is centred on the main activities of the Glaverbel Group. One BU covers one kind of activity (float glass, processed glass for construction, processed glass for the automobile industry, etc.) with its specific market, its particular technology and know-how; one BU can include several plants that produce the same kind of products. This system aims to generate more coherence and decentralization in decision, information and control processes. The business unit's managers and experts can rapidly put together a coherent set of information on the market situation and react appropriately with decisions on finance, human resource, marketing or production processes that affect the particular activity globally (even if this activity is carried out in different plants of the group in Belgium and abroad). With this management system, the emphasis is thus on rapid communication with the market and across the Group, so as to enable quick reactions.
- Finally, with regard to finance, it was a matter of reducing costs and increasing cash flow and capital, enabling the company gradually to ensure economic independence.

Putting these strategies into operation enabled the company to return to positive results in 1980, after five years of heavy losses. At the beginning of the 1980s these strategies were maintained and pursued further under the direction of the new Managing Director, Philippe Bodson. He continued the process instigated by his predecessor: industrial restructuring centred on specialization within the factories with the aid of heavy investment, concentrating sales in European countries, increasing sales of processed and specific products, reducing the number of employees, pay moderation and increasing turnover.

After becoming part of the Asahi Glass group, Glaverbel became the Japanese group's European centre for the company's activities. From 1983, the strategy had five central tenets:

- to pursue the development of European activities in the building and automobile industries (with new equipment, modernizing existing equipment, a partnership agreement with an Italian company for automobiles, and re-organizing automobile glass activities);

- to maintain the company's image as a leader in technology (by developing products with high added value, or those less subject to the vicissitudes of the economic situation, or products with special properties, such as glass for the electronics or computer industries or non-reflective glass, etc.);
- to increase sales of sophisticated products such as coloured float glass for export overseas (that is, outside Western Europe, where 80% of sales were concentrated);
- to achieve a cash flow which would enable industrial and research investments to be made (investments in new technologies, workshop modernization, development of sophisticated products, etc.) and to continue improving the structure of the balance sheet;
- to give greater job satisfaction to staff and enable them to increase their skills, while 'maintaining the payroll within limits which did not compromise the company's competitiveness'. The emphases were on individual motivation and job satisfaction, linked in particular to the launch of participative management; by the same token, shareholdings by workers in Glaverbel SA were encouraged.

In the years during which this redeployment strategy was being put into operation, the company saw its results improve and its introduction on the stock exchange in 1987 was considered a success.

In 1988, a new strategy for growth and internationalization was launched. This strategy aimed to give the Group a multi-national dimension, with a stronger implantation abroad, not only in Western Europe but also in North America and Central Europe, mainly by means of acquisition of existing companies and the construction of a new plant. More precisely, this strategy comprised five major orientations:

- maintaining competitiveness in existing activities (by investment aiming at continuously improving productivity in all types of activity: for example, investments in the latest float technology, improvement of thin and extra-thin glass processes, etc.);
- increasing specific activities: the need to strengthen the company's presence in buoyant activities or growing markets (such as the car industry, computer disks, etc.), supported by investments in equipment or for re-organizing production output and improving quality;
- the acquisition of already established companies with a view to responding to the globalization of markets for glass by establishing the Group's presence in the various large markets where it operates (in particular spinning off the Glavunion company, created out of a joint venture with a Czech glass manufacturing company, representing the first privatization in Czechoslovakia), and the construction of a float-glass factory in Quebec;
- the conclusion of partnership agreements, to set in motion a strategy of geographical diversification of the Group's activities (for example with a

German group, Schott Glaswerke, for manufacturing glass products for electrical household goods in particular);

- research on higher commitment, on the part of employees, to the organization and to the job, in order to stimulate the performance: instigating management and human resource policies aimed at 'greater self-fulfilment for everyone', participative management, training, communication.

Human resources and human resource management policies

In less than 20 years, Glaverbel has undergone some major changes. As far as human resources are concerned, these transformations have primarily been reflected in the considerable reduction in the company workforce and in the development of human resource management policies, among which communication, participative management and the specific concept of negotiation in collective bargaining hold pride of place.

Development of the workforce

The restructuring effected during the crisis years (1975–82) entailed a large number of redundancies in the company. In 1975, the Glaverbel Group employed 9400 people, of whom more than 8000 were in Belgium and of these 6300 were blue-collar workers (that is, 76% of the workforce).

In 1982, 5000 people were left in the Group, of which 4400 were in Belgium and of these, 3400 were blue-collar workers (or 77% of the workforce). In seven years, the number of company employees in Belgium had thus decreased by almost half.[6]

These large cutbacks were the result of the profound restructuring of company activities: a halt to activities, shutting down the glazing glass furnaces, factory closures, replacement of old production systems with new equipment, technological modernization, development of sub-contracting and a policy of reducing labour costs. In total, seven modern and specialized industrial units replaced 17 outdated workshops in 1982.

No part of the Group escaped redundancies: during the restructuring period, one person in two left the company at all levels. These redundancies were not achieved without opposition from the unions, sometimes involving fierce battles.

Union reaction to Glaverbel's decisions varied from one factory to another, depending on a range of factors which aroused varying degrees of vigorous opposition to the redundancies:

- The extent of the restructuring planned for the factory, and thus the number of redundancies envisaged by the management, naturally influenced the reactions of the workers. Shutting down the glazing glass furnaces in 1974 and 1975 (five furnaces shut down in two years), which was accompanied by a large number of redundancies and inevitable changes in jobs, gave rise to bitter conflicts (strikes, factory sit-ins, etc.).

- Union culture in the factory also played a role in the development and extent of the conflicts, as did regional union culture. For example, in the region of Charleroi, where there is a strong union tradition, certain factories experienced collective conflicts which were longer and more difficult to resolve than in other company factories located in other regions.
- The period in which the number of workers was reduced also influenced, to a lesser degree, the type of union reaction to management decisions: after the 'golden sixties', restructuring was an exceptional phenomenon, something new, not easily accepted by workers accustomed to relatively stable employment and regular increases in salary granted by an economy of growth and positive results. In 1975, Glaverbel was the first large company to close a factory and at that time 'the minds were not ready for it', said Mme Gillot, Director Corporate Management Development and Communication. For this reason, the restructuring was difficult to admit, by the company's workers as much as by the political authorities or the unions.
- The unions' strong reactions were also a result of the lack of a tradition of dialogue between company executives with workers' representatives and of communication within the structure as a whole.

The ensuing battles in the factories ended in the conclusion of collective labour agreements negotiated by the employers and the unions and, in some cases, the public authorities. In particular, these agreements set out the number of early retirements (for some factories, early retirement by the age of 50 for men, or by the age of 47 for women), the creation of social funds for workers affected by restructuring, retraining programmes or individual placement in other companies.

For the company, the bilateral (employer–unions) or tripartite (with the addition of the public authorities) agreements entailed considerable costs at the very time when its results were negative and it had to make investments in order to achieve recovery. It was during this period that the company's management began to introduce and develop a communication policy aimed initially at restoring the external company image and regaining the staff's confidence, while other human resource management policies were gradually being organized for the Group as a whole.

Human resource management policies

In 1975 the company management decided to develop external and internal communication strategies systematically in order to explain both the urgency and necessity of the restructuring on which they were embarking. Simultaneously, other human resource management policies were being developed and systematized across the Group under the impetus of general management: management by objectives, permanent training for all staff categories, participative management (from 1982). A systematic policy of dialogue with the unions was also gradually implemented throughout the Group. These policies were based on three key themes: communication, participation and partnership.

It is important to note that from 1975 to the present these policies have accompanied the transformation of jobs and a general increase in qualifications in the glass-making industry, together with numerous changes implemented in the products and methods of production.

Communication During the worst part of the crisis, in 1974–5, a general climate of mistrust with regard to company management set in, both among the staff and the public at large, and this was sustained by the unions and the media in particular.

As a reaction to this, the general management decided to implement a policy of communication designed to restore confidence. It must be noted that 'communication' here does not only refer to information 'tools' or techniques but also, and mainly, to a global process, generated by the top management in relation to the company's strategies, including the content of messages and policies implemented in the firm in terms of information and interactions between its members.

As discussed above, this preoccupation with communication arose after the closure of a factory. At that time, Glaverbel was the first company in Belgium to restructure and close a factory, and this unfortunate privilege met with no sympathy and caused negative reactions from all quarters. Assisted by an external consultant, the Group's management instigated a policy of communication in 1975 which was to develop from 1977 onwards. This policy was primarily geared to external relations: it aimed to explain to the press and the public at large the necessity and reasons for restructuring.

In 1977, the communication department was expanded to handle both external and internal communication. Up to that time, it was the unions and the press who mostly enjoyed the confidence of personnel. During the first few years of restructuring, the executives became aware that the changes would fail if staff opposed or did not support them, just as they could not be accomplished without at least a minimum of confidence in relations with the unions with whom they had to negotiate and consult. From that time on, communication was to be considered a necessary condition for implementing the changes.

Under the impetus of the new Managing Director, the communication department acquired a 'strategic' role in 1977: it was henceforth to have direct representation on the Executive Board, and its mission was to transmit the messages and actions of 'top management' throughout the organization. From this perspective, communication was not only considered a human resource management policy, but more generally a global policy for supporting the company strategy.

Thus a policy of systematic information was developed by the management, on strategies, policies and results, for the personnel as a whole, including executive staff, those in the various factories and the union representatives. Different media were used (written 'flashes', written documents, slides, meetings, etc.), whose main focuses were speed and keeping in touch with people. According to Mme Gillot, 'we had to be in close contact with people all the time and perform as well as the press', in order to be perceived as credible among the staff and facilitate a quick implementation of the changes required by the restructuring programme.

Today, it is generally acknowledged that communication played a crucial rule during these changes because it helped the various members of the company to understand and accept the strategies. For instance, the systematic informing of union representatives generated interactions between management and unions which sometimes led to negotiations on the conditions of change before its implementation (and not only on its consequences), allowing conflicts to be avoided.

The efficiency of communications remained nonetheless dependent on certain details in the process which required particular attention: the necessity to monitor components of the information process (validity of information, methods used, results obtained); the importance of consistency between the information issued by executives and staff's perception of their work situation; the necessity of considering communication as a continual process that had to be sustained and stimulated incessantly.

Thus, from 1977 the company implemented a staff communication policy. In 1978, an important change in the management system also had substantial consequences for communication: management by business units. It became important to communicate results across the Group rapidly, facilitating immediate reactions. Management by business units was therefore accompanied by direct communication between factories and with head office, enabling the Group and the factories to react faster to the results obtained. For example, each month the BU managers would meet in an 'Operational Committee' in Brussels to exchange information and make decisions concerning the company's situation, product lines, factory results, etc. In parallel with this, direct departmental liaisons were developed. For example, sales executives from different business units could establish direct relations with each other, without necessarily going through their superiors or through head office as had been the practice before.

Overall, a global information and communication process was gradually put in place between the different factories and with head office, parallel to that between management and personnel in the Group.

'Participation' as a managerial approach At the beginning of the 1980s, the company management realized that communication was not enough to make Glaverbel recover; what was primarily required was the support of the people at the bottom. At the same time, management wanted to prepare itself for the 'new worker', based on the conviction that the expectations and qualifications of the industrial workers of the 1990s would be different from those of workers before the crisis.

Company executives decided at the beginning of the redeployment phase to instigate 'participative management'. Its objective was to 'link everyone to the realization of fixed objectives, by involving his/her creativity and thus providing for greater personal development and job satisfaction'.

This would be implemented gradually, with one basic principle: at all levels (factories, departments, services, individuals) employees were free to choose whether or not they wanted to participate. The idea of 'participative management' was first to be tested in two pilot factories before extending it to the Group as a whole.

The 'tools' of basic participative management were 'progress circles', envisaged as a means of promoting active participation by all the collaborators in the Group's redeployment, aimed at encouraging individual responsibility simultaneously with the decentralization of management.

Progress circles are composed of three to six people, all volunteers, with a leader, who choose a problem to deal with that they have encountered in their work and who meet during working hours to work out a solution to it. In the words of Mme Gillot, 'The interesting thing about this formula is studying a problem with a method, offering solutions, presenting them to the managers and, after a decision has been made, participating in their implementation and assessing their efficacy. It's therefore a motivating way for getting a thorough grip on a problem and dealing with it efficiently.'

In the factories, co-ordination of progress circles is ensured by a 'pilot committee' and a 'facilitator'; at the Group level, general co-ordination of the programme is run by an 'orientation committee' and a 'co-ordinator'. In this way, the work in every progress circle is supported by a structure that can assist it in case of difficulty and that guarantees the homogeneity of the participation experience in the various production units of the Group. The Board of Management, the highest managerial organ in the firm, is considered to be the initiator of this project of primary importance.

At the launch of these progress circles and during their gradual implementation, participating employees and leaders received training (on team working, problem-solving methods, etc.).

But how did the unions react to the project and to the introduction of participative management? At the beginning of the 1980s, the unions admitted that restructuring was essential for survival. The search for consensus guided relations between management and the unions on the participative management project, and the unions committed themselves to supporting the management project with a series of conditions aimed principally at maintaining the specific roles and responsibilities of the management and the union representatives. Thus it was possible to put the whole project in place in the Group without any strikes.

However, the difficulties came mainly from middle management who feared that they might lose some of their authority. If the workers they are supposed to command meet together in progress circles to analyse production problems and send on solutions to the top management, what will be the role of middle managers? Is it possible for them to reconcile a management and commanding role with workers' participation and expression? The implementation of the participation programme thus brought questions and some uncertainty for this category of employees and, for this reason, it received little support from them.

In 1988, participative management was integrated in a project entitled 'Quality and Participation', launched throughout the Group with a view to 'strengthening economic performance by performance in labour relations'.

At the beginning of the 1990s, participative management was considered by its instigator as a great success: 'We never envisaged participative management as a production technique; . . . the reference was the role of the company and the new worker. That's the reason why it has worked. People's support resulted from the conviction that the top management's priorities were the respect and the integration of individuals.'

Nevertheless, at this time the experiment was only being extended gradually and not all the personnel chose to participate. Moreover, certain limits on participative management have not been ignored:

- according to factory managers, participative management does not mean participation in decision making, and one should not be confused with the other: problems must be discussed, but the final decision rests with the superior, whatever level he or she is at;
- it also appeared to certain factory managers that a human resource management policy by itself could not change the performance of people if there is not an environment at work that offers the employees the chance to improve their performance.

Finally, it appeared to everyone that, in a project such as participative management, what was important was not having a large number of progress circles, but implanting the change on the shopfloor, in the daily routines and practices for this, a continuous effort over the long term was necessary. In parallel with this, a 'participative spirit' was created, which expressed itself in daily activities, independently of the progress circle procedures and the guidance structure: for example, when there was a problem, the people concerned met directly with each other to try and resolve it, 'and that comes from the close-knit framework of the progress circles'.

Partnership Collective labour relations in the 1960s and 1970s were characterized by peaceful co-existence: 'those were the good old days', said one factory manager. A growing economy and a favourable situation enabled factory managers – who at that time were much more isolated in relation to the Group – to satisfy the unions: 'labour relations were good because the situation was good and we were able to agree on everything with the unions'. Peace was maintained in labour relations in exchange for increases in pay and guaranteed employment. The unions, being satisfied with the state of affairs, received minimal information on economic development from the management.

The company survived the crisis with thorough restructuring, accompanied by a large number of redundancies and a policy of pay restraint. But redundancies and pay restraint could not have been achieved in any of the Group's factories in Belgium, bearing in mind the industrial relations framework in that country, without the consultation and co-operation of the unions. This is why, from the end of the 1970s, general management noted the importance 'of a policy of dialogue with the unions for establishing a consensus in labour relations. The search for consensus was henceforth to be given priority in the human resource and labour relations strategy in the firm.'[7]

From 1975–7 onwards, after a period marred by labour disputes which were sometimes very bitter – particularly in the region of Charleroi – the search for consensus and a systematic policy of dialogue with the unions were defined as components forming an integral part of the Group's policy.

In reality, consensus is almost obligatory in the Belgian context:

- labour relations are to a large extent determined and strongly regulated by collective agreements concluded after negotiations between employers and unions within individual companies, but also and above all within industrial sectors and at national level covering all sectors;
- the glass manufacturing sector has a workforce which is 90% unionized;
- if there are to be collective redundancies, the employer is obliged to negotiate terms for them;
- Glaverbel moreover had several factories in the region of Charleroi during the 1970s, a region characterized by a strong union culture and powerful control by union organizations over the personnel in those factories.

Group management and factory managers were therefore not in a position to carry out restructuring without negotiating the conditions with the unions.

Glaverbel's originality resides primarily in the fact that the search for consensus was defined as a component of the strategy and this brought about an important policy of information with regard to the unions, which has been systematically practised since the beginning of the 1980s.

Under the impetus of the Director of Human and Labour Relations, Robert Wauters, the unions were regarded, among the various Group factories, as 'economic partners and competitors in labour relations'; and as reliable mediators, whose logic for functioning was geared towards success, as was that of the company. According to Wauters, 'union activity is a commercial business whose success is measured by the number of members'.

From this perspective, important information practices were developed during the 1980s:

- information given to all the executives throughout the Group, with the purpose of altering their perception of union activity and to get them to consider that 'the union is a partner just like any other';
- development of contacts between factory managers and union representatives (factory delegates, but also members of union bodies at regional or national level). The aim of these contacts was to exchange points of view and respective concerns of the representatives, and to try to reach a common standpoint;
- systematic information given to workers' representatives: for example, the 'permanent' union representatives automatically receive any information destined for factory personnel; there are meetings between the regional and

national 'permanent' union representatives, to present the main strategic directions to them, with the participation of the Director General of Glaverbel.

All of these practices made it possible to create and maintain a climate of confidence between factory managements and the unions, in which relations were established between representatives who could be mutually trusted to look for consensus in labour relations.

The factories

How were the general strategies and human resource management policies, as defined by Glaverbel's management, implemented in the various factories at the ground level? What changes did the restructuring and redeployment phases entail in the Group's production and processing units? The main changes effected in three of the Group's factories in Belgium are briefly described in the following pages.

Each of these factories, through the nature of its products, customers, etc., has its own characteristics or specific circumstances. Throughout the modifications effected between 1975 and 1992 in each of these factories, their specific characteristics were maintained, sometimes amplified, sometimes reduced. The strategies defined for the Group as a whole were applied by each factory in accordance with local requirements.

However, the implementation of the changes in each of the units cannot be understood independently from the rest of the Group. The operation was therefore dual: on the one hand, the main directions for change were decided on and implemented for the Group as a whole; on the other, each factory integrated these directions at the ground level in accordance with its own particular characteristics – for example, by emphasizing certain human resource management policies. At the same time, we can see an integration of the factories in relation to the Group and a real autonomy for the factory managers on the ground. How can this be explained?

First of all, this duality is linked to the possibility for factory managers of negotiating in part the implementation of the changes with general management: the latter defines the strategies for the Group as a whole, but the factory managers can negotiate their implementation taking local circumstances into account (for example, when introducing participative management each factory emphasized different topics or decided to start the progress circles later than others). In other words, general strategies only make sense if they allow for effective application on the ground, which requires allowances to be made for each factory's individual limitations and opportunities. The three factories presented below exemplify this approach.

Secondly, the introduction of management by business units in 1978 had an important impact on relations between the factories and the Group. At the beginning of the 1970s, the various factories functioned in an isolated way. Management by business units strongly reduced this isolation, even if it was only because one type of activity (one business) does not necessarily correspond to a single glass production or processing site. That is, a business unit corresponds to a specific product line (for example, double-glazing), which has a well-defined market and the same kind of customers. Management by business units was accompanied by a greater decentralization in decision making linked to development in lateral communication – between factories – and vertical communication – between factories and head office. As a result, the factories lost their autonomy as distinct entities within the Group, but they gained autonomy as sources of special knowledge available to the Group as a whole. This relative autonomy enabled them to put into operation the orientations defined by general management in accordance with their particular situations.

We might note that Glaverbel was able to make these very profound changes and succeed particularly because a clear 'vision' formulated by general management was accepted at ground level, and precisely because this vision could be translated and adapted to the local situation.

Moustier: 'float glass production at the service of the Group'

Some figures In 1975, the factory at Moustier was producing about 1000 tonnes a day of float glass, with two float lines (the first built in 1964 and the second started operating in 1974). At that time the factory employed 956 people (Table 2.1).

In 1991, 774 remained working on three float-glass production lines (632 blue-collar and 142 white-collar staff), producing about 1700 tonnes per day (the third line was started in September 1989). By December 1993, there were 650 people working on the three floats. In four years (from 1989 to 1993), BF 6.5 billion was invested in this unit.

In terms of markets, Moustier is the primary glass supplier for all the manufacturing and processing units of the Glaverbel Group and its subsidiaries (building and automobile). Float glass is also sold directly to customers outside the Group, essentially in Europe. With three float-glass lines, this factory is the Group's largest glass production unit. It is also the largest in Europe.

Developments since the beginning of the 1970s During the 'golden sixties', when all the Group's units were making large profits, Moustier was the only factory to produce very high-quality cut glass, but the manufacturing processes were extemely energy consuming (fuel) and labour intensive (unskilled labour/

Table 2.1 *Moustier: workforce evolution*

Year	Workers	Clerical and executive staff	Total
1975	811	145	956
1982	763	124	887
1991	632	142	774

'strong arms'). At that time there were two ways of making glass: 'glazing glass' (window glass), and 'cut glass' (in French, literally 'polished glass', *verre poli*) which gave a distinguished product, although it was more expensive because of the polishing operation it required.

Pilkington had invented a new method for glass manufacturing – float glass (glass floated on molten tin) – which was going to revolutionize the glass industry; the first production of this kind was launched in England in 1961. In 1964, Moustier acquired its first float unit to replace its cut-glass process.

The float process had been perfected to replace 'cut glass', but after some development it would also be competing in a few years with the 'glazing-glass' process. However, it was not until 1970 that everybody realized that the future of the glass industry, and Glaverbel in particular, could not be planned without float technology, despite the very considerable investment cost of installing it (BF 3.5 billion for one float). According to the Director of the Moustier factory, 'it's never easy to want to change when everything's going well . . . It's even more difficult to actually do it.'

When Glaverbel joined BSN, it was decided to build a second float, which began operating at Moustier in 1974. At that time, Glaverbel lagged considerably behind its competitors (Saint-Gobain in France and Pilkington in the UK), who had had to replace their cut-glass furnaces and who, because of this, had the edge over Glaverbel, which was still strongly rooted in glazing glass. The oil crisis dealt a severe blow to the company which was then still using many traditional furnaces which were heavy energy consumers. Furthermore, labour costs, which were very high in Belgian factories compared to foreign competitors, was yet another obstacle for the company in keeping an even footing and caused a considerable loss of competitiveness in exports. Under these very difficult conditions only one factory in the Group – Moustier – managed to make a profit, thanks to its two floats, enabling the Group as a whole to survive. In the mid-1970s, this factory was therefore the company's 'cash cow'. 'At Moustier, we had a spirit of independence from the Group', noted one of its members.

For these reasons, the Moustier factory escaped the heavy restructuring (changes in technology, massive redundancies) and closures which affected other factories in the Group, some of which were located only a few kilometres away. In spite of this, however, it still had to take part in the restructuring by closing a double-glazing unit; its activities were transferred to another site. According to Mme Gillot, 'That unit was relatively small and closing it down was in some sense a symbol of solidarity.'

In contrast to other factories in the Group, labour relations were usually good and discussions were possible, even though union membership was as high as in the other Group factories in other regions of the country (about 90% of the non-executive workforce). This state of affairs was very different from that which operated in certain other Group factories at the time, where violent confrontations were not uncommon, and it is fundamentally attributed to three factors by Glaverbel's members:

1. a difference of attitude in workers coming from a region where there is less opposition between workers and management, Namur (situated less than 25 kilometres from Charleroi where restructuring and redeployment were implemented in an extremely difficult climate for labour relations);
2. a situation which required fewer radical changes in activities (for example, while other factories were closing down the glazing-glass furnaces, Moustier was expanding);
3. an existing tradition of discussion, onto which were grafted the policies of communication and participative management initiated by the Group.

Thus, in terms of labour relations Moustier 'was in a class of its own' – which is apparent in the fact that this factory never experienced serious strikes.

Keeping its own culture while integrating with Group objectives The Moustier factory therefore suffered less from the effects of restructuring than did other Group factories. However, rather than shutting itself off with an attitude of independence and paternalism, Moustier – strong in its technology and its support for others during difficult times – was to integrate the new objectives defined by the Group's general management by applying the following policies:

- concentrating activities on float-glass manufacturing, which in the factory meant increased sub-contracting, outsourcing certain jobs and thus reducing the workforce;
- strengthening sales policies for Europe, with help from the Group in finding new European markets;
- a noticeable increase in the qualifications of its personnel, which was achieved at Moustier through important training programmes, retiring unskilled workers early (early pension at 52) and taking on much better trained young people;
- the definition in the Group of a system of management by business units, in consequence of which the strategic choices and localization of new investment were approved or orientated by the Group's general management. Once these were decided on, however, the factories enjoyed greater autonomy in running their own affairs.

All these policies gave Moustier more advantages than disadvantages:

- recognition of its role of principal float-glass producer in the Group;
- recognition of its greater know-how in matters of float-glass production over other factories, in the Netherlands, Quebec and the Czech Republic;
- relative autonomy of the factory's management and facilitation of relations with head office.

The application of Group strategies, however, was not achieved without difficulties for the factory. Management and factory personnel had to accept:

- redundancies linked to a re-centering on the basic job and modernization of equipment (the new floats produced greater output with fewer personnel);
- the limitation and obligation of being the glass manufacturer for all the

factories (for glass working) of the Group and of being subject to their quality requirements, which became increasingly stringent;
- international competition within the Group itself, in particular after Glaverbel was joined by the Czech factory Glavunion, where labour costs were lower overall but productivity was also lower.

Human resource management policies From the mid-1970s onwards, the Group's general management insisted on strengthening communication with and giving information to unions and workers, as well as on participative management. What did this mean for Moustier?

Here, as in other factories, members of the Group management team (General Manager, Head of Communication, Director of Human and Labour Relations) came to explain the main thrust of their policy: the importance of communication; dialogue with union representatives ('the union is an economic partner and a competitor in labour relations'); an end to unrealistic, and therefore unrealizable, promises and collective agreements; raising qualifications and job adaptability; quality management; participative management.

If, in other Group factories, considerable work had to be done in terms of communication to restore the confidence between workers and management which had largely evaporated, at Moustier the efforts made towards communication mainly brought about the practice of reciprocal information and discussion on the strategic choices implemented by general management, as well as a clarification of the factory's situation within this general policy.

Management by business units was accepted rather easily for several reasons: the desire to communicate the objectives was manifest within the Group; Moustier's position had not changed; and the acceptance of the 'BU system' permitted more autonomous management in the plant within the framework of the objectives determined for the factory.

As regards collective labour relations, dialogue with union representatives already existed, but went from being conducted in a paternalistic, easy-going way (in the context of a favourable economic situation the management, in order to preserve real peace in labour relations, granted many advantages) to a more rigorous fashion between partners mutually regarding one another as equals ('Knowing all the details of the economic situation, let us find a mutual consensus which will enable the factory to survive.')

As for participative management, its success and impact at Moustier will have to be qualified. For the factory managers, it was not the number and activities of the progress circles as such which were important, but rather the 'participative spirit' which was created – that is, the search for dialogue, the desire to discuss in order to reach the best solution to problems: 'When there is a problem, we get round the table to resolve it.' The increase in qualification levels and the precise definition of everyone's tasks facilitating the sharing of responsibility was a distinct advantage to this mode of operation. For those same managers, the limits of participative management were to be found in a very clear explanation of the concept, itself to the benefit of good communication. According to the Director of the Moustier factory, 'The management hierarchy, thanks to participative management, must have access to the maximum amount of pertinent information possible, so that the decision reached will be the best possible – technically and in terms of acceptability – but it is the line manager who takes the decision and who monitors its execution.'

The introduction of participative management at the factory met with some difficulties, however:

- The tools of participation (progress circles) ran out of steam. What was important was to maintain the 'spirit' of the initiative, for instance forming groups to solve problems or to prepare projects, without necessarily respecting the procedures of progress circles.
- There was fear on the part of middle management that they would lose authority and see their role reduced in the proposed new way of operating.
- Constant involvement by all the levels of the hierarchy was required in transmitting information from top to bottom. Management and middle management had to explain and translate the general policies and the 'Group notion' on the factory floor; they were also responsible for warning the factory director's team about sensitivities, incomprehension, or demands coming from the factory floor.

Finally, since 1988, these policies have been implemented in parallel with the strategy of internationalization for the Group and the investments made in Quebec and the Czech Republic, which aroused new fears among the personnel at Moustier as to their continued employment.

Lodelinsart: 'in difficult situations, seize the opportunity to regain confidence'

Some figures In the mid-1970s, the factory at Lodelinsart was strongly affected by the restructuring imposed by the Group on its various production units. Its main equipment, a vertical-drawn glazing-glass furnace, one of the oldest manufacturing processes in the industry, was finally shut down in 1975 and gradually replaced by other activities generating higher added value.

The consequent reduction in the workforce (Table 2.2) was achieved in a very difficult climate of labour relations and accompanied by many disputes, which established for the Lodelinsart factory a reputation of being the 'black sheep' in the eyes of the Group's top management.

By 1993, after a 'turbulent adventure in labour relations' (in the words of

Table 2.2 *Lodelinsart: workforce evolution*

Year	Workers	Clerical and executive staff	Total
1975	457	84	541
1982	432	74	506
1991	295	76	371

Mme Gillot), Lodelinsart had gradually been divesting itself of this negative reputation and was concentrating its activities on glass processing, in particular double-glazing and special glass (vacuum-sealed double-glazing), mainly for the prestige building market.

Specifics of the Lodelinsart factory Since the beginning of the crisis, the factory has been in a state of 'permanent restructuring': it has had to accept numerous transfers of its activities to other sites, just as it has had to integrate a certain number of new activities involving radical changes in technology and qualifications.

The concentration at Lodelinsart of activities coming from other factories has been coupled with the re-integration of groups of workers coming from factories about to close down and who found a chance to remain employed at Lodelinsart. As the Head of Human and Labour Relations at the Lodelinsart factory noticed, 'These transferees often had a difficult time, the factory no longer had its own culture but an agglomeration of sub-cultures very much closed in on themselves.'

In addition to this, Lodelinsart is located in the Charleroi region, well known in Belgium for its strong traditions of union activism. The crisis years exacerbated the tensions and conflicts in all the firms of the region. At that time, the majority of personnel employed by the factory were largely unskilled and the unions wielded considerable power over them. The unions, represented by both factory union delegates and permanent representatives (belonging to the union structures outside the company), were the obligatory intermediary (and the only ones) between the management and the workers. It was impossible at that time for the management to address the workers directly and stoppages were the daily routine.

This climate of labour relations was further aggravated by the very acrimonious after-effects of the closure in 1975, in difficult conditions, of one of the Group's factories located some kilometres from there, at Gilly.

Furthermore, the factories at that time were living in a 'socio-economic ghetto', with little contact with head office, and the local management team, as much through fear of acts of violence as to maintain peace with the workers, became involved in a series of 'arrangements' with the unions which gave rise to a personnel policy characterized by a certain laxity and lack of clarity.

Major changes The restructuring and redeployment implemented by the Glaverbel Group entailed the following major changes at the Lodelinsart factory. In 1975, the main furnace was shut down and replaced by double-glazing work, which already meant a considerable change in terms of jobs. The Director of the Lodelinsart factory stated that, 'At that time, no workers in this factory had previously seen a sheet of glass more than three metres long.'

There was a considerable number of redundancies among the least skilled workers, either through early retirement or voluntary resignation. The changeover in activities was met with considerable resistance by the transferred workers who could no longer use their know-how in the new jobs in glass making.

In 1988 and 1990, two very sophisticated pieces of equipment were installed, magnetrons which add special insulating layers and other coatings to the glass. This equipment demanded high levels of skill (and radically new skills) from the workers. It was therefore necessary at the same time to take on highly qualified personnel and to lay off other workers who even after training did not have sufficient competence to work with such tools.

The 'restructuring' continued in 1990 and 1991 with the transfer of compound glass work to another of the Group's factories and new difficulties linked to the collapse of the world market.

Human resource management policies The changes imposed by the Group's general management and all the difficulties alluded to above might have led to a situation where anomie replaced the previously anarchic situation. Perhaps more than with the other factories studied, it was its capacity to seize on these upheavals and turn them into opportunities for change which enabled Lodelinsart to extract itself from trouble.

Human resource management in the broadest sense – carried out by the personnel department, although also by the managers, middle management and engineers – was a powerful lever for transforming the climate of labour relations. This translated itself into the following directions, especially in the late 1980s:

- Considerable improvement in qualifications. At the beginning of the 1970s, the work still demanded 'muscle power'; now, the factory's work consisted of manufacturing products of high added value for which much higher qualifications are necessary.
- Re-positioning of middle management, who have more autonomy in their relations with personnel and more confidence in dealing with technical and human problems at their level of responsibility.
- Implementation of a project aimed at 'transforming people into entrepreneurs'. The emphasis was on collective success in mollifying in time the 'gut' reactions of opposition or withdrawal (lack of commitment). The password has become: 'from the Director down to the cleaner, nothing can stop this factory'. The common objective, shared by the union delegation, is to 'make the factory profitable through a constant care for quality, with equipment which works better and self-fulfilled personnel'.
- Continuous insistence on strengthening the practice of communicating, to achieve more transparency with regard to the economic objectives to be attained and the changes to be made. Communication makes the changes less difficult to accept by the personnel, but requires an indispensable coherence between words and deeds. Communication further permits everyone to identify his or her role within a group of activities which is becoming more complex and abstract. It is in fact essential for every member of the factory to recognize themselves and to be recognized in their role to ensure collective success.

- Development of a partnership with the unions. The purpose is gradually to restore relations of confidence between the representatives, while having regard for everyone in their own role. According to the Head of Human and Labour Relations at the Lodelinsart factory, 'everyone must negotiate responsibly, which means fairness and understanding on all sides'. The aim is therefore not to get rid of the union delegation but to maintain the credibility of the union delegates.

Progress circles have never really been implemented in Lodelinsart. The various and continuous changes in the 1970s and 1980s, combined with a very hard climate of industrial relations, did not constitute favourable conditions to introduce the same methods as in other Group factories. 'We are not pre-occupied with having progress circles, but with getting people to co-operate with each other', noticed the Head of Human and Labour Relations at the factory. That is why a different kind of work team is preferred: when new methods or equipment are introduced, a cell is created, independent of the existing structures, which includes all the representatives concerned. The only criterion for determining who will belong to that cell is the person's competence in relation to the project. The cell studies all the aspects of organization for the purpose of gathering all the opinions, asking all the necessary questions to find the best solutions to the problems and anticipate any difficulties through the agreement of the personnel. This is considered at the Lodelinsart factory as a form of participation, but the factory's Director insists on the boundaries: 'we have to take care to maintain participation within the limits provided: opinions must be noted, explanations given, but the decision always rests with the person responsible, at whatever level he may be'. For the Head of Human and Labour Relations, participation depends essentially on 'collective maturity' and it is necessary 'to go as far as possible – this is imperative for maintaining his management's credibility in difficult periods'.

To promote such a slow and gradual change, the human resource department tries to reinforce the influence of middle management on personnel (in reaction to the unions' influence), to ensure continual contact with workers' representatives with a view to establishing 'fair and just' labour relations centred on the company's collective objectives. Finally – although this is not the least of its roles – the human resource department has to maintain the dynamic of communication throughout the process to ensure the viability of the change.

Mol: 'change in continuity'

Some figures In the early 1970s, the factory at Mol still had three 'traditional' glazing-glass furnaces, and was gradually specializing in thin and extra-thin glass as well as in manufacturing double-glazing. This factory was then the uncontested leader in quantity and quality of thin and extra-thin glass, which could only be produced at that time with the traditional process of drawn glass.

Nowadays, the factory at Mol has modernized all of its equipment and even the thin glass is produced by float. All of its products go either to other

Table 2.3 *Mol: workforce evolution*

Year	Workers	Clerical and executive staff	Total
1975	1487	201	1688
1982	941	152	1093
1991	750	138	888

Glaverbel subsidiaries and establishments or to outside customers (more than 50%): the building trade (double-glazing), the automobile industry (special glass) and the medical, photographic, electronic and computer industries (thin and extra-thin glass).

Since 1975, the number of personnel has been reduced by almost half (Table 2.3) but, contrary to the majority of factories in the Group, this reduction was achieved gradually, involving neither disputes nor massive redundancies – mainly through early retirements and natural attrition spread out over time.

Important but gradual changes in both equipment and qualifications In this factory, the changes imposed by new technologies (float) were implemented gradually. In fact, float technology did not lend itself immediately to the manufacturing of all thicknesses of glass and Mol was a leader in making thin and extra-thin glass with traditional equipment.

In 1985–6 it was finally decided to abandon drawn-glass technology and a float producing very thin glass (1 mm), perfected by the Japanese Asahi Glass, began operations in 1988. 'It was the Belgians who taught the Japanese how to make fine drawn glass, in the seventies; but the Japanese developed floats and they succeeded in perfecting a float for thin and extra-thin glass,' the Director of the Mol factory explained.

At that time, the manufacturing process for double-glazing was also changed but, there again, the change was effected 'gently' and with a plan for the restructuring which 'made it possible not to throw out the past altogether and to avoid the dramatic situations in other factories in the Group', according to the factory Director.

However, in 1977 the quest for higher productivity involved reducing both costs and labour. In 1977 and 1978, agreements were concluded with the unions making it possible to reduce the workforce and improve competitiveness, which could no longer satisfy the traditional criteria expressed in terms of production quantities.

This concern with competitiveness went hand in hand with the arrival throughout the Glaverbel Group of management by business units. This system entailed that each factory, in accordance with its business unit or units, had to take into account the real cost of production. If suddenly warned by head office of any unexpected rises in the market or the competition, it had to correct the differences in a reduced time.

The changes implemented in the factory at Mol (increased productivity, reduced workforce and, later, technological changes) were facilitated by several elements:

- they were effected in a less brutal way than in other factories in the Group and could be anticipated over a period of time;
- the factory's management had always made it a point of honour to prepare for these changes by compiling dossiers for each of them which fully set out the arguments from both the technical point of view and that of the repercussions on employment;
- the unions were informed as a matter of priority of the necessity for these changes, as well as their negative consequences (loss of employment) and their positive ones (maintenance of competitiveness). 'We tried to find any solution that was acceptable to both parties, even if it meant slightly delaying the plans envisaged by the Group', said the factory Director.

It is clear that these changes required personnel with higher qualifications than previously. Effecting the transformations in stages enabled some of the personnel to be trained in the new technologies, to engage better-qualified workers and to provide for the reduction in the excess workforce by early retirement or voluntary redundancy. However, even though the transition was carried out gradually, the factory at Mol encountered certain difficulties: there was particularly a paradoxical situation in the fact that a certain number of workers were allowed to leave at the same time as new personnel possessing different skills (technicians, electronics engineers, etc.) were recruited – occupational groups that were not necessarily connected with the old glass-making jobs. For the rest, the difference in qualifications between old and new sometimes caused new staff to leave the firm because they could not integrate and utilize their skills as fast as they would have liked.

Human resource management policies – 1. Communications which crossed the divisions between factories Even though Mol transformed itself gradually, the implementation of management by business units induced important changes for personnel, particularly at the management level. This type of management favoured communication between factories within the Group, reduced the isolation of Mol in relation to other units in Wallonia and stimulated direct departmental liaison between all of the Group's units.

Previously the factory at Mol, which was fairly isolated, only communicated with head office or other factories through its Director. Nowadays, also taking account of the higher qualifications and personal autonomy, every technical Head, for example, can communicate directly with his or her peer in one of the other Group factories. Although top management kept its decision-making power, several cross-organizational networks were created (sales, technical, etc.) which came out of the framework defined strictly by the organization chart. For example, certain investments are now being proposed by the departments, to be studied further by head office.

Human resource management policies – 2. Participative management In 1983, the factory at Mol accepted the experiment of participative management proposed but not imposed by Glaverbel's general management as one of the central tenets of its human resource management policy. Thus the factory became one of the two pilot factories in the Group for implementing participative management.

Participative management was envisaged in the continuation of organized communication – putting as much reliable information as possible at the disposal of middle management and the workers about the factory's position in relation to its market, its quality requirements and the optimum use of its equipment – with the desire to 'get people to work better together'. However, for the factory Director there is a difficulty for participative management – there is a limit to what one can ask of the workers without 'pulling the wool over their eyes'; that is, without hiding from them the fact that the economic environment remains largely unpredictable. Furthermore, even within the Group, the recent policy of internationalization has meant giving priority to investment outside Belgium (and obviously outside the Mol factory).

Ten years after the start of participative management, it appears that, in the words of the factory Director, 'You cannot change people's behaviour if a favourable environment is not created, comprising better working conditions, increased responsibility and greater capacity for self-expression, which would give them the desire and motivation to change their own behaviour.'

In participative management, the continuity of a policy in time and the example given by top and middle management are two essential elements. 'The example must come from the top . . . It's absolutely on the shop floor, every day, that results are achieved and victories won!', said the factory Director.

Additional data

Unionization rates in Belgium, 1982–91

Percentage membership of unions is shown in Table 2.4.

Table 2.4 *Unionization rates in Belgium (%)*

1982	1983	1984	1985	1986	1987	1988	1989	1990	1991
79.80	79.05	79.03	79.01	77.44	76.90	75.37	75.40	76.29	77.44

Unions: CSC +FGTB + CGSLB.

Source: Arcq, E. (1993) 'Le taux de syndicalisation 1982–1991', *Courrier Hebdomadaire*, CRISP, no. 1386

Some figures

Glaverbel in 1991 (in Belgium, not including the Group's subsidiaries) consisted of:

- Factories: Lodelinsart, Mol, Moustier, Roux, Seneffe, Zeebrugge

- R & D centre: Jumet
- Head office: Brussels

Table 2.5 *Financial data (in BF millions)*

	1975	1982	1991
Turnover	5,397.5	11,242	30,765
Equity Capital	1,950	1,889	19,478
Loss	(2,135)		
Net profit		243	799
Cashflow	negative	854	5,761
Industrial investment	336	884	2,885

Other financial data are given in Table 2.5. For the first time in 1982/3, the company established consolidated accounts: consolidated turnover BF 12,447 million. In 1991, the data cited above are the consolidated data for the Glaverbel Group. In 1991, of the BF 2,885 million of industrial investments, there are BF 2,769 million invested in European activities (Western and Central Europe).

Workforce evolution in the Group and in three factories

Table 2.6 shows the evolution of the workforce. In 1991, the employment structure was greatly altered by the integration of the Czech firm; in total, the number of people employed by the Group rose from 6,364 at the end of

Table 2.6 *Workforce evolution*

	1975	1982	1991
Group total	9,414	5,120	10,001
Workers	7,237	4,090	7,928
Staff and middle management	2,177	1,030	2,073
Total for Belgium	8,286	4,405	4,523
Workers	6,325	3,392	3,325
Staff and middle management	1,961	1,013	1,198
Total outside Belgium	1,128	715	5,478
Moustier	956	887	774
Workers	811	763	632
Staff and middle management	145	124	142
Mol	1,688	1,093	888
Workers	1,487	941	750
Staff and middle management	201	152	138
Lodelinsart	541	506	371
Workers	457	432	295
Staff and middle management	84	74	76

December 1990 to 10,001 at the end of December 1991, of whom 3,630 were in the Czech Republic. 'As a comparable structure, the global workforce remained more or less stable, the reductions in personnel made in the Benelux countries following the restructuring measures implemented at Lodelinsart, Mol (Belgium) and Hardmaas (Netherlands), having been partially compensated for by the new staff taken on in the Spanish subsidiaries and at Glaverbec in Canada' (1991 Annual Report).

Themes/issues to consider

In analysing themes highlighted by this case for discussion, you should consider one or several of the following issues:

- Consider the nature of industrial relations in Belgium. Identify the various partners, analyse their role and their relations. Analyse the key elements and implications for organizational change, as illustrated by the Glaverbel case. Compare them with your own situation in your country.
- The relationship between environmental change (economic, technological, labour relations, financial) and organizational change – what were the main effects in this case?
- The interactions between strategy, organizational change and human resource issues: analyse the relations between strategy and human resource policies, in terms of personnel planning, staffing and development (including participative management and communication).
- Discuss the processes and mechanisms of change illustrated in this case in terms of shift in organizational structure, organizational culture(s), communication policy.
- Participative management as an employer's initiative: analyse the potential competition/interaction between different types of workers' representation (participative management, representation by unions, etc.).
- Organizational culture and sub-cultures: what cultural elements can you observe in the Glaverbel company and factories?
- Implementation of general management's decisions in organizational reality: how can coherence be maintained between the top management's decisions and the situation on the shopfloor. Examine the key elements that influence the way changes defined at general management level are adapted in the factories.
- Analyse the role of middle management in organizational behaviour and change.
- The problem of downsizing and restructuring: what are the difficulties related to personnel planning in a crisis situation?
- The role of the human resource management professional: is it possible for human resource managers to reconcile contradictory activities (such as downsizing vs participation)?

- Evolution in the representation of individuals at work: has the place of 'human resources' in the organization changed since the late 1960s? How can you observe it in the Glaverbel case?

Assignments

In organizational change and behaviour or in human resource management, there are no universal, unambiguous answers – no 'magic formula'. But, in a given context with specific opportunities and constraints, there are more suitable responses. It is in this frame of mind that we advise instructors and students to remember that finding the best solutions requires one to ask the right questions. That being said, you can work on the following assignments.

1. As a member of Glaverbel general management, in charge of human resource and labour relations issues, explain to the other members (the managers in charge of production, technical, financial or marketing), what key elements must be taken into consideration to define the change projects for the company, and why. The following sub-questions could help you, if necessary:
   - Why in Belgium in general, and in the Glaverbel company in particular, do all innovative human resource management policies have to take into consideration the union representatives?
   - What are the limitations of a decentralization policy and of autonomous business units with respect to human resource management?
   - What are the areas of responsibility of human resource management in maintaining central control of the Group and why?
   - How can you explain the fact that each of the factories interprets the corporate objectives differently?
   - What reason does human resource management have for maintaining distinctive sub-cultures in each of the factories?
2. As the Human Resource Manager of one of the factories (Moustier, Lodelinsart or Mol), analyse the key elements affecting the factory's human resource development and management and, keeping these elements in mind, think about actions you could take (also paying attention to consistency with the corporate objectives of the Glaverbel Group). For instance:
   - As the Human Resource Director of the Moustier factory, what actions would you take with respect to the employees who are concerned about competition from the factory that was bought by the Group in the Czech Republic, where the labour costs are much lower than in Belgium?
   - As the Human Resource Director of the Lodelinsart factory, what actions would you take with respect to your employees who are developing internal rivalries because of former memberships in

different areas of the business which now no longer exist (competing sub-cultures)?

- As the Human Resource Director of the Mol factory, what actions would you take with respect to the concerns of your employees about the technical changes developing in the near future (for example, liquid crystal in double-glazing for applications in the computer and audio-visual industries)?

Be prepared to negotiate and to justify your point of view in meetings with the union representatives and with Group general management.

Suggested reading

Arcq, E. (1993) 'Les relations collectives du travail', *Dossiers du CRISP*, no. 39, Brussels: Centre de Recherche et d'Information Socio-Politiques. A synthesis of the industrial relations system in Belgium, showing the specificity and complexity of the different levels of negotiation, and the role of the different actors in this system (employers, unions, government).

Baglioni, G. and Crouch, C. (eds) (1990) *European Industrial Relations: The Challenge of Flexibility*. London: Sage. To quote from the book: 'The last decade has seen a remarkable change in the balance of power in industrial relations throughout European countries after the period of industrial militancy and union strength during the 1970s. A widespread political shift to the right, high unemployment, and a restructuring of the labour force have all contributed to a change in the context and content of management and workforce relations.'

Crouch, C. (1993) *Industrial Relations and European State Traditions*. Oxford: Clarendon Press. Using a combination of rational choice theory and historical analysis, Crouch traces the development of industrial relations systems in Western European nations from the 1870s to the present. He seeks explanations for differences further back in time, showing that longer-term historical explanations of contemporary institutions are more necessary than most exercises in policy analysis prefer to accept.

Schein, E. (1988) *Organizational Culture and Leadership*. San Francisco: Jossey-Bass. Organizational culture has become a major theme in recent best-selling books. Indeed, culture is often used to explain everything that happens in organizations from successes to failures. Schein carefully defines 'organizational culture' to make it truly useful in understanding and managing organizations.

Strategor (1988) *Stratégie, Structure, Décision, Identité*. Paris: InterEditions.This book presents the most recent developments in strategy and business policy. The main chapters are dedicated to the analysis of strategy, structure, decision and identity.

Notes

This case is based on a wide range of documents and statements collected in the company. We would like to thank the following in particular. At Glaverbel's head office: Mme Gillot, Director Corporate Management Development and Communication; M. Wauters, Director of Human and Labour Relations; M. Toussaint, Industrial Director, Blank Glass and Construction Division; M. Cobut, Head of Industrial Relations; M. Thiry, Head of Collective Relations. At the Moustier factory: M. Delisee, Plant Director; M. Cavrenne, Head of Human and Labour Relations; M. Demoulin, Head of General Services. At the Lodelinsart factory: M. Lambert, Plant Director; Mme Devillers, Head of Human and Labour Relations. At the MOL factory: M. Feyen, Plant Director.

The initial idea of carrying out this study came from reading the work by G. Warnotte and E. van Haelen entitled *Approche des politiques sociales en entreprise* (approach to company social policy), published by the University Press of Namur in 1988.

Finally, this case study could not have been undertaken without the financial support given by the Interuniversity College of Doctoral Studies in Management Sciences (CIM), Brussels.

1 Arcq, E. (1993) 'Le taux de syndicalisation – 1982–1991', *Courrier Hebdomadaire*, CRISP, no. 1386; Ferner, A. and Hyman, R. (eds) (1992) *Industrial Relations in the New Europe*. Oxford: Blackwell.

2 See, on this subject, Spineux, A. (1990) 'Trade unionism in Belgium: The difficulties of a major renovation', in Baglioni, G. and Crouch, C. (eds), *European Industrial Relations: The Challenge of Flexibility*. London: Sage, pp. 42–70.

3 Storey, J. and Sisson, K. (1989) 'Looking to the future', in Storey J. (ed.), *New Perspectives on Human Resource Management*. London: Routledge, pp. 167–83. See also Salaman, Graeme (ed.) (1992) *Human Resource Strategies*. London: Sage; Ferris, G.R., Rowland, K.M. and Buckley, M.R. (1990) *Human Resource Management: Perspectives and Issues*, 2nd edn. Boston: Allyn & Bacon.

4 'Si GLAVERBEL m'était contée . . . ', internal company document, p. 2.

5 Ibid., p. 3.

6 It should be noted that in 1991, the Group again had 10,000 people on the payroll, but only 4500 were employed in Belgium. In reality, the employment structure was greatly altered between 1990 and 1991, through integration with the Czech firm: in total, the company workforce went from 6364 in December 1990 to 10,001 in December 1991, of which 3630 were in the Czech Republic.

7 'Si GLAVERBEL m'était contée . . . ', p. 3.

3

The Humanitarian Foundation (HUF)

Revitalizing an old organization

Søren Christensen and Jan Molin

The Humanitarian Foundation (HUF) is an international aid and disaster organization based in Denmark. HUF was founded in 1876 and is now organized in 250 local branches and 17 county districts. The head office is based in Copenhagen. In 1990 HUF spent some US$ 40 million on international activities and US$ 35 million on a programme caring for foreigners asking for political asylum in Denmark; 85% of the budget was funded through government sources in Denmark.

In 1990 the President and General Secretary of HUF felt that it faced major organizational problems. On the one hand, the increase in international aid programmes and refugee camp administration had forced HUF to employ an additional number of professionals. On the other hand, the governing bodies of the organization – the General Assembly and Central Committee were recruited from the members of HUF elected through the 250 branches and 17 county districts. These members do not have a professional background but are responsible for governing HUF's activities. The bi-annual General Assembly involved 350 people and the Central Committee had 41 members.

The issues in HUF had to do with the structure of the organization and the decision-making processes of the governing bodies. The democratic structure of the organization has always been important – at least symbolically – to the members. The representative democracy of the organization is complicated and most members do not play an active part in the governing of HUF. The majority of members are motivated by its good cause and activities, and have no desire to participate in its leadership. Since the 1980s many of HUF's tasks have become highly professionalized, and the number of professional staff has increased. This, in the eyes of the Secretary General and the President, calls for a more 'business-like' organization, stronger leadership, and a more efficient decision structure.

Cultural context

In this section we will briefly set The Humanitarian Foundation in its cultural context. This means trying to understand its institutional origins and how it relates in modern times to the values, institutional context, and history of Danish society.

The Humanitarian Foundation did not have an easy birth. In 1864 the Danish government had signed the Geneva Convention on the treatment of sick and wounded during war. For the next 12 years, the Geneva Committee tried to put pressure on Denmark to create an organization to deal with the Geneva Convention and finally public opinion realized that 'it does not look good if our nation is the only one – among civilized nations – that is not part of the movement'.[1] In 1876 'The Society for the Improvement of the Conditions of the Sick and Wounded during War' was founded in Copenhagen.

At least formally, the society was organized democratically with members paying an annual membership fee. However, the Executive Committee – consisting of prominent conservative citizens drawn from the army and the bourgeoisie – assumed power and controlled the organization until it was reorganized in 1917.

But why was there a controversy over its foundation? In 1849 Denmark gained its first democratic constitution. Therefore, the choice of organizational form in all parts of Danish civil life was as much a political as a practical question. There were opposing forces: the enlightened citizens who wanted to express themselves as 'modern' and 'civilized', utilizing their newly won democratic rights of assembly to form a member-based 'society'; and their opponents – the conservatives drawn primarily from the bourgeoisie – who did not favour the new democratic constitution. Involved in the struggle was also the army, which felt that the creation of an organization was indirectly a criticism of its ability to deal with 'the sick and wounded during war'. The solution to this controversy was the creation of a society which was organized as a voluntary association where the members elect the leadership. At this point this was the only legitimate organizational structure to choose. But membership fees were comparatively high and citizens were not used to playing an active part in public life. This made it possible for a small military/bourgeios élite to take control of the organization and protect their own interests.[2]

This tight control lasted until 1917, when the army apparently lost interest in the issue. In 1917 HUF was re-organized and turned into a country-wide organization with regional offices and local branches.

Since its foundation and until the present HUF has been performing a variety of activities. Since their establishment in 1917 the local branches have engaged in activities such as caring for the poor, childcare and nursery homes. The head office has taken on a variety of tasks, such as international humanitarian aid in connection with situations of war or natural disasters. From around 1980 the Head Office was professionalized and HUF took on two major tasks financed primarily through government funding: international aid and disaster work, and refugee administration in Denmark of foreigners seeking political asylum. This led to a growing professionalization of the head office and a growing cleavage between the professional staff and the local branches which consisted of volunteers.

From a sociological point of view, Denmark today is a remarkably homogeneous society. It is a small country with a population of 5,146,000 covering 43,000 square kilometres – about the size of Switzerland.

Denmark is a highly industrialized country. In 1990 only some 6% of the labour force were employed in agriculture, which is roughly the same size as the construction industry. Some 20% were employed in manufacturing, whereas 67% worked in services (including public service).

There are virtually no religious, ethnic or language cleavages. Although the society is stratified through economic, cultural and educational criteria, the equalization policy of the welfare state has softened this stratification compared to most other Western countries.

Important aspects of the welfare system are the free health service and education. As Fivelsdal and Schramm-Nielsen suggest,[3] the educational system is possibly closest in revealing the operative values of a society. In Denmark general compulsory education was introduced as early as 1814, well ahead of the first democratic institution which was introduced in 1849 when the King was convinced to relinquish his absolute rule. The Danish educational system is free of charge, that is, virtually no tuition is paid in any part of the system, from primary school to university education. All the way through the system is based on egalitarian and democratic values.

From the middle of the nineteenth century education has played an important role in shaping economic and political life in Denmark. N.S.F. Grundtvig (1783–1872) played a particularly major role as a clergyman and educationalist and opinion former. His main opponents in religious as well as educational matters were the classical Latin culture and authoritarian belief structure. He was in the forefront in establishing folk high schools, farmers' co-operative dairies, slaughter houses, savings banks, etc. in Danish society in the latter half of the nineteenth century. The Grundtvigian movement played a significant role in shaping the anti-authoritarian and democratic values now embedded in the educational system and in society at large.

At present Denmark is striving to modernize its welfare system. The tax burden is heavy and growing as the unemployment figures have been increasing since 1980. Professional values of efficiency and effectiveness are now competing with the democratic and anti-authoritarian values in society. Government services are being privatized or outsourced, and HUF – like other non-governmental organizations (NGOs) – has developed into an international NGO receiving most of its funding from the Danish International Development Agency (DANIDA). Since around 1980 HUF has gone through a period of professionalization. The structure of the organization – a voluntary association with elected grass-root leaders – has not changed. What was found in 1990, when the Secretary General and the President wanted to modernize the governing structure of HUF, was a basic struggle between two sets of deeply rooted values: democratic and anti-authoritarian versus professional.

Such an issue is not unique to HUF. The whole society is addressing similar discussions, and the antagonism between these two sets of values is not easily resolved.

HUF in 1980

The Humanitarian Foundation (HUF) is a relief organization founded in the late 1870s. During the twentieth century HUF expanded into a national organization, establishing local committees across the country. Since the Second World War HUF has engaged in general humanitarian tasks and relief work in third-world countries.

In 1990 HUF had 66,000 members, 35% less than in 1986 when it had 102,000 members. HUF is organized in 250 local branches and 17 county districts. Traditionally it acquired its funding through membership fees, fundraising, lotteries, etc.

However, since 1978 the government has increased its financial support dramatically, reflecting the important role that HUF has come to play in international relief and disaster aid in the third world. In 1990, the government financed some 75% of HUF's total budget for international activities, corresponding to about US$ 30 million. In 1984 HUF was requested by the government to assume the task of administering the reception, housing, provisioning, etc. of foreigners asking for asylum. In 1990 some 4000 foreigners applied for asylum. At that time, HUF had established 24 centres across the country and was reimbursed with US$ 34 million to cover the expenses of this, amounting to 45% of its annual budget. This meant that in 1990 85% of the budget was financed through government sources and only 15% through traditional sources: fundraising, membership fees, lotteries, etc.

As a consequence of this shift in activities and in financial profile, HUF has been experiencing some major difficulties. On the one hand, the increase in international aid programmes and in refugee administration has forced HUF to employ an additional number of professionals. On the other hand, the governing bodies of the organization – the General Assembly and the Central Committee – are recruited from the members of HUF. These members do not have a professional background in international aid or refugee administration, but are responsible for governing these activities. The bi-annual General Assembly involves some 350 people and the Central Committee has 41 members. This situation is not unique to HUF. Many Danish non-profit organizations have the same governance structure since they draw on the Danish tradition of democracy in governance.

Organization

Members The organization is based on the idea of membership and is run according to democratic principles. The members are attached to the individual

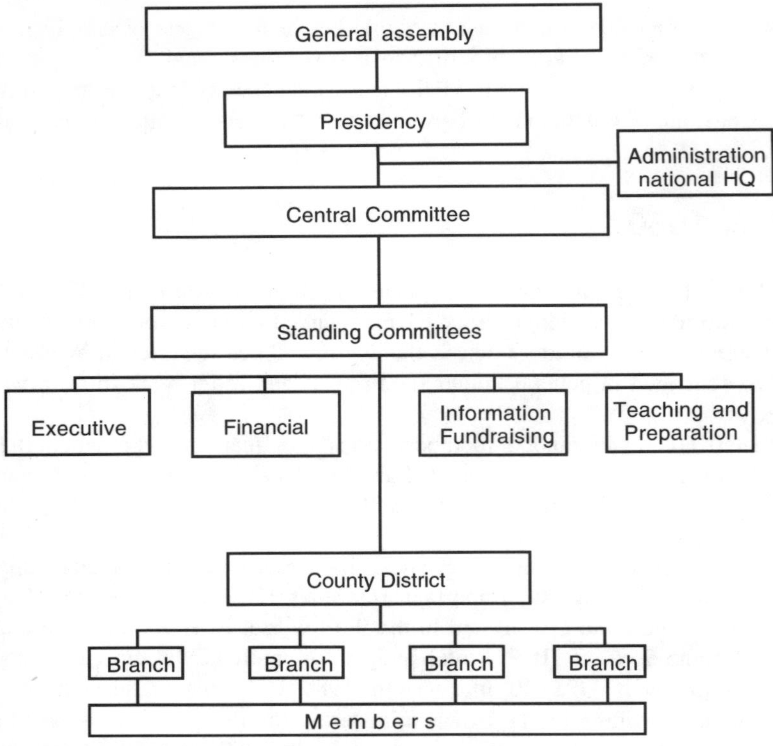

Figure 3.1 *Organization of HUF*

local branches. In 1992 the annual subscription for single members was US$ 11 and for families US$ 20.

Branches The total number of branches is 250. The branch committee is responsible for all HUF activities in the area, such as recruitment and service to members, fundraising and social and educational activities including first aid training. The branches are managed by a committee, headed by a chairman. The committee is elected by the members of the local branch.

County districts The county districts follow the public administrative structure of Denmark (public counties). HUF has 17 county districts in Denmark (plus one covering the Faroe Islands, and one covering Greenland). The county district is managed by a committee elected by the branches within the district. The county district is in charge of co-ordinating and supporting the activities of the local branches.

General Assembly The highest authority of HUF is the General Assembly, which convenes bi-annually and is open for representatives from all branches and for the Central Committee. Total number of participants is approximately 350.

Presidency The Presidency covers the President and the three Vice-Presidents.

Central Committee The activities of HUF are directed by the Central Committee. The Committee consists of 45 members, primarily elected by the county district committees. Furthermore a number of members are elected by the Central Committee in special consideration of their expertise. The period of election covers four years. The meetings of the Central Committee are chaired by the President. Major decisions in HUF are made by the Central Committee. They are often prepared by the Secretary General and his Administration and preliminary discussions take place in the Executive Committee (see below) before they are put before the Central Committee.

Standing Committees The Central Committee has appointed a number of Standing Committees in special consideration of their fields of activity. The most essential Committee is the Executive Committee, comprising 16 members.

Secretary General The Administration of HUF is headed by the Secretary General. The administrative structure is detailed below.

Administrative structure

National and international activities are directed by the national head office in Copenhagen, with approximately 130 employees. The Secretary General is responsible to the Central Committee for administration. The President of HUF controls the activities of the national head office on behalf of the Central Committee (see Figure 3.2).

Although Refugee Administration is a separate division of HUF, headed by a manager and situated in a different building in Copenhagen, it is subject to the Central Committee, President and Secretary General, as are the other parts of the administration.

Members and economy

The total number of HUF members amounted to 102,000 at the end of 1986; by the end of 1990 this had decreased to 66,300. Plans were made for a number of member recruitment initiatives in 1992, in which it was hoped that all branches would participate. The members are distributed over the 250 branches, five of which are situated in Greenland and one in the Faroe Islands.

Figure 3.3 shows the development in number of members between 1986 and 1990.

HUF's activities are mainly financed through fundraising and government and EU contributions. To this must be added income from its own handicraft, lotteries, second-hand shops, sale of articles, external training activities, institutions and financing.

During the last few years there has been a distinct increase in income, which can be seen from Figure 3.4.

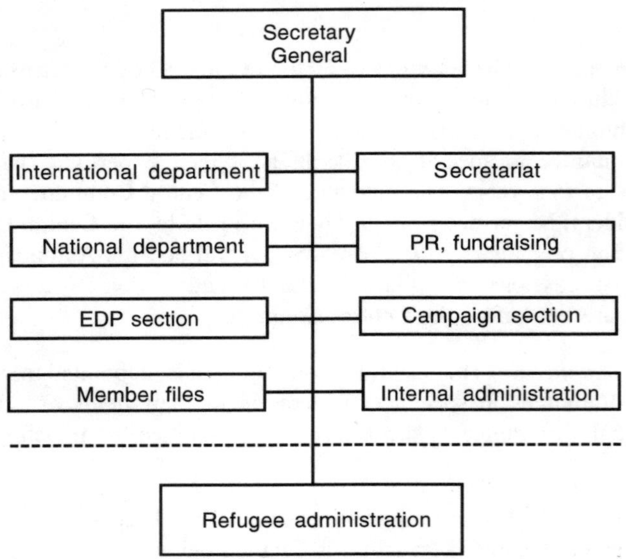

Figure 3.2 *Structure of the national head office*

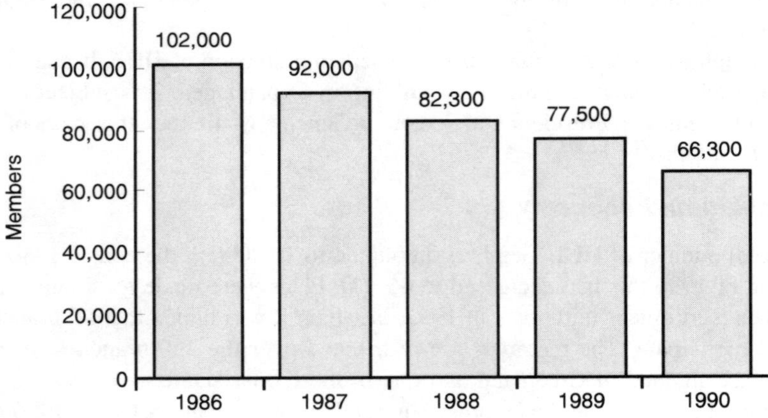

Figure 3.3 *Membership 1986–90*

Table 3.1 shows the distribution of net income in 1990. When leaving out of account the expenses in connection with asylum administration and activity, which are covered in full by the Danish government, the expenses are distributed as in Table 3.2.

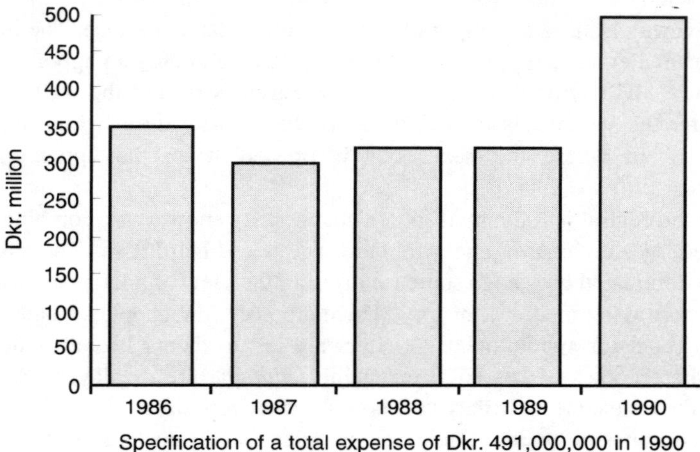

Figure 3.4 *Annual turnover 1986–90*

Table 3.1 *Distribution of net income, 1990*

Asylum administration	45%
International assistance and development projects	40%
Administration	4.5%
Fundraising	3.7%
National activities	2.8%
Production of articles, institutions	2.8%
Financing	0.5%
Information	0.4%
Net result	0.3%

Table 3.2 *Distribution of income excluding asylum administration*

International activities	74%
Administration, etc.	9%
Fundraising, information	7%
National activities	5%
Production of articles, institutions	5%

Life in the organization

Head office

HUF head office is situated in the exclusive north-eastern part of the Copenhagen, surrounded by embassies and similar prestigious buildings. On an impressive avenue lined with old trees and broad sidewalks, the HUF building presents itself with unobtrusive grandeur behind a wrought-iron lattice and a small driveway leading to a flight of steps up to the main entrance. The building itself is a smaller-scale replica of the Queen's Castle and only a flagpole with the well-known HUF symbol flying reveals the activities behind the walls.

To enter the visitor has to be cleared at the security desk behind the main entrance, from where the next door is opened when the appointment is confirmed.

Inside the central hall the atmosphere changes. It is now a rare combination of a reserved, wealthy charm, and a forward, warm and helpful air. The hall itself is totally dominated by a huge staircase offering the view of a large stained-glass window portraying medieval history. There are very few people around waiting to be collected for appointments. Visitors are left to themselves at a table and chairs where copies of the HUF magazine *Dialogue* are displayed. Browsing through the magazine it strikes you how much it resembles the well-designed airline magazines normally found in an aeroplane's seat pockets. The expensive layout and colours serve as an invitation to browse and not to read too seriously.

Administration, EDP (electronic data processing) and Information are located on the ground floor and at the end of the right-hand hallway is the library, which is used every day for meetings. It is a beautiful room cutting across the entire building, offering a view of the avenue at one end and of the small park behind the building at the other. With a high ceiling and bookshelves covering one of the walls from floor to ceiling, the room is important and solemn in its own right. At the far end a picture gallery of all HUF's presidents hovers over a huge working desk. In the middle a long meeting table sets the scene, and at the other end a sofa and a group of chairs around a small table offer space for more relaxed negotiation. This is a room for serious talk or for quiet reading of the many volumes on human rights or the Geneva Convention.

The first-floor offices are occupied by the National Department and the Secretariat. The rooms are large but crowded, with too many people working at too many desks in too little space. The atmosphere is one of busyness, extreme cautiousness and quietness at the same time. At the far end of the corridor, at the end of the Secretariat, in a bright, spacious and well-furnished office, the Secretary General (SG) resides. He is a modern, well-educated and experienced technocrat in his late forties. With an academic background, a career in the Ministry of Foreign Affairs and years of diplomatic service, he has built an image around himself of intelligence, effectiveness and ambition. The HUF organization has grown dramatically during his reign. As a professional the SG has clearly demonstrated to the public that HUF is a well-administered and efficient relief organization – and internationally he has succeeded in making HUF projects appear high-status operations.

To people working in head office there is little doubt that it is the SG who runs the organization. There is a democratically elected president but he is old and has primarily symbolic duties. The Head of National Department is concerned with activities in Denmark, but his power only reflects how little interest the SG takes in national activities. There is a Head of International Department, concerned with relief and disaster operations and to an increasing degree with development aid to countries in the third world, but he has to share his power over the international programmes with the SG, since the latter sees these as the core of HUF. As the Head of the Secretariat sees his job as carrying out orders in a resigned and bureaucratic fashion, there really is no one in head office who poses a challenge to the SG's reign. On the contrary, he receives a lot of respect from many of the ordinary employees who recognize the possibilities of an expanding organization. Most of the employees have a background similar to that of the SG. They have graduated from university and made a career either in public administration or in one of the NGOs (non-governmental organizations) dealing with relief projects. These are trained professionals who have been carefully selected to fit HUF's needs for reliable bureaucratic routines matched with commitment and experience in working with foreign aid programmes. They believe in the overall humanitarian purpose and they have individually combined this belief with a personal career that has brought them to HUF. Once inside HUF very few leave again as they pursue further advancement in the HUF world: either as delegates or consultants in another country, or as section-leader/head of department in head office.

On the surface, then, HUF appears to be a well-run organization without open conflicts or internal problems to address. Life in head office is smooth, busy and rewarding, as the attention to international catastrophes has a profound motivational effect on people fighting to organize prompt and substantial disaster relief. Even the day-to-day administration of development aid programmes in the third world offers this feeling of importance and personal satisfaction.

This is, however, only the picture seen from head office. As the main entrance closes behind the visitor, HUF becomes an organization to be read about in the newspapers when a new relief project is initiated, or a new conflict occurs in one of the refugee centres – or it becomes a number of voluntary first-aid people at a local rock concert. HUF is a versatile organization and, although there may be difficulties *within* the different fields of activity, the most characteristic aspect of the organization is the differences *between* the respective types of national and international activities.

Activities

HUF is concerned with three kinds of activities: international, national and refugee administration. In terms of money (that is, turnover and funding) the international activities are most significant. In terms of people involved the national leg is the largest, since all the members are involved in some kind of activity (collecting money, running second-hand shops, serving as first-aid volunteers etc.). In terms of being controversial the refugee administration is most often ahead. Problems in the refugee camps often make headlines in the newspapers, and since HUF is administering the government's policy in this area, political controversies are often debated also among HUF members.

Refugee administration

The Refugee Administration has its own location in Copenhagen not far from head office. Its task is to run and support the many refugee centres throughout the country. At these centres the guests can stay as long as they are formally recognized as political refugees applying for a provisional residence permit. This may take one to two years and as such the refugee centres experience many conflicts rising from insecurity, fear, uncertainty and restlessness. Some of the problems develop inside the refugee centres, between the refugees themselves – and other problems develop between the refugees and people in the local community. The whole operation is organized centrally from the Refugee Administration, which has direct communication with the government bodies dealing with political refugees. The Ministry of Justice pays HUF to handle the administration and the refugee centres. This is an economic arrangement that is not integrated into the ordinary budgets and accounts of HUF, but is kept as an independent financial operation.

The centres provide spare-time activities and medical aid for the refugees and the employees at the centres are mostly people trained in the field of social work and daycare. They are generally easy going and flexible, which is important as the intake of refugees changes over time, demanding occasional lay-offs. Many of them have only little formal training but possess a good deal of genuine humanitarian tolerance.

At the central Refugee Administration only a few dozen people carry out the co-ordination and financial transactions needed to make the 25 centres work according to the agreement with the Ministry. The atmosphere in the office is very relaxed and unpretentious, and people come and go very much of their own accord. The day-to-day routines work impeccably, not least because of this self-sustained unit's ability to combine control and bureaucratic procedures with a casual, flexible and human face. To people working in the refugee centres or in the Refugee Administration, the Director of the operation deserves credit for the apparent success in carrying out this enormous task. The refugee issue arose out of the blue and soon grew to be a major humanitarian and administrative-political effort – and HUF became the organization to take this demanding task off the shoulders of the Ministry.

The refugee centres represent a humanitarian problem to be catered for, but in many of the country's 250 local HUF branches members tell their local committees that the refugees constitute a controversial problem. In many places refugees are seen as a threat to the 'Danish way of living'. They are mistaken for foreign workers and subsequently perceived as potential competitors for scarce resources in a society in recession. These local members play a major role in the life of HUF. There are a total of 66,000 members in the national organization. Only 8–10% of members take an active part in the local work of the branches or the county districts, but still this amounts to more than 5000 people.

Local branches

Life in a small HUF branch is very different from that of the employees in head office. International disasters are very far away – catastrophes are serious but something that comes to you by television. HUF relief projects make everybody proud in the local branch, but still their agenda consists of a whole different world of issues. Who are these people setting this agenda and why is it so different from the issues of the international relief projects and the refugee centres?

Generally, the members of a local branch are people well into their fifties and sixties. Most of them are women and only a few are working full time. They belong to the middle class of their local community and they focus by tradition on the needs and prospects of this community. Their world is to a large extent evolving around life in the small town, where people meet when shopping to discuss what was in the local paper that morning. Most of these members are anonymous citizens converting their own bad conscience towards their fellow man into an annual donation to HUF. But a small number of them are active in the organization, giving life to the whole variety of local HUF activities.

Some take part in the leadership of national HUF activities as they become elected to the branch committees, the district committees or the Central Committee. But most of the active members help with different local activities such as first aid, visiting service for the elderly, second-hand shops, sewing and needle groups, fundraising, recruitment, telephone chains, beach watch, etc. These active members have a long history in HUF. They have been in the organization for 15 to 20 years or more, and they do not seriously consider the possibility of leaving it. They are loyal, serious and caring as they give a hand once or twice a week, year after year. To these people HUF *is* the local activities. They see the branches as the foundation of the international relief projects and they take great pride in the contributions that their branch makes to the central HUF disaster fund each year.

Coming to a small country town there is no immediate sign of HUF having a branch there. Like the other humanitarian organizations HUF does not care for a shiny surface or flashy billboards. The local branch committee holds office in the private home of the chairperson or in a borrowed room at the local school. No two local branches are alike in the sense that the committee members determine the profile of activities, the line of administrative procedures, and the relationship with the local community at large. This is not because these committee members seek to have influence, nor through power vested in them by HUF. It is a consequence of the decentralized organization which depends entirely on the energy and motivation invested in it by the chairperson, the cashier, the committee members and the handful of ordinary members constituting the branch. And yet this also makes the branches somewhat alike. However different they may be on a day-to-day basis, covering very different types of activities, almost all of them share the same basic features of the local committee meeting in the chairperson's kitchen trying to build a local HUF branch around very local needs and preferences.

Going up the main street of the town, the only visible sign may be the second-hand shop with the familiar HUF symbols. In the shop, the elderly women sorting out recently collected material and displaying the best clothes on hangers are only too happy to give you information about what HUF does in the town, and how to become a member or volunteer without official membership. At the chairperson's house conversations start in the living room over coffee and home-made cookies and there is no rush or strings attached. Joining a local HUF branch starts by walking into the private home of a person who may work part time in the district hospital or be an independent craftsperson, who may be on a pension or a laid-off unskilled worker. Anyway, this is the person whose spouse or neighbour is the cashier and whose friendly hospitality symbolizes what HUF is all about. No one is expected to do as much as the chairperson, the cashier or the committee members, and normally nobody does. In most branches it is the work of a handful of active individuals that generates the platform for all the local HUF activities – and the down side of this is seen in continuing and increasing problems of recruiting new committee members and younger members. The local branches shut themselves off as they rely on the old and experienced members who faithfully and well intentionally carry on year after year.

As the day-to-day work is carried out by the members and the committee, head office becomes still more distant. A strong local chairperson creates a local HUF branch with very little contact with the National Department, the SG, or the President in head office. Seen from the small branch, head office appears as a body whose interest is directed towards voluntary national money collection (fundraising by ringing door bells) and the enormous funds provided by the Ministry of Foreign Affairs. So the chairperson and the local committee soon learn to mind their own business. They comply with the few prescriptions and procedures called for by the National Department concerning accounts and donations, and otherwise spend their time on doing locally what they like, keeping a low profile. Most branches are creative in generating additional funds, some of which are used locally to sustain new initiatives. No one would dream of using HUF funds for personal purposes – and no one would dream of transferring it all to head office.

County districts

This is not the case at county district level. People in the district committees are recruited from the branch committees. They are members who see HUF as a means of exerting influence. They enjoy the power and influence vested in them by their constituency and they demonstrate a lot of energy in their attempts to treat political and administrative decisions as important and meaningful steps in the democratic processes of HUF. On the one hand, they see themselves as safeguarding HUF democracy and decentralization – and on the other hand, they see these democratic processes as means to promote their own political career, aiming at a seat in the central committee, the post as vice-president, or chairperson of the district committee; whereas the local branch committee ignores much of what is going on in the district and the central democratic processes. The local committees prefer to spend time on generating local activities, whereas members of the district committees turn much of their attention away from the branches and focus on head office and the Central Committee – in pursuit of their own political careers.

Attending a district meeting is an enlightening experience. It is held in the local nursing home for severely disabled and as usual it is based on coffee and cookies. Before the official opening, the various branch committee chairpersons and their cashiers arrive. Nobody sits down. People stay outside the room, walking slowly up and down the corridor greeting each other quietly. Obviously, most of the people present have been chairpersons and cashiers for many years. When the meeting is officially opened the first five to ten minutes are spent on getting coffee for everyone, cookies are passed around the tables, more coffee is fetched from the nearby kitchen and so on.

When the time is right, the chairperson of the district committee opens the meeting and reads the agenda. A couple of controversial issues have been carefully prepared in a small informal session before the official meeting: one dealing with branch participation in the international project in Africa, 'A Source of Friendship', and the other with second-hand shop collaboration at the district level. Slowly, the discussion starts. The chairperson invites participants to voice their opinions and stresses the democratic process as fundamental to HUF activities. The first few comments are offered by some of the participants – and in each case the chairperson makes an explicit effort to refute the remarks. Apparently people seem to accept this violation of the alleged democratic discussion, as they continue to voice opinions and be brushed away by the chairperson or one of the core group committee members.

To the outsider this is clearly a case of manipulation more than a process of democratic dialogue. Yet people appear reasonably satisfied as they declare the continuing need to get together and support the decentralized, participative ideals of how to organize HUF locally. A couple of hours later the meeting is adjourned. People leave the premises as quietly as they arrived. Only a few decisions have been made and the district committee seems to be content that the controversial issues have been dealt with and decided on without creating major changes in existing routines. Concerning the issues of 'A Source of Friendship' and the second-hand shops collaboration, the district policy continues to be non-committal.

Over a beer people praise the democratic processes and the commitment demonstrated by the participants. The meeting is considered a success and an example of the HUF tradition of participation and dialogue.

So different, and yet alike

Travelling the country in this way a picture emerges. There are major differences between head office, Refugee Administration and local committees. There are also significant differences between the many local branches, as there are differences between what takes place at branch and district level. And still, there appears to be something intangible, a kind of common denominator, running as an undertow throughout HUF regardless of where you enter the organization. Behind the controversies between professionals and volunteers, despite conflicts between local committee members and head office professionals, there seems to be a core of basic values that people adhere to. People are proud to be part of HUF. They take great pride in their affiliation with an organization that rests on humanitarian, democratic and participative ideals. People may disagree but they still see themselves as belonging to a collective, working for a good cause.

Central Committee in session

Two months after the district committee meeting the Central Committee has its quarterly meeting. Topping the agenda (distributed with only a few supplements three weeks ahead) are three issues, of which two appeared at the district meeting, although at district level in more detail. In addition to the issues of 'A Source of Friendship' and the administration of second-hand shops, the third important item on the agenda concerns a proposal to move out of the present head office premises. Among the 20 issues on the agenda these three appear to draw all the attention of the 45 elected representatives and several different observers/representatives of head office (including the SG). The way the central committee deals with these three issues is interesting.

In the middle of the morning session, it is time for the 'Source of Friendship' question to be addressed. The SG gives the necessary briefing as he recalls the discussions in the bi-annual General Assembly, where the National Department proposed these small-scale international schemes involving a direct relationship between local branches and a local recipient in the third world. Such initiatives, it was suggested, should be financed by the branches and supported administratively by head office's National Department. To the SG the issue at this Central Committee meeting is to discuss how to bring life to these projects which apparently 'don't work'. At the General Assembly as well as in the different Standing Committees no one had spoken against the idea; and yet nothing has really happened. Again the discussion is timid, few remarks are made and consequently no decisions are taken. Like the discussion at the general assembly, the issue is closed with a 'declaration of intent'. During lunch, however, the issue is discussed in a great deal of detail as the representatives are sitting next to people they know well. This time the opinions are far from timid: remarks describe the lack of support from the National Department, the insufficient information initiating the 'Source of Friendship' scheme, and the resentment that the International Department shows when branches approach head office with ideas for possible projects.

The next item on the agenda is the proposal for a large 'second-hand centre' in a branch in the Copenhagen area. The idea of the centre is to co-ordinate much of the second-hand business in the district – building a large 'shopping centre' with a selection that the individual branches could never provide for their own shops. A written proposal was sent to head office more than six months previously and has so far received positive reactions from the Standing Committee for finance and economy. At today's Central Committee the SG introduces the discussion by indicating concern that the guaranteed sum needed for the project could not be provided by HUF, as this would be too big a financial risk to take. Furthermore, members of the Executive Committee argue that head office is planning to employ a second-hand co-ordinator, a consultant on a six-month basis, to organize the second-hand shop activities on a national level. Naturally, it should be left to this consultant to deal with the idea of a centre. Again, only a few representatives comment on the issue, even though it is apparent to everyone present that the committee member who launched the proposal feels that his case is being given poor treatment and that earlier promises are being set aside.

Over lunch this called for a number of candid comments as some of the committee members tried to raise the necessary guarantee funds among district representatives, but without success. Much of the lunch gossip at this stage suggested that the reason for head office's intervention against the proposed centre was the possibility of 'losing' a profitable HUF national project to a local branch/district.

So far, the Central Committee meeting has been conducted in the usual neutral and passive atmosphere. Despite the controversial issues and the way they are handled, the level of discussion resembles that of the district meeting two months earlier. The people in power at the district meeting, however, are now the people without power – discussing the very same issues at the Central Committee level. But when the last item on the agenda is reached the atmosphere changes totally. 'A new location for head office' was added to the agenda only a few days before the meeting and with only scant background information to support the discussion. The SG presents the problems of working in the present building with too little space – and describes the new possible solution brought forward through negotiations with the Ministry of Defence (the formal owner of the present head office building). Moving to new premises will involve a US$ 5 million investment. However, it is pointed out that in the long run HUF will be reimbursed for this investment by the Ministry of Defence under various financial arrangements. Consequently, HUF would lose no money by moving to new premises. HUF's (central) administration would gain more space, and would be able to integrate the Refugee Administration at the same time.

This proposal causes an enormous reaction. Representatives reproach head office for being ready to invest US$ 5 million with little guarantee that the money will actually by reimbursed by the Ministry. People are furious that they only received this fundamental information a few days before the committee meeting and much of it at the meeting itself. It is argued that the public and the local branches will interpret this message as a signal of a growing HUF administration where support and funds are eaten up by prestigious administrative ambitions. The discussion goes on and gets out of control and finally the SG has to withdraw the proposal, commenting that negotiations to buy new buildings have to be swift and more or less secret. He cannot hide his disappointment at having invested resources in analysing the proposal and calculating the financial consequences in vain. The meeting is adjourned, but the discussion continues over lunch and is characterized by individual emotional and aggressive arguments.

After lunch the HUF staff members go back to their jobs, having been confirmed in their prejudices about the decision-making capacity of the Central Committee. Once again it is demonstrated to representatives of head office and the local branches/districts alike that committee meetings do not work. The elected representatives go back to their home base with yet another story to tell about head office manipulation; and head office representatives tell their colleagues new stories about how rigid and disinterested the local representatives are in the fundamental issues of HUF, focusing only on their petty arguments against a sound administrative move of location. As no one seems to know how to untie this social deadlock, life goes on in HUF as it has done for years.

Analysing the problems

Based on the recommendations of the outside anthropologist, the General Assembly decided to initiate a study of the current problems. A group of independent researchers was asked to suggest alternative models for organizing HUF. The administrative set-up at head office as described above was, however, not part of the task.

The researchers' report consists of four sections:

- Section 1: Strategic analysis of HUF.
- Section 2: Paradoxes in the HUF organization.
- Section 3: Paradoxes and organizational perspectives.
- Section 4: Three alternative organizational models for HUF.

Strategic analysis

Like any other organization, HUF has its strengths and weaknesses, and parts of the environment in which it operates have unexplored potential, whereas other parts pose threats. These two perspectives on the organization and the environment formed the basis for the strategic analysis.

Strengths and weaknesses The strength of the HUF organization is its flexibility. It comprises a well-functioning network which has succeeded in developing administrative routines which keep down costs. The network represents ample and multi-faceted human resources and the members are both loyal to and engaged in performing the activities stipulated in HUF's action programme. In general, the basic attitudes of the members can be described as loyal and the structure as efficient.

The weaknesses of HUF concern the various sub-structures which are necessary for operating the organization, especially since the tasks performed involve both attitudes and interests. It is difficult to make the various decision-making bodies fit the spectrum of activities undertaken by the organization.

Different interpretations of the concept 'representative democracy' do not always match the demands which arise from the nature of tasks and activities. On the one hand the administrative systems are simple, low cost and efficient, and as a consequence also restrictive and standardized. On the other hand, the needs of the elected members for discussions on principles, attitudes and ideas and for analysis of various alternatives in decision making are not well served by the administrative apparatus.

There is a lack of leadership in the sense of participants who are willing to take responsibility for co-ordinating interests and ideas for future activities to be carried out by the organization. Being an efficient and professional organization does not suffice among the members if HUF is incapable of utilizing its potential by finding ideas and attitudes to develop the organization.

Potentials and threats On the whole, HUF's position in society provides many opportunities, especially in relation to the citizens of local communities. Recent political, economic and social trends have provided HUF with a central position – nationally as well as internationally. Historically, and by tradition, HUF is well equipped to undertake both national and global aid activities and perform the role as society's 'watchdog'. The organization is showing a growing understanding of the necessity of guarding basic social and humanitarian values.

However, being part of the 'social ecology' also poses a threat to HUF's status. Its current position of esteem is extremely dependent on its ability to maintain the image of a true relief organization. This image stems from the complex combination of local activities, international disaster aid and state-subsidized aid programmes in the third world; from basing its activities on a mixture of employees, volunteers and politicians; and from being able to find the right balance between contributions, collections, state subsidies and administrative costs. HUF is a rather conservative organization based on 'grass-roots' support and a rather complicated democratic system. Its future position will depend on its ability to adapt to changes in the external environment without betraying the complex network of agents which constitutes its base.

HUF's current situation and reputation can be summarized as follows (based on an opinion survey of the Danish population):

- HUF is one of the best known relief organizations.
- HUF is perceived as a traditional, somewhat old-fashioned organization.
- Many people, even those who are members of the organization, hold a passive attitude towards HUF. They are positive but not actively engaged in the organization.
- HUF particularly attracts older (rather than younger) citizens, and people with lower (rather than higher) educational backgrounds.
- The population finds it difficult to distinguish between HUF and the other major Danish relief organization, Dan Church Aid, since they perform the same activities and often co-operate.
- In general the population's attitude is that HUF should continue to engage in both national and international activities.

The possibility of HUF gaining support from new groups in the population depends on its ability to attract younger citizens with a higher level of education. However, to reach these groups HUF must be able to present itself as a more modern and interesting organization than is currently the case. Not that such measures will immediately reduce the current attitudinal conflicts characterizing the organization, but in the long run they might result in a more uniform and harmonious organization.

Paradoxes in the organization

A paradox represents different perceptions of fundamental issues. Thus, a paradox reflects organizational conditions which do not seem to fit together or which appear to be mutually impeding. Such paradoxes are, of course, 'a product' of how situations are perceived. The following three examples reflect some of the paradoxical patterns identified in HUF.

Paradox 1: 'The local branches are not interested in international tasks' This paradox is related to the decision-making processes of the Central Committee, which finds it difficult to discuss international disaster and relief work.

Strategic decisions have been made regarding the economic commitment to international tasks. Nothing seems to indicate any opposition within HUF against these decisions:

> The proposal to put priorities to our tasks was presented by the International Department. The local branches were invited to participate in a workshop to do this – an initiative which the participants perceived as very informative. (Head office statement)

On various occasions attempts have been made to create more interest in international work. Employees from the International Department have visited local branches and told them about international projects. But the various initiatives have been in vain – international projects still attract little attention locally. The meetings between head office employees and local members have been characterized by a lack of interest rather than disagreement or opposition from the members:

> The geographical structure creates a narrow local patriotic attitude. Local citizens meet to solve local problems. (Head office statement)

Once a year HUF's head office submits a detailed report on its international relief work which is included in the local branches' annual reports. But the report does not seem to give rise to any debate. The Secretary General presents reports on international tasks at Central Committee meetings and General Assemblies – but they never cause any discussion.

The project 'A Source of Friendship' was established to strengthen the local branches' engagement in international work. However, the initiative did not achieve the desired effect. Head office regards it as yet another example of local branches lacking interest in international work; and members of the local branches conceived it as yet another example of activities which are not sufficiently supported by head office.

Local branches that have been engaged in international projects for a long time wonder why they are not informed about the status of these activities. They have asked if it would be possible for a representative of the local branch engaged in a mini-project to visit the project and thus be able to provide the other members with an 'eye-witness' report on how the project is progressing – something which might also create greater local interest in HUF's national and international work:

> We are engaged in a small international project . . . but we are never informed about how it proceeds. Actually, we do not even know if the money we collect is allocated to the project.

The paradox is evident. The discussion about HUF's international commitments and the priority of this work demonstrate consensus. But when it comes to the concrete activities related to the establishment and maintenance of projects, the situation is characterized by significantly different perceptions of why it is so difficult to establish a dialogue.

Head office, represented by the Secretary General and the Department of International Relief, complains about the lack of interest in and support for decisions concerning international activities. Local and county districts complain about their international activities not being taken sufficiently seriously by the head office employees. But behind these statements, blaming head office and local branches respectively for the lack of interest in international activities, the parties have conceded that international activities should be given high priority in the action programme. An opinion poll reveals that 85% of the local and county districts find that aid and disaster activities should be given first priority; correspondingly, 67% find that local and county districts should be given greater influence in international activities. This support undoubtedly conceals different attitudes towards balancing disaster relief and development aid.

More generally, however, the paradox has to do with professionals and volunteers. They share an attitude that supports the international work of HUF. The professionals (the International Department) want to involve the volunteers in supporting this work, but they do not want to have the local branches actively involved, since the work is highly professionalized. The volunteers feel cheated by the professionals. They want to be able to demonstrate to their local branch that they are actively involved. At best they would like to 'adopt' small projects in third-world countries. So the paradox reflects differences between professionals and volunteers and between head office and local branches, rather than differences in attitudes towards international tasks.

Paradox 2: 'The General Assembly is expensive red tape' It is interesting to note the status which is attributed to the General Assembly. Most participants describe the basically democratic platform in very tentative terms:

> To most members the general assembly is a question of having a good time with other old-timers in HUF.

> Arriving at the general assembly you find all the important people sitting on a platform at one end of the room. The scene resembles a meeting in the former Soviet central committee.

From an outside perspective the different opinions presented can be characterized as:

- formal and symbolic;
- devoid of content;
- social.

The paradox is again evident. In general, none of the participants experiences the meeting as important. Furthermore, there is broad consensus about much of the criticism, but not when it comes to assessing the legitimacy and potential significance of the meetings with respect to the organization's future activities.

Much seems to indicate that the General Assembly represents a self-fulfilling prophecy in HUF. Its democratic structure is based on the idea that the local branches are represented according to their membership basis, in spite of the fact that in HUF there are different methods for calculating the number of members. The popularly elected members of the Central Committee, who in day-to-day management safeguard local interests, are elected by the county districts which are not represented at the General Assembly. Therefore, the relationship between the 'grass-roots' members and the Central Committee is characterized by scepticism.

The General Assembly is attributed significant formal competence. However, with bi-annual General Assemblies attended by a large number of participants, it is difficult to imagine it as a platform for making the necessary strategic decisions. It is almost to be expected that everybody expects everyone else to produce content, efficiency and basic beliefs.

Again, the paradox reflects profound dilemmas in HUF: between the democratic structure which places the (formal) decision-making power in the hands of the General Assembly and the professional discretion needed to make decisions of a highly complicated nature. The representatives feel manipulated by the professionals, who for their part claim that the representatives are there for all the wrong (local, status) reasons.

Attempts by head office to calculate the costs of organizing the General Assembly have recently been subject to much debate. In line with the general trends in HUF (and society), attempts have been made to figure out the exact costs of this activity. The representatives are reimbursed for their travel expenses and do not pay for room and meals during the two-day meeting. But they contribute their energy and do not receive any financial compensation for participating. Rumour has it that the 1990 General Assembly was extremely expensive. However, this economic rationality colours any discussion of the organizational outcome of the General Assembly (social, symbolic and official), as well as any debate about what HUF potentially might be able to gain from such meetings – possibly because the gains cannot be stated in dollars and cents.

Paradox 3: 'Head office does not provide an adequate service' Behind many of the problems described in connection with the above paradoxes are a number of unformulated expectations related to the roles and distribution of tasks in the organization. These expectations reflect two parallel developments in HUF. Simultaneously with the content of the action programme shifting focus from the historically conditioned aid to victims of war to more broadly based relief and development aid activities, it has been increasingly difficult for members to 'see' the connection between international and national activities. Concurrently with HUF parting from an epoch of activities based on local branches collecting funds for international disaster programmes, the gap between international and national activities has become increasingly visible. For a number of years HUF has increasingly focused on undertaking government-subsidized development aid programmes, which are not necessarily initiated on account of visible disasters and which are only slightly dependent on local contributions. This adheres to government development policy: that it is important to do development work since that will reduce disaster and relief operations.

Recent changes have made it possible for local activities and international aid and disaster programmes to develop independently of each other, thus escaping interaction, co-ordination and coherence. The action programme is sufficiently broad and spacious to harbour everybody. Nor does any acute market or competitive pressure exist that calls for co-ordination of local and international activities.

Against this background it becomes extremely difficult to narrow down exactly what it is that employees and volunteers expect of each other. For many years each party has been handling its own affairs and has not intervened unnecessarily in each other's domain. However, this predicament is aggravated by the fact that international activities have grown tremendously in recent years, at the same time as it has become increasingly difficult to recruit members for voluntary activities:

> The organization has been divided into head office and local branches.

> Many local branch members do not like to contact head office . . . and probably vice versa. Another problem is that members earn their living during day time and do HUF work in the evening – and head office closes at 4 pm.

To the employees in HUF local activities are currently characterized by 'crisis'. They find that volunteers are raising their expectations that head office will engage more actively in the branches' activities in terms of counselling and administrative support.

The volunteers have an image of uncontrollable growth in international activities, of which 10% is financed through local activities. They find that the employees have greater expectations of the local branches in terms of their being willing to undertake still more burdens – financially as well as workwise.

> Head office is convinced that it 'allocates' money to the local branches . . . while we feel that we are 'allocating' money to head office that spends it on activities on which we have no influence. (Interview with a local branch chairman)

It is a situation of undocumented assumptions. Nobody seriously dares to start the discussion, even though both parties feel that their prejudices have been confirmed. They both have difficulties in facing the fact that they hold unrealistic expectations of and prejudices against the other party.

Thus, the employees find it legitimate to expect positive support from the volunteers regardless of the services that head office is willing to give the local branches. The prevailing prejudice is that the volunteers merely want to exploit head office resources without being willing to support its international activities.

Correspondingly, the volunteers find it legitimate to expect concrete and efficient support from head office employees, independently of how much money the local branches are able to allocate to international activities. The prevailing prejudice is that the employees are merely interested in 'thrusting the costs onto the local committees' without being prepared to allow them a minimum of influence.

It is a matter of clashing interests – who is to service whom. Everybody is ready to discuss the question only in their respective 'home groups', a fact which poses an almost insurmountable barrier to a discussion which might lead to future co-operation based on a dialogue between the groups.

Paradoxes and organizational perspectives

The three paradoxes represent widely different problems and conflicts in HUF. The core of several of the descriptions is identical, but each paradox has its own nature.

Applying Leavitt's[4] model to HUF and adding the culture variable (see Figure 3.5), we see both positive and negative flows.

Some of the problems are not solely caused by the structural configuration of HUF, but just as much by the technology (the 'toolkit' applied to relief, disaster and development work by the professionals), the participants (volunteers and professionals) and the choice of and nature of tasks.

The first two paradoxes concerning the international work and the General Assembly strongly illustrate the relationship between structure and participants.

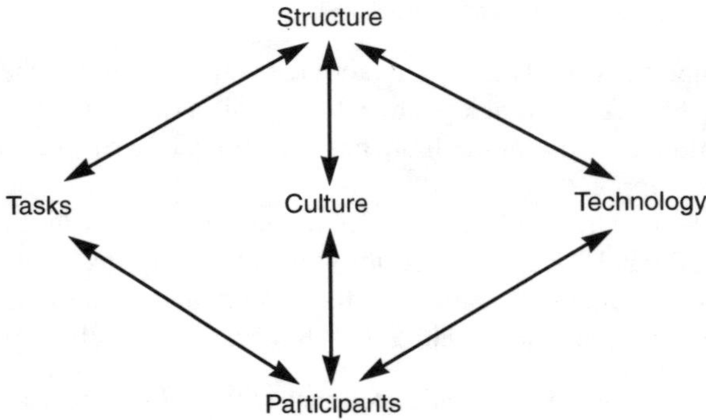

Figure 3.5 *Leavitt's model*

The paradoxes not only touch upon HUF's structural model, but also illustrate how this is affected by the participants and how it affects their attitudes towards the principles of the action programme.

The third paradox, on the other hand, describing the relationship between local branches and head office, signifies the importance of technology to the participants' experience of HUF's structure and functions (communication, administrative routines, member services, etc.).

It is characteristic of all three paradoxes that they are linked directly to the participants. Applied to Leavitt's model it is striking how the paradoxes almost form a fan anchored in the participants. This picture is hardly surprising – organizations are inhabited by people to whom structures and processes must be adapted if they are to give life to the organization and 'fill in the holes'.

Much seems to indicate that previous debates about organizational changes in HUF have concluded by being referred to committees or turned into proposals for regulatory amendments – because nobody took into account the 'human factor'. If proposals for change are to become something other than a piece of paper and evolve into actual change processes, they must take into account the values and capacities of the members of the organization. We can ask why committees did not work towards such an end, but apart from providing general insights into HUF, we do not have the answer.

Three alternative organizational models

The following three alternative organizational models are each aiming at strengthening certain aspects of HUF. They are very different and merely represent precepts. None of the models represents an ideal solution to the problems raised.

Model 1: The 'company' and grass-roots organization The starting point of this model (see Figure 3.6) is the fact that a growing number of activities are subsidized by public funds (Ministry of Foreign Affairs, Ministry of Justice). Therefore, HUF could be divided into two independent units – a professional organization (the company) and a popular (grass-roots) organization.

The company will be organized as three divisions headed by a manager. Each of the units will have an advisory committe. The company is headed by a Managing Director who is the Chief Executive Officer and refers to the Executive Committee.

The grass-roots organization is a voluntary association and the organizational set-up will facilitate the involvement of volunteers in its activities.

The model does not imply that HUF ceases to be one organization, rather that the two units are designed to function relatively independently of each other without any prescribed collaboration. Not that collaboration is excluded, but it should grow out of the participants' desire and need for collaboration on issues they find relevant.

Model 2: The regional model The regional model (see Figure 3.7) does not distinguish sharply between activities undertaken by HUF volunteers and those

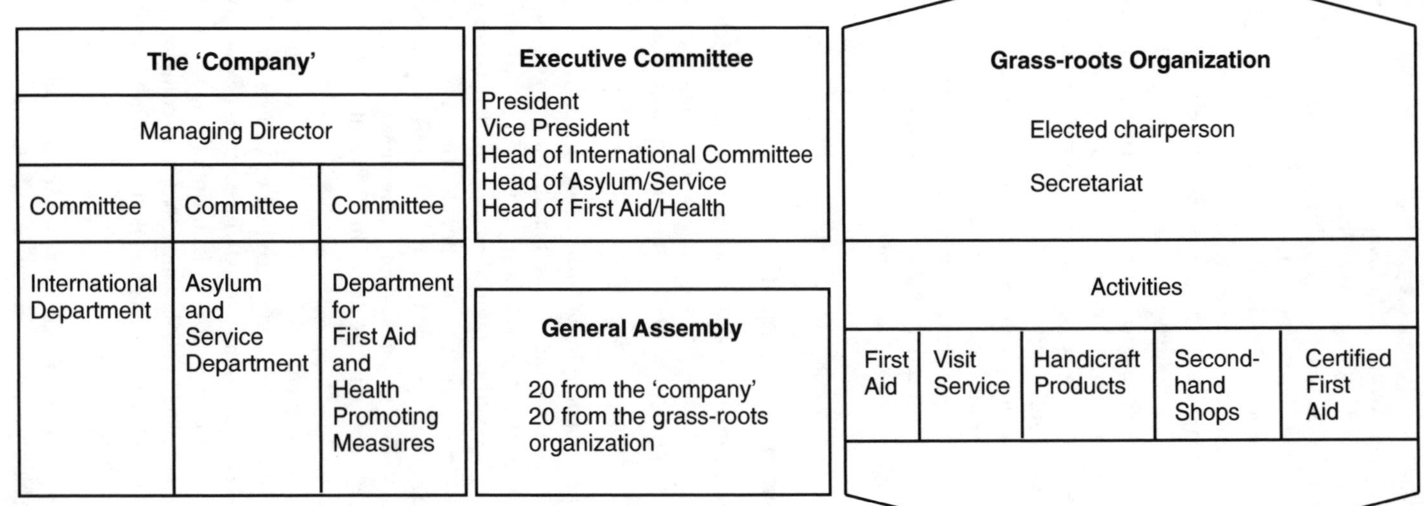

Figure 3.6 *The 'company' and grass-roots organization model*

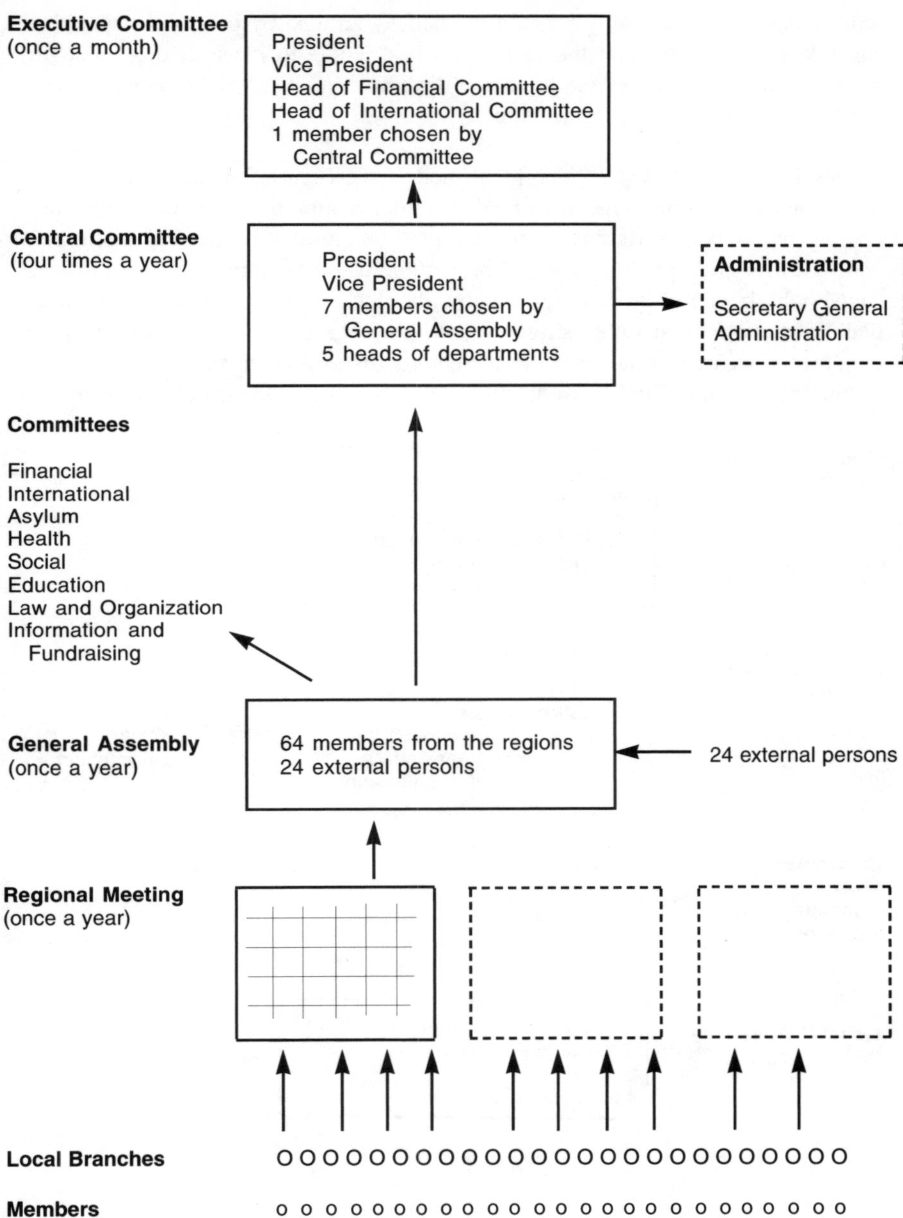

Figure 3.7 *The regional model*

undertaken by employees. In line with the current organizational model, the regional model retains HUF as one organization. Compared with the current model it does, however, contain a number of radical changes. The number of county regions is reduced and given a stronger position. The activities will be carried out not only by local branches, but also by county districts that can take on activities that the local branches decide to place at this level for purposes of co-ordination and to ensure developments (first-aid groups, second-hand shops, international projects, etc.)

Model 3: The local model The local model (see Figure 3.8) does not operate with county districts. The model takes into account that the local branches operate under very different local conditions (size, activities, local traditions) and that this great variation should be exploited to strengthen HUF. Activities can/should be co-ordinated directly by the local branches that jointly may undertake projects, share experiences and advocate new ideas for activities. In the current organizational structure the county districts seem superfluous for co-ordinating activities, and consequently are removed as an organizational unit in

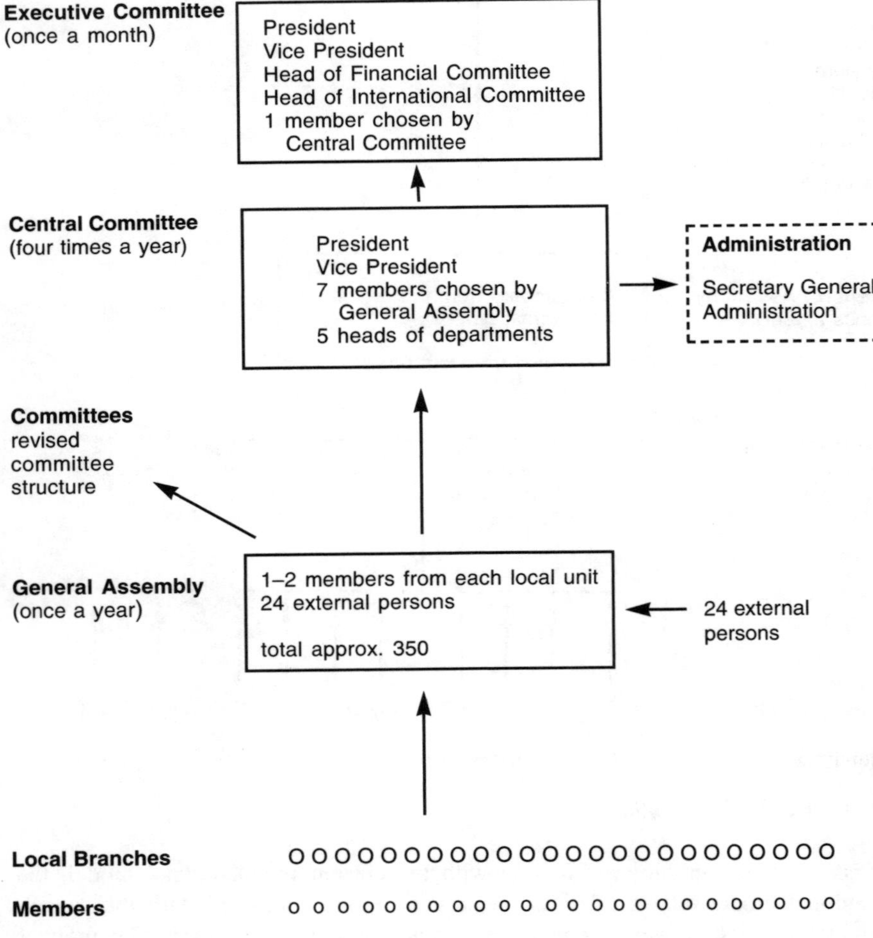

Figure 3.8 *The local model*

this model. Head office could, of course, function as the co-ordinator, but the model is operational without this link.

Advantages and disadvantages of the models The *'Company' and grass-roots organization* model turns HUF into a more efficient disaster and relief organization – nationally as well as internationally. But efficiency is achieved at the expense of the popular democratic element which strongly characterizes the organization today. This model may prove to hamper the possible synergetic effects of forcing volunteers and employees to work together. And HUF's legitimate position in society to a large extent rests on its broad popular basis, which this model partly removes.

The *regional model* retains the organization as one comprising both professional and popular aspects. The model links HUF activities to the regional level as a means to achieve greater effectiveness. Regional branches are given a crucial position. The question is, however, whether it will be possible to breathe sufficient new life into the regional branches to make them fill the role stipulated. If not, the regional branches will become an organizational barrier impeding the necessary co-ordination of HUF activities.

The *local model* preserves vital parts of the present organization, in spite of the fact that it is not functioning optimally. There are great variations in how the local branches function, but many branches operate well and several others possess the potential of doing so. The idea behind excluding the county districts is to leave it to the local branches to initiate co-ordinating activities. So far such activities have been undertaken by the county districts, but it is assumed that local branches will continue this task at an informal level and that new types of collaboration will emerge. In this model the structural interplay between local branches and the General Assembly is simplified and all branches are represented at the General Assembly. Consequently, the General Assembly will contain as many members as the current one – and the inherent problems of a meeting of this size.

All three models seek to exploit the strengths of HUF and subdue its weaknesses. They are very different and each has its advantages and disadvantages. None of them represents the optimal organizational model for HUF. When choosing an organizational model it is imperative to ask: Which problems in the current organizational model do we want to get rid of and which new problems are we willing to shoulder in a revised model?

Themes/issues to consider

Structural redesign

What are the likely consequences for organizational efficiency and effectiveness and for participant motivation of choosing one of the models or a combination?

Cultural analysis

What are the strengths and weaknesses of the HUF culture? What should be done (if anything) about this culture, and how is it possible to intervene? Please specify ways of intervening as well as the process (e.g. who should be involved) in the intervention process.

Assignments

Structural redesign

1. What are the likely problems that HUF will face if it chooses model 1, model 2, or model 3?
2. What is your suggestion to the Central Committee about redesigning the structure of HUF?
3. Which of the models (or combinations/other alternatives) will you propose to the central committee?
4. How will you propose to implement the structural redesign in HUF?
5. Decide how you want to make the presentation in the plenary session.

Cultural analysis

6. Make a diagnosis of the organizational culture in HUF.
7. Discuss a presentation to the Central Committee emphasizing what you think are important features of the culture in HUF (strong/weak points, differences and similarities in different parts of the HUF organization).
8. What is your suggestion to the Central Committee regarding what should be done about the culture in HUF (if anything), and how will you propose to intervene? (Do *not* consider any structural redesign of HUF.)
9. Decide how you want to make the presentation in the plenary session.

Suggested reading

The reading suggested here is related to different parts of the HUF case.

HUF in its cultural context

Christensen, Søren and Molin, Jan (1994) 'Origin and transformation of organizations: Institutional analysis of the Danish Red Cross', in Scott, W. Richard and Christensen, Søren (eds) *Advances in Institutional Analysis of Organizations: International and Longitudinal Studies*. London: Sage. Gives a historical account of a non-profit organization from its founding in 1876 until the present. The perspective is institutional and tries to understand the foundation and reorganizations of the organization in a wider social context.

Fivelsdal, Egil and Schramm-Nielsen, Jette (1993) 'Egalitarianism at work: Management in Denmark, Chapter 3: Denmark', in Hickson, David J. (ed.) *Management in Western Europe:*

Society, Culture, and Organization in Twelve Nations. Berlin: Walter de Gruyter. An up-to-date and excellent short presentation of Denmark. It provides an understanding of the particular national culture which is an important part of the cultural context of HUF.

Zalewski, Barbara (1992) 'The history of the Danish Red Cross' (unfinished manuscript for a PhD dissertation), Copenhagen. The historical analysis of HUF is partly based on this manuscript.

Analysis of organizational culture

Frost, Peter J., Moore, Larry F., Reis Louis, Meryl, Lundberg, Craig C. and Martin, Joanne (1985) *Organizational Culture*. London: Sage. This book offers different theoretical perspectives on organizational cultures and is particularly useful in discussions of how cultures can be studied and understood.

Schein, Edgar H. (1985) *Organizational Culture and Leadership*. San Franciso: Jossey-Bass. This book is a classic in organizational culture analysis and offers a functionalist perspective on culture and leadership.

Organizational redesign

French, Wendell L. and Bell, Cecil H. Jr. (1990) *Organization Development: Behavioral science interventions for organization improvement*. Fourth edition. Englewood Cliffs, NJ: Prentice-Hall. This book covers a wide array of approaches to organization development and could been seen as a source book on OD.

Mintzberg, Henry (1983) *Structures in Fives: Designing Effective Organizations*. Englewood Cliffs, NJ: Prentice-Hall. Gives a precise and useful discussion of different structural configurations and how these may be appropriated for different task environments.

Notes

This case is based on a research project running from January to October 1991, conducted by Søren Christensen, Jan Molin, Ann Westenholz, Finn Borum (Copenhagen Business School, Insitute of Organization and Industrial Sociology), Peter Gundelach (Aarhus University), and Bjarne Ipsen (Danmarks Højskole for Legemesøvelser) in collaboration with the following students: Toinni Snellman, Jorgen Foley, Lene Lund Hansen, Per Hansen, Helle Slott Jørgensen, Niels Keller-Larsen, Helle Strand, Henrik Andersen, Linda Evald, Jen Hall-Andersen, Gitte Højen, Lizi Keinicke, Maj-Britt Bregnegaard Knudsen, Søren Kraglund, Ulrikka Mikkelsen, Anders Schoubye, Kim Schrøder, Gry Stenkilde, Anette Toft.

Results from the project are presented in *Dansk Røde Kors Undersøgelsen* (1991), Bind I (125 pp) and Bind II (221 pp). Copenhagen Business School, Institute of Organization and Industrial Sociology.

1 Zalewski, Barbara (1992) 'The history of the Danish Red Cross', unfinished manuscript for a PhD dissertation, Copenhagen.
2 Christensen, Søren and Molin, Jan (1994) 'Origin and transformation of organizations: Institutional analysis of the Danish Red Cross', in Scott, W. Richard and Christensen, Søren (eds), *Advances in Institutional Analysis of Organizations: International and Longitudinal Studies*. London: Sage.
3 Fivelsdal, Egil and Schramm-Nielsen, Jette (1993) 'Egalitorianism at work: Management in Denmark' in Hickson, David J. (ed.) *Management in Western Europe: Society, Culture and Organization in Twelve Nations*. Berlin: Walter de Gruyter.
4 Leavitt, Harold J. (1965) 'Applied Organizational Change in Industry: Structural, technological and humanistic approaches' in March, James G. (ed.) *Handbook of Organizations*. Chicago: Rand McNally & Co.

5 March, James G. (1994) *A Primer on Decision Making: How Decisions Happen*. New York: The Free Press.

Appendix: Role playing exercise

As a general background you may wish to refer to the excellent book by James G. March, *Decisions and Organizations* (Blackwell, 1988). In this book the author not only presents his own work, but also gives a good summary of decision-making theories.

You may wish to conduct a role playing exercise addressing group decision making and leadership issues, drawing on some of the data in relation to HUF. The session should have a time frame of approximately two hours.

You will need a total of 6 actors:

- Robert McGuire, Head of Secretariat
- Adam Grant, PR and Fundraising
- Freddy Johnson, Campaign Section
- Eric Blackwell, Member Files Section
- Bart Kelly, Internal Administration
- Edward Green, EDP – Logistics

The remaining students observe the role play. All actors and observers should receive the following handouts: General instructions and Layout of the offices (Figure 3.9). The actors should receive their individual handouts with their role; the observers should receive the handout titled Observer instructions (see p. 106).

General instructions

For a number of years the head office has been putting up with poorly equipped offices. The ground-floor activities have suffered with very small offices. Recently, the Secretary General gave in to the demand for better working conditions and agreed to create two new offices. One of the offices is ready for occupation and the other one will be ready in a year. The new office measures 47 square metres and is larger than the existing offices. Furthermore, it is much better located and equipped.

The question is: Which of the five sections will move into the new office?

The ground floor is divided into five sections:

1. Campaign. Johnson manages this section with four employees.
2. Member Files. Blackwell manages this section with three employees.
3. Information, PR and Fundraising. Grant manages this section with five employees.
4. Internal Administration. Kelly manages this section with seven employees.
5. EDP – Logistics. Green manages this section with two employees.

Robert McGuire, head of the secretariat, has invited the section leaders to a meeting in order to discuss which of the five sections should be allocated the new office. All five section leaders participate in the meeting, which is conducted by McGuire.

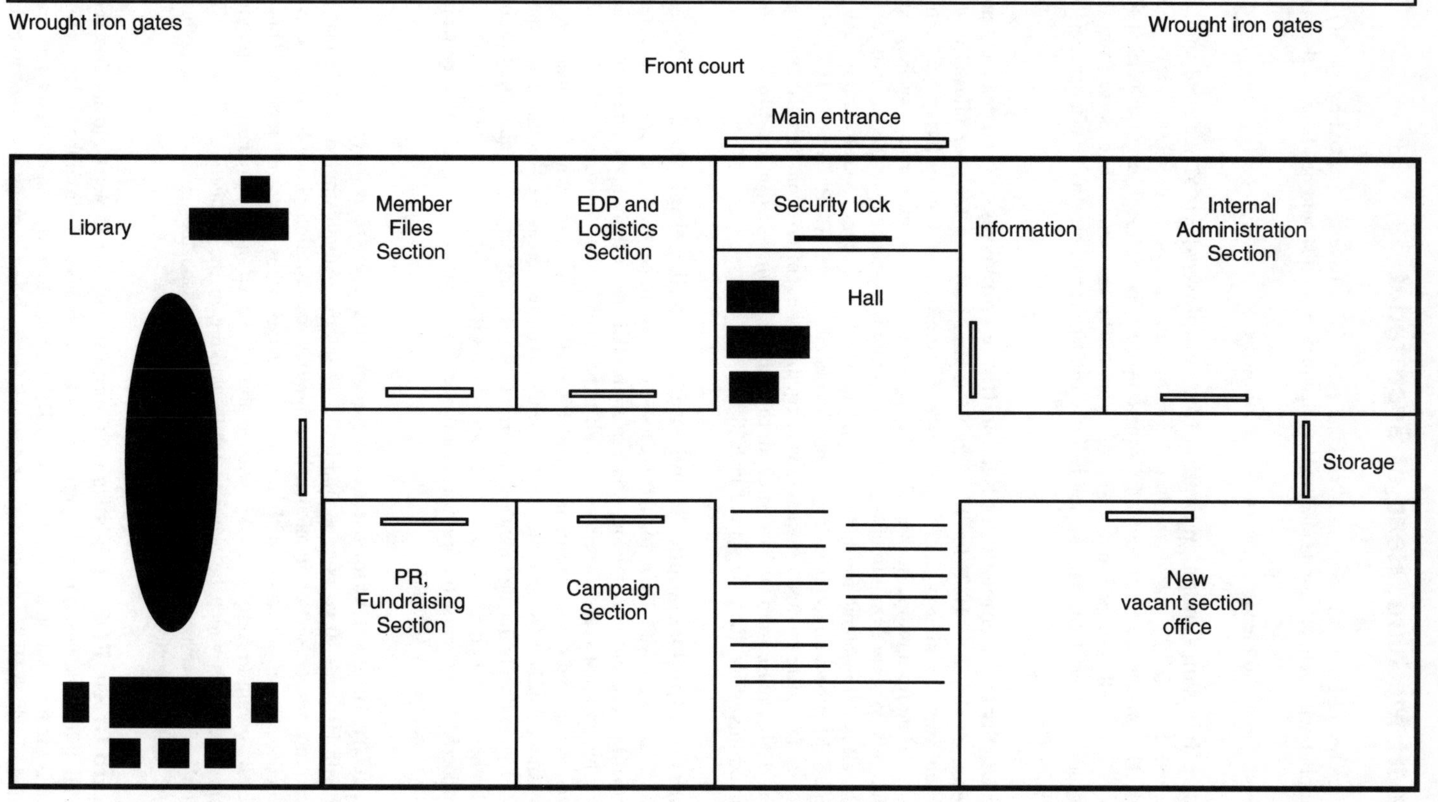

Figure 3.9 *Layout of HUF offices*

Robert McGuire, Head of Secretariat

You are head of the secretariat in HUF head office. You have been asked by the SG to collaborate with your section leaders to decide which section should be allocated the new office.

About the section leaders you know the following:

Freddy Johnson, Campaign Section (four employees) is 52 years old and has been with HUF for 20 years – the last 10 years in his present position. He enjoys good health. His present office measures 28 square metres. Even though it is not perfect for visitors it is well equipped and sealed off from traffic disturbance and noise from the downstairs canteen. Johnson's section is lively and has shown reasonable effectiveness in recent years.

Eric Blackwell, Member Files Section (three employees) is 60 years old and has been employed in HUF for 15 years as section leader of Member Files. He was recruited from a similar type of organization. During the last four to five years he has been suffering from failing health, which has upset him. Part of his current psychological condition is possibly owing to his section's declining importance over the last five years. Blackwell is not to blame for this development, which is brought about by technological changes. Membership registration is now handled by the EDP section. His office measures 18 square metres, is nice and well equipped but suffers from one disadvantage: a great deal of noise from both the street traffic and the downstairs canteen. Blackwell has occupied this office since he started in HUF.

Adam Grant, Information, PR and Fundraising (five employees) is 30 years old and has been with HUF for five years – the last three years as section leader of Information, PR and Fundraising. His career in HUF has experienced a meteoric rise. During his two first years he proved himself to be an excellent 'salesman', which is why he was transferred to the Information and PR section, a position which he handled so successfully that he was appointed section leader. The section as well as the results have grown tremendously during Grant's reign. His office is fairly large, 25 square metres, but in all other respects it is the poorest of the section offices. Grant's section has occupied the office for three years. Before that time the section occupied the smallest office which is now occupied by Green.

Bart Kelly, Internal Administration (seven employees) is 41 years old and has been with HUF for 10 years as section leader of Internal Administration. Before that he worked in a similar section in another humanitarian organization. Since Kelly took over the section, the effectiveness of Internal Administration has increased rapidly. This is especially owing to Kelly's vast knowledge about the need for and potential of applying simple procedures which he acquired while working in the Ministry of Defence. His section's office measures 26 square metres and is of a reasonable standard, but is nothing special. Kelly's section has had the office for three years.

Edward Green, EDP – Logistics (two employees) is 35 years old and has been with HUF for nine years. For six years he worked in Blackwell's Member Files section. Green is the first section leader of the new EDP section which was established three years ago and of which HUF expects a great deal. HUF has invested many resources in trying to develop competence within this field in an attempt to cope with increasing problems of national co-ordination. Green's office is the smallest of the section offices, 14 square metres. It is of a reasonable standard but troubled by quite a lot of noise from the street traffic.

If you together with your section leaders are unable to reach a decision on which of the sections the new office should be allocated to, the SG will make the decision.

Freddy Johnson, Campaign section (four employees)

You are 52 years old and have been with HUF for 20 years. For the last 10 years you have been section leader of Campaigns. Your working results have been reasonably stable during the last few years. Your office is the largest of the section offices. It measures 28 square metres and is the most well equipped. You are not bothered by any noise from the street traffic or the downstairs canteen.

You have good reasons for wanting to move to the new office. You hold seniority in HUF and together with Blackwell you also hold seniority as section leader. During your years in HUF you have proved yourself to be a stable and loyal employee. You have taken any opportunity to stress that your section office is too small for the many visitors you have in connection with the campaigns, but you have always done this without raising your voice.

Eric Blackwell, Member Files section (three employees)

You are 60 years old and have been with HUF for 15 years. During the whole period you have been section leader of Member Files. Before that time you worked with another humanitarian organization. For the last four to five years you have been suffering from failing health and find it increasingly difficult to handle your stressful job situation. Your personal insecurity has become evident to your surroundings and you are very sensitive to noise. Your disquiet is connected to the rapidly declining importance of your section. You know that you are a good clerk and that you are not to be blamed for this development, which stems from the introduction of new technology.

You are rather disappointed about the SG's decision to establish a special EDP section for member files. This section was established three years ago when HUF decided to develop its own technological routines combining the requirements of co-ordination, filing, forecasting and logistics in a new section. You find that the new section has been set up at your expense as your former subordinate Green was appointed section leader. It is your opinion that a political decision to start a central recruitment procedure is due – and this, in your opinion, will call for a larger Member Files section.

Your office is the second smallest of the section offices and measures 18 square metres. It is a very nice and well-equipped office which has only one major flaw: noise from the street traffic and the downstairs canteen.

There are several reasons why you should be allocated the new office. You are the oldest of the section leaders. Together with Johnson you hold seniority as a section leader. Your health is failing and you are suffering a great deal from the noise in your office. For the past five years you have been trying to get another office but have been unsuccessful.

Adam Grant, Information, PR and Fundraising (five employees)

You are 30 years old and have been with HUF for five years. Your career in HUF has experienced a meteoric rise. Three years ago you were appointed section leader of Information, PR and Fundraising. Before then you had proved yourself to be an efficient and competent PR officer. Fundraising has increased tremendously under your leadership and you have succeeded in gaining substantial financial support from different sources. Your section office measures 25 square metres, but is in all respects the poorest of the offices.

There are several reasons for your section being allocated the new office. Together with Green (the section leader of EDP – Logistics) you are the only one of the section leaders who has been able to demonstrate efficient and good financial results. Because of your section's external relations you have a great number of officials visiting you and your section leaves them with a bad image of HUF. Your primary argument is that from HUF's perspective it is imperative that you are allocated the new office.

You have occupied your present office for three years. Before then you occupied Green's office, which is the smallest one measuring 14 square metres. You asked for your current office only because you needed more space.

Bart Kelly, Internal Administration (seven employees)

You are 41 years old and have been with HUF for 10 years. You are section leader of Internal Administration. Before you got this job you worked on the same task in another humanitarian organization. During your time as section leader the effectiveness of administrative routines has increased tremendously, as you have been able to draw on your extensive experience from your work in the Ministry of Defence. Your section works very closely with the EDP section, since new technology was introduced in HUF partly to serve such purposes. Your section also functions as a kind of consultancy to local branches, which only to a very limited extent applies to the other sections. Your office is the second largest of the section offices, measuring 26 square metres. It is of a reasonable standard and fairly well equipped but certainly nothing special. You have had the office for three years.

You have ample reasons for being allocated the new office. Together with Johnson you are the only one of the section leaders who really needs more space for handling your daily tasks. Moreover, you often have to meet with individual employees in HUF who are in need of administrative help – as well as branch representatives calling for the consultancy tasks you are undertaking. And your current office is not suitable for such purposes.

Edward Green, EDP – Logistics (two employees)

You are 35 years old and have been with HUF for nine years. For the first six years you worked in Blackwell's section for Member Files. Three years ago you were appointed section leader of the newly established EDP section, incorporating a great deal of what Blackwell used to manage but which is now computerized. As a result of recent technological innovations and subsequent declining demand for conventional routines, HUF has chosen to invest its resources in your section at the expense of your former section leader Blackwell's domain.

You are working hard to develop your solutions to the growing need for national co-ordination and your small office is jammed with computers, printers, files, etc. The office is the smallest of the section offices, measuring 14 square metres. It is of a reasonable standard, but suffers some noise from the street traffic.

As your office is the smallest it is only fair for you to be allocated the new and larger office.

Running the role play

1. Place a table with six chairs in the room that allows the six actors to see each other and the observers to see all of the actors.
2. Prepare name cards for the six actors to be placed in front of them.
3. Give everybody the General instructions and the Layout of the offices, and allow five minutes' reading time.
4. Give the six actors their individual role instructions and the observers the Observer instructions. Allow 10 minutes' reading time.
5. Ask the actors to take their seats at the table. The Head of the Secretariat, Robert McGuire, chairs the meeting. You normally allow a maximum of 30 minutes for the role play.
6. When the role play has been completed the group may or may not have reached a decision. Ask the observers for their observations of the process as well as for their evaluation of the result(s).
7. Use this input as a platform for a more general discussion of decision-making processes and small group interaction and leadership. On decision making you could try to contrast rational decision models with 'conflicts and politics' and 'ambiguity and garbage can' models.

Observer instructions

1. How is the 'problem' presented?

   Who formulates the problem and how is the aim of the discussion emphasized?

2. Which types of information are included?

   Who decides which criteria are relevant?

   Do these criteria change during the process. If yes, why?

3. Which solutions are suggested?

   Who formulates 'solutions' and on the basis of which criteria?

   Who engages in a discussion of the various solutions and what are the arguments?

4. How is the process 'controlled'?

   What characterizes the social climate during the process and who assumes responsibility for it?

   How does the discussion start, who recapitulates during the process and who assumes responsibility for concluding the discussion?

4

Italdata Italiana

Learning from the chaos: the irrational in organizational change

Carlo Turati

In 1990, Italdata Italiana was one of the largest Italian software companies. During the late 1980s, it had impressive growth both in sales and employees. However, the company realized that its *ad hoc*, poorly organized structure was badly strained by its growth. Therefore, in 1989 Italdata developed a quasi multi-divisional organization built around its markets, products and clients. This required merging internal units as well as wholly or partially owned subsidiaries. New competencies were needed to manage the company, so employees were hired from other firms, notably from a large computer hardware company. This caused conflict between former employees and the new recruits. It was soon clear that the new size of Italdata would itself be a generator of complexity. This combination of factors resulted in the development of new organizational rules.

These problems were further exacerbated by ambiguous managerial attitudes *vis-à-vis* the need for more formal and explicit organizational rules; poor relationships with partially controlled external companies; a tendency toward 'balkanization' of the internal organizational structure; and strong resistance by managers against moving from the unprofitable mainframe rental market to more profitable project management.

A management consulting firm was hired to guide the change process. It assumed that some type of managerial development programme could solve the problems. The consultants found a very dynamic but culturally fragmented organization. This case focuses on describing the employees' perceived need for more organization without the accompanying restrictions on individual perspectives or freedoms. It also addresses the problem of, and need for, alternative methods of change.

Cultural context

Historical and social background

All over the world Italy stands for pasta, mandolins, 'O sole mio', the Pope, Venice and the Coliseum. Italy has a soul of art, a heart of passion, a reputation for shrewdness, and products which are unreliable. The 'art of keeping going' is a national slogan and a source of pride.

At the beginning of the nineteenth century Baron von Metternich remarked, 'Italy is no more than a mere geographical expression'. In many ways he was right. Divided into small kingdoms and tiny counties, Italy was just a geographically defined region with no political, social or economic integration. The Spanish domination of southern Italy declined only in 1860, the ecclesiastical state in middle Italy was finally disbanded in 1870, and the Austrian empire retired from north-east Italy only after the First World War.

In its past Italy knew years of impressive richness in terms of economic power, through the domination of the Mediterranean by the 'seafaring towns' – Genoa, Venice, Amalfi and Pisa – and of the fifteenth- and sixteenth-century bankers from Genoa and Firenze, as well as cultural influences stemming from the Renaissance era. But with the discovery of America, the strategic role of the Italian peninsula greatly lost its appeal to would-be Mediterranean rulers.

Despite Italy's reunification in 1870 it remained a very fragmented country. There was a common observation that northern Italy was highly developed, continental in attitude, had a good infrastructure, but had lousy weather. The southern region of the country, however, was rural, poor, poorly equipped to enter the modern industrial world which was developing at the turn of the century, but had great weather. Whether true or false, it is these stereotypes which seem to predominate even now after more than 100 years.

The First World War invigorated industry in the north. Then the two decades of fascist rule which restricted imports caused both a strengthening of Italy's production capacity and technological and managerial backwardness. At the end of the Second World War the Italian economy was in a shambles. But in the 1950s, under the financial aid of the Marshall Plan, Italy started a period of impressive growth, mainly sustained by both a complex mix of small firms and brutal exploitation of labour. Developing in this climate was a generation of humanistic, clever entrepreneurs. Men such as Mondadori, Olivetti, Einaudi and Ferrari created Italian capitalism and a humanitarian interpretation of the social role of economic institutions. Di Marzio, CEO of Italdata, was a follower of this new creed and he was inspired by the entrepreneurial style of Einaudi.

The distance between north and south became wider during the 1960s, a period of dramatic change also in the social structure of the country. The year 1969 signalled the start of 15 years of social tension and crisis. In 1970 workers achieved a new, more favourable *status quo* and trade unions became powerful institutions. The 1973 oil crisis hit the Italian economy, triggering unemployment, stagflation, a weak lira and an impressive public debt. This combination brought the country close to national bankruptcy.

The yuppy-dominated 1980s and the crisis of the early 1990s were common all over the Western world, but in Italy these years had a special uniqueness:

- public debt was never really brought under control;
- a corruption-collusion system developed between political parties and manufacturers (*Mani Pulite* inquiry, a police investigation into corruption in the late 1970s and 1980s that began in 1992. It led to radical change within political parties and at local and central government levels);
- only minor attempts were made to upgrade outdated public infrastructure in terms of organization and information systems.

By the end of the 1980s, the financial health of most companies dealing with the government sector was seriously jeopardized by political blackmail ('if you want us to buy, you have to pay us') and by financial blackmail, because the public bureaucracies were normally given up to nine months to settle accounts. The end of a decade of prosperity and the advancing international crisis were the main challenges for the 1990s: an era of problems for companies and prosperity for business consultants.

Computer services market

In 1990 the information technology market in Italy reached 17.29 billion lire, a growth of 15% on 1989, and with an expectation of further increases in the following five years. This happened because of:

- the low level of computerization in small companies;
- the demand by small firms for standard, low-priced solutions;
- new, large projects by large private and public clients;
- the need for more computing power and automation by medium and large companies.

The software and professional services share (Italdata's principal business) was 40% and increasing. This trend was owing to rapidly increasing demand for:

- integrated solutions (hardware, software, management consulting and training), rather than partial solutions;
- tailor-made solutions, customized for specific businesses (industry, retailing, local and central public administration, banking and finance, insurance);
- increasing sub-contracting of information system activities by larger companies.

Different business activities suggested different needs. The major need in industry was for design tools and manufacturing automation and control. The resulting technical demand was further enhanced by increasing managerial sophistication and greater diversification of applications (marketing vs decision-support systems vs integrated management of manufacturing), all of which acted to drive the market.

In banking the main differences compared to industry were the lower number of counterparts, and the higher degree of computerization. From a technological point of view, the demand was fed by the need to update existing applications; produce solutions suitable for new networking services; and provide multi-function, client-oriented, self-service solutions. The lack of proficiency of Italian banks, accompanied by increasing competition through the opening of national borders to foreign banks, promised a dramatic increase in demand.

The demand in the insurance sector was pushed by the needs to update internal information systems; to cover an extensive backlog in techno-commercial areas; and to speed up insurance and claims processing procedures.

The public administration sector was under-computerized. The backlog of needs in this sector was enormous and the current demand was mostly serviced by state-owned, low-quality software companies. The probable deregulation of the software market would open this market to Italdata.

Market growth expectations for the next five years were uncertain but generally positive. One scenario projected a stable decrease in demand of 11% to 15% during the next five years. A further projection was for an initial decline for two years followed by an increase. The final prediction was stable or increasing growth rates during the next five years. The market was shared among almost 4000 software firms, although the industry's largest 10 companies controlled 30% of the market (Italdata was the fifth largest). The other 70% was contested by small, poorly organized firms. These firms survived because they were able to exploit the immaturity of customer demand. They paid relatively little attention to the quality of their service, thus damaging the reputation of the whole industry. Forecasts predicted a substantial concentration of supply through mergers and takeovers by the larger software firms.

Italdata's competitors could potentially be any information technology firm, from hardware manufacturers willing to sell complete solutions to small consultants providing only software integration. Italdata's only direct competitors, however, in terms of size and strategic capabilities, were Finsiel (IRI) and Olivetti (OIS). Finsiel was ranked first in Italy, second in Europe, and ninth in the world. Olivetti was second in Italy, sixth in Europe, and thirteenth in the world. What worried the top managers of Italdata was that Olivetti openly proposed merging with Finsiel. Together they would create a global information services giant ranking first in Italy, second in Europe and third in the world. While Olivetti dreamed, Italdata pondered what to do. Its only chance to survive and realize its own dreams was to grow so rapidly that it would be impossible for its two giant Italian competitors to ignore its presence in charting the future of information services in the Italian market.

Prologue

Once upon a time there was an entrepreneur. He, a handsome Roman, was graced with the glamour of a Latin lover. He looked with sparkling eyes at every new secretary hired by his company, better, he contributed to her recruitment with the right of final choice. He believed that people were the ultimate resource of his company, a precious and unrivalled one. He had a dream, a democracy of people with a lot of open doors. His dream came with a tough will to succeed in the tough information technology industry. He loved Fellini's black and white movies.

Once upon a time there was a manager working at the Lega Co-operative. His bald head gave him the appearance of Yul Brenner except that his smile displayed twisted teeth yellowed from the 60 French cigarettes he smoked on an average day. He was, let us say, a pragmatic communist – his dream was to build a democratic, bottom-up, holding company that would not be called a business. This dream organization, an inheritance from his co-operative culture, would be a federation of companies, where everyone's voice would be heard in the imaginary parliament of his creation. He often read Calvino, the Italian writer/philosopher.

Once upon a time there was a former top executive consultant with the face of a bulldog and mannerisms which would be quite comfortable in a used car salesman. He hated bureaucracies and their paper traces. He was a tough vice-president with a genetic code made by unwritten, but very rigid, rules. He too had a dream, to became the greatest man in the greatest company. His favourite reading was Machiavelli.

Once upon a time there was a consultant. A professor with a little grey hair and a 40-year-old smile riding on a 50-year-old body. He was a master of both the theory and the practice of administration. He had a dream as well, that all companies had at least a bit of organization and that this bit mirrored his own ideas. His most admired author was Henry Mintzberg.

Once upon a time there was a crossroads where all these lives met. Just for a short while, of course. But enough to give life to this story.

Act 1: Introduction

Everything had started nine months before with a couple of phone calls. Mr Marinetti, Italdata Operations Vice-Chairman, had more than one problem. His problems were massive: a chaotic organizational structure, an unhealthy social atmosphere, a dissolving company culture, a deficit of positive managerial attitudes and a heavy balkanization in the firm; the last being a process of heavy fragmentation inside the company due to the excessive power held by Business Unit Managers. Strong middle managers, many only recently hired away from larger companies, spoke the language of local autonomy as they introduced new rules. Mr Marinetti needed help. He wanted advice on how to rank Italdata's main development goals; reassert organizational sovereignty over that of each manager; improve quality; identify and minimize the sources of inefficiency; and give legitimacy to the need for the new rules necessary to survive the 1990s.

Mr Marinetti was not the only power holder in Italdata. At the top were two other people. One was Nino Di Marzio, accented with an imposing moustache, tanned skin and Mediterranean features: he was the founder of the company. The other was Lucio Vomero, a former business consultant, fat, and just a bit hostile toward any consultant working for the company. He entered Italdata in 1987 to take charge of the corporate staff. Marinetti joined the firm two years later, bringing his experience as former manager of a co-operative located in northern Italy. He soon had the full support of Di Marzio, who had nurtured similar values at Italdata: a culture of social relationships, a policy of friendship among people, a company of friends rather than professionals or colleagues. This managerial triad dominated the firm and its members. It thought, it organized, and above all it managed public relations, a strategic resource absolutely necessary for a company whose principal strength was its good relations with its politician customers. However, by the end of 1990, the atmosphere within this triad was changing.

The triad agreed on goals but fought on methods. They agreed that they could only win in the IT business by having continuous corporate growth. Disputing how to achieve this growth created an acrimonious atmosphere. Marinetti was very sensitive to the potential risks of rapid growth. Di Marzio was very sensitive to the financial issues of growth, largely because he was the principal shareholder in the company. Vomero wanted time to study the issue, usually saying, 'On the other hand, you will agree, in this phase it is hard to understand the market.'

The three members of the triad also differed in personality. Di Marzio was the entrepreneur, the strategic navigator. Vomero was the rationalizer, the man of balance sheets, profits and costs. Marinetti was the dreamer, the man with the vision.

However, they all agreed that to succeed their firm would need to foster innovation and be able to catalogue and use the expertise held by its members. Di Marzio explained:

> We think that in this business, in order to attract investors, one must show a strong attitude towards innovation and technical excellence. That's why we built the new software factory in the south. We are also trying to encourage our people to innovate. I don't mean R&D, but a systematization of what we already know. We have been mainly individual craftsmen, but we must collect, catalogue and distribute our knowledge more effectively. In the old days when we were small this was much easier because everyone knew everyone. Today we are just too big.

A ringing phone interrupted and Di Marzio left the room. Vomero also left, explaining that he had a short but important meeting. Marinetti ended the presentation of Italdata by explaining:

> Honestly, we are a fragmented company. We have some problems with the integration of some of the units of our group. The principal problems come from TTI, our information systems subsidiary, and BIS, our banking unit. We own 51% of TTI and Di Marzio personally owns another 24.5% of it. However the remaining 24.5% is owned by an ex-partner of Di Marzio who also actively manages the unit. For a lot of reasons they have a negative attitude toward Italdata. BIS, our banking unit, speaks a different organizational language, making it hard for us to effectively co-operate. They are also losing money, which does not help the situation. The point is we are losing control over those two units and we want a sort of organizational solution able to bring them back under a central authority. We really want to keep the central government in Italdata.

Di Marzio's assistant informed Marinetti and Professor Angiolini that the

President had left because of an unscheduled meeting. So they decided to arrange a new date to discuss the company in more depth. Marinetti seemed quite happy about the chat and gave the consultant a dossier of internal documents about Italdata. They walked towards the lift where Angiolini left, unescorted, finding his way to the front door of the building easily. Just as he was about to exit Vomero appeared and gave Angiolini a menacing warning: 'By the way, Professor Angiolini, we don't like charts and papers. We are a living organization: structures are only a source of rigidity for us. Please, remember it.'

Act 2: Angiolini's homework

Studying the dossier he had obtained from Marinetti, Angiolini began to understand more about Italdata's history, future and problems. In the middle of 1990 Di Marzio began considering alternatives for organizational development in order to cope with the dramatic growth the company faced: a positive shift in income (+35% per year), people (from 400 in 1986 to an expected 2000 by 1992), and current debts and interests on debts (up to 10% of income). The confusion was serious. One person thought that the Group's sales were about 130 billion lire, someone else less than 100 billion. The rush to market also produced a dramatic change in the organizational climate of Italdata. It was moving from a small–medium-sized entrepreneurial firm of the early 1980s to a medium–large company. The rapid hiring of staff modified the natural texture of social relationships built up in almost 20 years of easy-going activity. In order to deal with the increasing need for room, manufacturing activities were transferred in a new building 20 km from the headquarters. This hindered co-ordination and communication.

Di Marzio was known to comment on these changes by saying:

> Once upon a time there was an entrepreneur able to call every person in this company by his/her nickname. Now the same entrepreneur is not only unable to remember all the names, but also has trouble keeping updated on exactly how many people are working here. We are losing our identity and a company without identity is like a car without a driver, it doesn't go anywhere.

Italdata had been born in 1971 in Rome when Nino Di Marzio, a charismatic entrepreneur, formed the firm with some friends. The company's first decade had been devoted to entering the local market, where it sold low-cost data processing. At the end of the 1970s a massive hiring, mostly from one bigger fierce competitor, gave Italdata an actual 'manufacturing' identity. It was clear that Di Marzio, the small businessman, had bigger things in mind. He often said things like:

> In this business you grow faster and faster. The market increases 30% a year and it forces you to become rapidly a giant or to die. If we grow less than the market, it is as if the market says to us, 'hey guys, you don't know your jobs!'

The second decade started with a strong impulse in three directions: to expand the company all over Italy; to define and reinforce the image of Italdata as a quality software manufacturer; to build and maintain a broad integration between ownership and employees. In the 1980s three main events occurred which both threatened and helped the company's strategies:

- the entry to the group of INA–Assitalia (an Italian insurance company) as a financial partner (20%);
- the starting point of an acquisition strategy designed to provide a superior visibility for Italdata, the main action being the acquisition of 51% of BIS, a software house in the banking niche;
- the hybridization of the structure of the company through a mix of 100% ownership by Italdata and majority or minority positions in several other, often competing, companies.

These events occurred simultaneously as Italdata started its dramatic growth, both in terms of economic results and in terms of new niches to be covered. When the company asked Angiolini to help it was operating in the following niches: insurance, banking, public administration, industry, consultancy; systems and intelligence building plus the previous data-entry business. In terms of geographical key areas, Italdata was heavily present in Rome, Milan, Bologna, Firenze, Palermo. In addition a software factory had recently been opened in the south of Italy to provide a set of pre-packaged software which could be sold by the firm.

Structure

Italdata looks like an organizational spider's web composed of both internal divisions (Finance, Insurance, Public Administration, Consultancy, North, South) and partially owned subsidiaries (among them BIS, TTI, Italdata Software, Italdata Services). Italdata was the centre of this web, controlling individual units, redistributing functions across units at will, sometimes creating true divisions or external companies, which often acted as subsidiaries. Italdata itself was owned 80% by Nino Di Marzio and 20% by Assitalia. The ownership of the subsidiaries is listed in Table 4.1.

Among all the external units, BIS and TTI were the largest. BIS employed 220 people and had sales in 1991 of 19.5 billion lire. TTI employed 330 people, and had 26 billion lire in sales for the same year. The year's results were positive for TTI (profits of 300 million lire) and negative for BIS (losses of 5.1 billion lire).

BIS was a recent acquisition, and the poor results were attributed to the

Table 4.1 *Italdata's major subsidiary ownership structure*

Company	Italdata's position	Others
BIS (banking software)	60%	40%
TTI (information systems and data processing)	51%	24.5% Di Marzio + 24.5% a former member of Italdata's board
Italdata Software (software factory)	70%	30% public investors

continuation of its inherited managerial attitude which was characterized as extremely bureaucratic. TTI, on the other hand, had long been the most profitable part of the Group. Its disappointing results were a consequence of delays in internal payments (Italdata was a large customer of TTI) caused by Italdata's cash flow problems. TTI mostly sold information systems and data processing and had a very broad and deep expertise in both of these markets. Tension between Italdata and TTI arose both from financial and personal problems. First, Italdata was an unreliable payer; secondly, bad 'vibrations' linked Di Marzio and Espositi (TTI active director and co-owner). In describing Espositi, Di Marzio recounted, 'He was part of my board, he was a partner of Italdata, and he was our Pole Star. But we did everything opposite of what he suggested.'

North Division, with 6 billion lire in sales, was situated in Milan in the same building as BIS. Employing 75 people (60 technicians, 3 marketing and 12 sales people) and spread between Milan, Torino and Bologna, it sold to the insurance, public administration and industrial markets. In competition with TTI, North Division also employed 20 systems specialists, whose sales totalled 1.2 billion lire. That income and all the systems business was part of a fierce debate between TTI and Italdata.

Finance Division was the biggest internal division and generated about 34 billion lire in sales from its insurance, consultancy and new applications markets.

South Division was in charge of the southern Italian markets which it managed through several small units. The biggest of these was Italdata Sicily, with 2 billion lire in sales and 15 employees. The division's most challenging problem was managing the new Italdata Software subsidiary which employed 70 people (expected to increase to around 400 in the near future) and no current sales. Italdata Calabria, Italdata Basilicata and Italdata Puglia were other small units.

Italdata was active in 12 different market activities from professional services to strategic consultancy. Table 4.2 details the sector sales generated by some of its principal units.

Quasi-captive markets based on long-term mainframe leasing generated most of Italdata's income. Both personal preferences and its already strong 'political' connections discouraged Italdata from embracing pure competition. Similarly, its cost-plus data-processing contracts and mainframe leasing contracts (70% of sales) provided enough security and sales to make the new project management approach undesirable. Project management contracts, although they are more profitable, are far more complex and risky than mainframe leasing. In a mainframe leasing contract the client expects to pay a certain sum for each man/day of work, while in a project contract the cost of the whole venture is pre-defined and the supplier's challenge is to make margins on such a basis. Of course, it requires good forecasting skills and a certain ability to assess the potential capacity of its own resources. Italdata was still not able to do this sufficiently well to take the associated risks, at least in the minds of many of its managers. They generally believed that the low level of co-ordination and

Table 4.2 *Sector sales for principal Italdata divisions and subsidiaries*

	Public Administration	Insurance and Banking	South	North	Total
Professional services	23.00	41.95	1.77	5.00	71.72
Systems assistance	4.80	1.21	0.49	1.40	7.90
Expert systems	0.40			0.09	0.49
Integrated systems	0.72			0.26	0.98
Training	0.02		0.43	0.02	0.47
Logistics services		6.89			6.89
Hardware		3.87			3.87
Hardware maintenance		0.23			0.23
Software		2.89		0.01	2.90
Marketing	0.04				0.04
Software translations	2.20				2.20
Consultancy	0.60	0.56	0.72	0.08	1.96
Total (billion lire)	31.78	57.60	3.41	6.86	97.65

Note The remaining 2% is not mentioned in any official document from Italdata.

planning, coupled with competing interests and territories, hampered Italdata's ability to succeed in the profitable project management market.

The future

According to both internal and external sources, the future of the business was on the borderline between the large positive jump of the 1980s and the emerging crisis of the 1990s. Demand was stalling and changing at the same time. Older technological demand had levelled off, but demand for new technology was rapidly increasing.

Demand was stalling from a merely quantitative perspective. But it was in a phase of deep change in qualitative terms: the rapid evolution of knowledge, the diffusion of IT competencies, and some basic changes in hardware–software relationships produced a different attitude in customers' expectations.

The market was demanding fewer custom-designed applications and mainframe leasing contracts, both of which were strengths of Italdata. In their place the market was demanding:

- more standardized programs;
- more open standard hardware systems;
- a dramatic reduction of costs in standard software and hardware.

During 1990–5 the market was predicted to grow by 6% per year in the hardware business and about 14.5% in software. More precisely, 17% in the application tools area and 11% in system software and utilities. In the services segment the growth rate should be 20.3%, with professional services around 24%, and tailor-made solutions and network services both around 10%. Public administration, banking, insurance and finance sectors were estimated to grow at about 20% per year. Other sectors would grow at about 18% a year.

People

Italdata's organization was growing in an unplanned way. It was simply reacting to the market and hired people when contracts were obtained that required competencies not already present in sufficient quantity within the company. Its strategy was simply to hire the competencies needed rather than develop them inside the firm. 'We suffered from accelerated growth, so we had no time to develop internal competencies', Di Marzio used to say.

This strategy resulted in the rapid hiring of managers from other companies by offering them better salaries and/or more authority. These new managers were recruited from large computer technology companies such as IBM and Olivetti, and were primarily specialists in the marketing and sales areas. Of course the 'big company' orientation, youth and high salary/status combination clashed with the existing, small company, technical culture of Italdata. While the new managers generated impressive growth, they also generated massive problems for the company.

Di Marzio had always stressed that, 'People are our major resource. Our starting team of 5 entrepreneurs and 25 programmers had grown to 350 at the end of the 1970s. We remained more or less 400 people until 1986. It was during the last three years that personnel reached an unmanageable level: 800 persons in 1988, 1200 in 1989, 1600 in 1990.' Di Marzio predicted that the company would have 2000 employees by the end of 1991. He divided Italdata's employees into four different cultural groups.

The first were roots of the company, basically the ones who joined the firm during the 1970s. They represented about 10% of the company. The second group were the technical people who entered the firm during the 1980s. They represented the technical core of Italdata (analysts, systems specialists, programmers and consultants) and comprised 50% of the employees. The third cluster (about 20%) included all managers. This group had no homogeneous culture since they had mostly entered the firm directly from its competitors. These managers however were more marketing oriented than the older employees and held strategic positions in the corporate staff and other functional areas. Di Marzio believed that this class represented the values of a modern corporation. The fourth group was the new generation of young, educated, technically-oriented employees who used Italdata to start their careers in a fast-growing industry. They profited from the training and experience available, but left when their career paths were blocked or slowed by intra-company conflicts.

Of course, these strata brought them differing cultures and attitudes toward the business. 'They only talk about market surveys,' was a common complaint voiced against new managers. 'They don't understand that we must reach new economies of scale, software is a commodity market so we must adapt', was the typical response.

The response to this growth and lack of common culture was very distressing to many of the older employees. One, a manager who had joined the firm in 1985, recounted his bitterness:

> Nobody knows how many people are working here now. The growth is so fast that it is difficult to keep track of what the various divisions and subsidiaries are doing. I believe that the company is really held together by perhaps 30 people. The other 1600 are scattered around with no real sense of belonging to the core of our group. When I joined the company I knew everyone. We were a real team, almost a family. Now I know only about 15% of the people working here. We have really lost something.

Act 3: The second meeting

A few weeks after the first meeting Marinetti called Angiolini and suggested a new meeting when the three triad members would be available in Milan. Vomero left a message that he would be late, so they started the meeting without him. They again sat around the table in the boardroom and talked about the future of Italdata.

'I would like to go deeper with you about our expectations', Di Marzio interrupted what to him was a boring set of questions by Angiolini, 'because we are not in agreement about our future. First, myself. Of course I would like to make money through Italdata, but I'd also like to go back and enjoy my work. I want to play with my "toy" [the company] but not be always bothered by its problems.' He continued, 'The second group of stakeholders is represented by our managers who are demanding several things. First, they want a real delegation of responsibility. Second, they want their remuneration to be based on some kind of concrete basis, not simply on their good or bad relationships with the top managers. Third, they want to increase their own professional value by building up the company's image of excellence. They believe that if the company's prestige drops so will their future market value.'

Marinetti interrupted, 'I think they also want to be freer from the influence of the triad. The same can be said for the technical people who want more autonomy to develop their ideas.'

Di Marzio continued, scarcely pausing for Marinetti's comment, 'We want to grow faster than the market and not only by buying other companies. We also want to develop our managers. Right now, I don't think they are mature enough to accept real financial [responsibility].' Then standing up rapidly, Di Marzio shook the consultant's hand and excused himself because he had an important meeting.

Marinetti apologized for Di Marzio's abrupt departure, explaining that he was incredibly overworked. He went on to explain Di Marzio's personal philosophy, 'He has a strongly ethical approach to both work and people. His main goal is to protect them from the hurricane of wild capitalism. To him capital has no value, he loves to protect others' commitment to the company.'

The phone rang and transmitted the message that Vomero would not be able to come after all. Marinetti, a little embarrassed, finished by promising to arrange another meeting as soon as possible. He gave Angiolini some more documents about the company.

Act 4: 'Is this an organization?'

At Angiolini's third meeting the entire triad was available and the conversation centred on the organizational structure of Italdata.

'Do you have any organizational chart of your company, let's say something describing the financial and task relationships among the different internal divisions and subsidiaries of Italdata?' Angiolini asked.

'Of course we don't', Vomero answered. 'A chart would be too rigid for us. Can you imagine how many times we would change it during a single year? And can you imagine how much managerial time we would devote to publishing a reality that every manager already perfectly knows on a real-time basis?'

'Of course you're right', Marinetti quickly interjected, 'but I think that Mr Angiolini was asking something different. Am I right?'

'Well, basically yes', Angiolini answered. 'I'd like to know, for example, which are the current logics of Italdata, that is to say who depends on whom, and why. Or who makes . . . '

Vomero interrupted. 'Oh sure, we know it. I'll tell you, I don't like to formalize everything, but of course sometimes it's better to be clear, if we want someone else to understand our organization.' He continued, 'Honestly, we have only tried to tackle the challenges presented by our rapid growth. Before that we simply did not have enough time to bother with writing things down. We are essentially a network group, you know the virtual organization all those theorists write about. In fact, in 1989, we decided to make deep changes in the organizational and institutional structure of Italdata based on three types of business unit.'

Vomero handed the consultant a formal internal communication to managers explaining the new adopted structure. It described these units as follows:

---

1. *Market* units, interacting with the main vertical markets of the group, that is, the different categories of customers interacting with Italdata currently handled by BIS Ltd, Italdata Insurance, Italdata Public Administration, Italdata Industry, and other internal divisions.
2. *Product* units, centres of technical and specialist skills necessary to supply market and geographical units with assistance. Product units are responsible for developing products and services specific to their mission. These include TTI Ltd, Consultancy Division, Eltecne Ltd, and Italdata Software.
3. *Geographical* units, intended to cover the geographical markets as Italdata sales agents. These include Italdata North and Italdata South, including the sub-units, Italdata Sicily, Calabria, Puglia, Basilicata, and Veneto.

After the consultant had read the two-page memo Vomero continued, 'Market units are intended to keep us in touch with the different niches of the market. Every market has its unique needs and through such units we can better and more rapidly understand them. On the other side, the market units allow us to keep together all the knowledge and skills related to a specific market. So we can react more easily to every change.

'Geographical units are responsible for developing and managing all Italdata activities in their territories. For example, they propose the start-up of new sub-units, identify alliances and minority ownership able to favour local penetration, and represent our Group's products and services across the board to new customers.'

'Product units are companies or divisions developing specific competencies available to every Group unit to sell through their sales network. The product units don't have an exclusive market. As a consequence, their commercial activity is developed in strict co-ordination with the geographical units. The product units' main tasks are to develop competencies in their technology area which are coherent with market needs, and to develop economically new products and technology.

'We evolved this structure because of its capacity to support market segmentation, its financial and organizational flexibility, and because of its speed to create or throw out new strategic business units.'

'I agreed with this strategy,' Marinetti added in a tone of disagreement with Vomero's words. 'But we should not forget that it costs a lot more in terms of co-ordination mechanisms to define, manage and audit the roles and the relationships among the units forming the network.'

'In my opinion you need to identify the main interdependencies, not simply the areas of responsibilities, between these units', Angiolini said.

Marinetti pushed a piece of photocopied paper toward Angiolini, saying, 'Here is some of what you are asking.' Angiolini scanned the document.

TTI vs Italdata TTI depends on Italdata for all commercial services and acts as an Italdata supplier of computing services. Of its sales 32% are made to Italdata and Assitalia. Furthermore, Italdata often demands TTI specialists (never the reverse) to assist other divisions. TTI can only market Italdata's products or services to its old customers. For its new customers it is restricted to marketing only its own products. Italdata can directly target TTI's clients but it must first notify the unit of its planned sales campaign. TTI uses Italdata's corporate Personnel Department.

TTI vs Italdata North TTI sells consultants to Italdata North. The value of the transfer is about 200 billion lire a year.

BIS vs Italdata BIS and Italdata have common budget and accounting procedures. BIS uses Italdata corporate staff as external consultants.

BIS vs TTI BIS exploits both TTI's data-processing centre and its experts.

BIS vs Italdata Sicily BIS lends technical people to Italdata Sicily, for about 240 million lire a year. Italdata Sicily also uses TTI specialists.

Italdata North vs Italdata Italdata North exploits both Italdata competencies and image. They have a common marketing responsibility and planning.

Italdata North vs BIS Italdata North lends technical people to BIS. It also uses the BIS building.

After Angiolini had read the document Di Marzio added, 'Actually, we have three devices to help co-ordinate everything. First there is the Group's Strategic Committee, in which all the general managers of the units and companies of the Group participate. Its goal is to oversee the growth of all the Group and to align the rules and behaviours within Italdata. Secondly there is the Operations Committee composed of the same people plus some *ad hoc* invitations. For example, in order to build a stronger link with our peripheral units, every month a different manager from the geographical units is invited. Finally there is the Project Assurance programme. This is actually a written agreement between the sales people and the technical specialists outlining a project's cost/price, resource requirements, and unit responsibilities. It is required by us before we approve new contracts with customers.'

'And does it work?' Angiolini asked.

'Well, not really', Marinetti replied. 'But this depends a lot on the fact that individual division and subsidiaries are very different from one another. For example, TTI always tries to go ahead alone. They don't accept much central authority and they don't want to lose their independent market presence. I can understand them, because if they lose visibility they lose their chance to survive if we decided to sell them.'

Di Marzio added, 'And, given the financial situation, this is more than likely . . . '

'I don't understand how you can easily manage three dimensions together . . . ' Angiolini started a little lecture, as if he was merely discussing with a few of his university graduate students. He ended a few minutes later concluding, 'When an organization doesn't communicate clearly, it drives in no particular direction. To be honest, I can't say that I can understand its usefulness.'

Act 5: The consultant's interviews

During the next three months Angiolini's team interviewed managers at Italdata and its subsidiaries. The interviews produced a large amount of information, most of which conflicted even on key issues. This created a little confusion in his mind. For example, one manager believed that Italdata employed 1600 people. Another thought there were no more than 1200. No internal document shown to the consultants included a reliable figure. Italdata sales were similarly inexact, depending more on perceptions than numbers. Other important facts were also unclear, even after many interviews. This appeared to underline the amount of disorder within the company. Finally the consultants tried to go deeper into understanding the different cultures co-existing in Italdata. Some transcripts of their interviews are included below.

'But we are an organization, anyhow!'

Mr Ombroni (former IBM sales manager, joined Italdata in 1988) is in charge of the Organization and Personnel department at the Group's headquarters:

> I think Italdata has an ordinary history. It was a simple organization until it reached 200 employees. Before this it had a technology-oriented structure under the direction of a bright entrepreneur. In 1988 Italdata decided to reinforce the quality of its management team by hiring experienced managers from other firms, mostly large IBM-type companies. It also moved towards a multi-divisional form with an expanded central staff under the supervision of Mr Vomero. From 1988 until now, the organizational strategy has been to strengthen the relationships among the different units of the group, each of which is assigned to cover a specific niche of the market. We have some problems, however, in the allocation of niches among the units.
>
> I'm in charge of both the Organization and Personnel (O&P) and the Planning and Control (P&C) departments. O&P is responsible for the design and review of individual and global procedures. We have only this year established Group-wide personnel policies. We are trying to implement them now but find incredible resistance from everyone but the youngest managers. I believe we can only change the situation if we introduce some internal turnover among the middle and upper-level managers, that is, ask some of them to leave Italdata.
>
> P&C is developing a common budget structure for the Group which has been operating in Italdata since 1990. But not everybody has taken it seriously. For some a budget is not a useful tool but a constraint on their freedom. We still have cheating on both targets and results. Furthermore the reporting system is still not able to help the managers to change their behaviours during the year because the feedback channels often break down. Other budgeting systems still survive in some units and subsidiaries and I am not optimistic about being able to have only one system for several years.
>
> Another example is our lack of co-ordinated data processing, which is rather odd since we sell information technology. The Information Systems department has been trying to create a common structure for information processing and transmission, but still has not entirely succeeded. For example, can you believe that many of our reports must be printed in a building located 20 km from our headquarters, and that our data processing is actually done by our subsidiary, TTI?

Mr Mengarini, (formerly a consultant and manager in a multi-national chemical company, joined Italdata in 1984) is in charge of the Group's Accounting and Finance (A&F) department:

> I left my old employer because there was no room to create. When I arrived at Italdata there were only 200 employees and a lot of things needed to be created and organized. Technically speaking our current situation is not so difficult although the speed of our growth makes everything more complex.
>
> We moved from local accounting to centralized, mainframe-based accounting in 1990. Although it reduces flexibility it increases the quality of our accounting procedures. Of course, we are only beginning to expand implementation of the system. The procedures are still quite poor and only TTI and Italdata are using them. All the other units still work on individual, non-networked personal computers.
>
> On the other hand our staff integration is good. Only the group's Purchasing and

Logistics (P&L) department remains unconnected. However, the system is only just barely running and many basic problems must still be solved. For example, at the moment all corporate printouts are done in a building 20 km from our offices and the format of screens and printed pages is not homogeneous. So, when I ask to print something, I cannot be sure about what I'll receive.

Mr Muflone (joined Italdata in 1980 after graduation) is in charge of the Group's General Affairs (GA) department:

I was on Italdata's headquarters staff until the re-organization of 1988–9. I was mostly doing the jobs now done by the O&P and P&C departments. Now I am responsible for General Affairs, which essentially means I do everything and nothing at the same time! My department's involved in logistics, purchasing, legal affairs, finance, merger and acquisitions, and general services.

After 1990 we are going to be a more centralized organization and local units will no longer be responsible for the tasks we are being assigned. But the process has not been completed yet and currently we are just internal consultants with no reward or punishment power.

Our problems can be illustrated by our experience with purchasing procedures. We are responsible for everything Italdata buys, including human resources and consulting services. We gather the information necessary to approve the terms of purchases and pay suppliers. We check that all required documents, including the supplier invoices, follow our standards before transmitting the 'OK for payment' to the accounting department. We are not in charge of buying decisions, we simply assess the procedures. We can't control everything and we can't impose our decisions.

But we're trying to change this situation. Local managers must understand that we can help them. First, we have more technical expertise than local managers for whom a purchase is just a small task among many others. Second, from the centre we can exploit economies of scale to save money. If a local manager can obtain 1% discount, I'm sure we can negotiate 1.5%. They continue to ask for more autonomy, but it is simply a disguise to have bigger budgets.

'What? I'm not Italdata!'

Mr Pulici (joined Italdata in 1984, formerly from IBM) has been the Director of Italdata's TTI subsidiary since 1988:

Our major problem is the commercial relationship we have with Italdata. Information systems sales were about 17 billion lire in 1990. We earned another 10 billion lire from mainframe leasing. Of our leasing market 80% is in Rome, which we consider a difficult market because the Roman clients are slower to use information systems and are less sophisticated than the Milan market. So in Rome we really sell a total package. In Milan, however, the client is more likely to need a consultant to solve limited technical problems. Therefore when Italdata North needs specialized expertise, they call us to help. We 'sell' about 150–200 million lire a year to the Milan market through the Italdata North division, but we don't buy anything from them. It is a one-way commercial relationship.

Another problem we have is career development and staff turnover. My people should be able to grow on the job, developing a deeper and deeper knowledge of the hardware on which they work. Their career growth should allow them work on the same hardware but progress from simple clients towards more complex ones. Of course, our rapid growth makes it quite difficult to train people. If only we could grow 10% a year things would work, but the rate is never less than 30–40% a year.

'We are the money!'

Mr Benvoluti (joined Italdata in 1986) has been the Commercial Manager of the Public Administration division since 1990:

> We made a lot of money, going from 100 million to 2 billion lire in only one year. I have no secrets, only skilful people. I push them towards a market, not simply a client, attitude. I think that in this way they learn to generalize, which helps them increase their skills faster. We have internally 90% of the resources we need in order to produce and sell our products. This is fortunate because any inter-unit relationship creates problems. Nevertheless I must deal a lot with other units.
>
> First, I must deal with the local subsidiaries of Italdata. That is an important condition for the success of my unit. They have their job, I have mine. The territory should mature in terms of contacts, but we must also develop product sensitivity. By this I mean business/client competencies and a specialist attitude *vis-à-vis* both techniques and functions. Second, we interact with the corporate staff members. Each has very different attitudes about this interaction. For some a simple uninvited knock at the door is enough to get some help. Others need to be warmed up in advance by a phone call. The most formal require a fixed appointment in advance for a meeting. They are also different in terms of managerial style.
>
> For example, purchasing, logistics and finance are the closest to the free, messy Italdata style. General Affairs is the most formal and Personnel and Organization are always repeating, 'You must do this, you must do that'. That's great! I want some norms. I can use some standards and precise criteria for behavioural assessment. I can also use procedures to analyse investments and production processes. But I'm also a manager. They upset me when they deal with me and my people as if we were kids.

Mr Fruttosi (joined Italdata in 1988, educated as an electronic engineer) is in charge of the Finance division of Italdata:

> My division used to be bigger, but when BIS was purchased we had to turn over our banking customers to them. We now concentrate on three main areas: insurance, consultancy and innovative technologies. In the near future we will lose consultancy since it will become a new division. We are also losing about 4 billion lire in sales (out of 30) to Italdata North because these customers were located within its geographic territory, Still, being Director of the Finance Division is a good position since we sell about 27 billion lire a year through applications for insurance, as well as cross-selling TTI's products, consulting and Eltecne (site preparation and intelligence building).
>
> We are constantly wondering what we should try to keep control of and what might be transferred to other divisions. But really we simply do not have a homogeneous culture, or even for that matter a culture! Nor do we have a common organizational language or a spirit of inter-unit co-operation. We do have some very competent technical individuals, but so many different mindsets. For example, the technical people are good but extremely risk adverse. They prefer a safer mainframe leasing approach to more risky, but more profitable, project approach. The commercial people are good too and currently are the most respected. They are able to sell anything. I don't know what to say about the marketing people. They should help us to develop the market but, honestly, I don't see what they have added to our culture.

'The bank, c'est moi!'

Mr Benazzi is Chairman of BIS, the banking unit of Italdata:

> We employ 210 people, 75% with less than 2 years' seniority and 80% who are less than 30 years old. They are well educated (40% have university degrees) and seem to exploit our training system, since we have an annual turnover rate of 30%. I don't see how we can develop the internal technical competence the banking market demands. Last year my staff interviewed about 500 candidates just to hire 50. We have similar trouble attracting and keeping project leaders.
>
> Overall our level of management is poor and we are not able to maintain or increase the managerial competencies we need. Managerial tasks and internal careers suffer from poor images and are not appealing to our young recruits. That makes it quite difficult to have better resources, aligned with the level of the demand, even if we pay them a lot. Don't forget that the banking market is one of the most developed in terms of sophistication of both offer and demand. I think we must look for something to allow us to develop resources internally. The increasing formalization of personnel policies demanded by the Group central staff is not helping to solve our real problems.

'From Caserta we manage the future'

Mr Giannini (joined Italdata in 1981) has been CEO of Italdata Software, a partially owned subsidiary, since it was formed in 1991:

> We were born from a government aid programme designed to develop the poorer regions of Italy. Our financial partners are various government agencies which are willing to accept a lower rate of return to help re-industrialize certain regions. So Italdata is developing its first software factory, promising employment for 400 people in 4 years. We are currently (1990) at 70 people and we plan to be at 200 before the end of 1991. We want to create a new market somewhere between tailor-made products and Microsoft or Lotus-type standard software. Here we manufacture the 'bricks' of the basic software, I mean the standard procedures for every new package at Italdata. It is a new software philosophy, object-oriented programming, made in mainframe environment.
>
> A big problem we have is that the headquarters asks us not only to write software, but also to develop the local market, selling all the products of Italdata. So we must balance two extreme cultures: the sales people pushing us to sell everything, but not our new programming products which are reserved for Italdata, and the other side represented by our technical people who are investing time and money to develop a new methodology.

The staff

Mr Mengarini is an Italdata Staff Manager. 'We must create a homogeneous environment where everybody can feel at home anywhere in the Group.'

Mr Muflone is an Italdata Staff Manager:

> We must strengthen our relationships with the line so we can understand the nature of their projects and of the way they work. As we increase our own expertise we begin to lose contact with the product. But, in spite of this, we still heavily contribute to the

bottom line of the project balance sheet. For example, when we rent external resources (which is 95% of the time for the companies within our group), we are indirectly responsible for productivity. Or by centralization we can help our line departments save a lot of money. For example, when we convince them to use us as a central purchasing unit.

On the other hand, we must also have an evaluative role. All projects appear profitable on paper and the local staff can see the negative trends only afterwards. But from my Purchasing and Finance department I can see it in advance. I require more centralization of those kinds of activity. Unfortunately I can't have a complete picture of the situation because of the lack of standard procedures. I can only have a basic idea. For example, when the line needs tools, I buy them but there is no report telling me if they actually use the tools.

Us and TTI

Mr Orsi is Systems Specialist Manager, Italdata North:

Italdata's organizational history is quite complex. Based on my skills I should be attached to TTI as it was when the unit was first bought by Italdata. But headquarters preferred to transfer my unit to Italdata North. My main mission is to find new people, build a team, and conquer the northern market. I have complete autonomy. That doesn't mean that in the near future TTI cannot ask for my unit to be returned. It's a mess!

On the other hand, the split was justified by the need to grant autonomous development to the northern areas. Furthermore there is no room for true competition among us, because of both the distance and the customers' needs. Rome offers a few large clients for large plants, plus the captive market, of course, and a lot of routine tasks. Milan is different because we don't have room for any mainframe leasing, nor for routine. They ask us to design and install innovative projects. The split, of course, explains the absence of a common marketing and image strategy, a poor cross-fertilization of ideas, a duplication of research and development effort. It also keeps me in my market niche.

If I need a highly specialized technical person I am obliged to 'buy it' from TTI at an inter-company transfer price which is often higher than the market rate. Why should I use people from TTI? They are more costly to me and they prevent me from developing my own people or hiring someone new. Of course, if we were combined a lot of administrative and economic problems would automatically disappear every time there is an exchange (about 15% of my whole business). But for now I have little economic interest in TTI.

Mr Casella is Technical Manager at TTI:

It's well known that we have no real exchange with Italdata. We sell them our specialized resources but we don't buy or sell theirs. My personal feeling is that the Italdata management view TTI people as parasites completely lacking an entrepreneurial attitude. The TTI professionals look at Italdata as a structure exploiting their expertise and productivity, but excluding them from any consequent benefit.

Us and BIS

Mr Mengarini is an Italdata Staff Manager: 'BIS is something different. They have a banking culture and you can recognize it easily from the way they prepare their balance sheet report; we just make photocopies, they hard-cover theirs.'

Mr Ampia is Commercial Manager, BIS:

> I was a manager in Italdata Banking South, but was transferred to BIS in order to reduce the shock of transferring all banking business to BIS from Italdata; assist some of our long-term clients in the change to a new supplier; and reinforce the integration process. In my new unit there is dissatisfaction among the people moved from Italdata. We don't have any power and are not trusted by BIS's central administration. Furthermore, we have a different history from BIS people, so we don't have any feeling of belonging. In my unit I don't have slow people, just frustrated ones.

Centre and periphery

Mr Davi (joined Italdata in 1990, formerly with IBM) is General Manager, Italdata Sicily:

> I've been in Sicily since 1990 when Italdata created a joint venture with some local entrepreneurs. Now, we have 40 people and 1.3 billion lire in sales. We have a sales target of 2 billion lire for 1991 and great expectations in the Public Administration area. However, my margin this year was only 13 million lire. The low margin is caused by logistics problems. I must 'import' much of the talent I need from the Italdata headquarters, which is OK because if I were to hire all the talent needed to get this operation working well I would be stuck with expensive, long-term labour contracts. While headquarters generally charges me too much for intra-group personnel transfers, the real problem is communications.
>
> They are too poor and limited to my personal network (which is still small) up and down the organization. Sometimes it seems almost impossible to ask for collaboration from the centre. Quite often it happens that I call someone, don't find them, leave a message and, of course, nobody calls you back. There are no rules of communication, no 'post-it notes', no memos. Furthermore I do not belong to any group committee. Sometimes, I am invited to a meeting in the Public Administration division. This is often a real chance which I exploit to do thousands of other things. But too often there is no culture of team work, you know, there is poor scheduling and poor preparation, both at middle and top management. Sometime I go to Rome just to meet them and they tell me, through their secretaries, 'Sorry, but it is a mess here, I can't stay with you.' It is not only a problem of strategic co-ordination but of basic co-ordination between myself, the technicians and the marketing people. As a consequence our new project assurance promises are empty of content, of learning, and of co-ordination capacity. I believe project assurance will not work because people can avoid accepting specific responsibility, even though they know that they should contribute.

Mr Venturi (joined Italdata in 1989) is General Manager of Italdata Bologna, a small subsidiary of Italdata North division:

> My job is to develop this subsidiary, but I must do this ambiguously because some of the decisions I take depend on the co-operation of the Public Administration division which is mostly located in Rome. Formally we are a commercial unit but we also manufacture. The ambiguity generates an atmosphere of distrust where we are uncertain about the future of the unit, burdened with a heavy bureaucracy, find it difficult to remain committed to decisions, are unclear about our career prospects, and resent the strong interference of the centre in our decisions. Every time I ask for

more certainty, the response is that, 'we are not bureaucrats'. Of course, my unit pays the price for these failings in terms of a high turnover of people.

In terms of relationships with the centre, there are no rules and my lack of autonomy makes it truly difficult to lead both commercial and technical activities. I always must ask permission but, without any frame of formalization, I am left to discover my range of autonomy day by day. Nobody explains anything to me. Furthermore, the absence of a clear budgeting policy doesn't help in the definition of the unit targets. Finally, there are some overlaps. For example, Public Administration is responsible for south Italy but also has some interests here in Bologna.

Mainframe leasing

Mr Rampelli is Technical Manager, Italdata Public Administration:

We mainly do mainframe leasing where our people are assigned to work full time at the client's site and the customer pays for presence not results. However, mainframe leasing is less profitable than project management. We avoid project management contracts basically because we don't have any idea of how to manage projects where it is the results that count. Project management requires entrepreneurs who can maximize profitability. They have another style of life where there are real targets which must be reached to receive payment. This not only increases risk, it also increases the pressure on people and managers. If I had the temperament, talent and resources I could make big profits with projects.

Mr Truffucci is Commercial Manager, Italdata Finance:

Mainframe leasing is almost a need for us because our clients are too poorly prepared to takeover completed installations designed on a project management basis. In insurance business clients are at least 10 years late when compared with any other niche of our operations. Even banks are better! Furthermore, from our internal perspective, in order to work on a project basis we would need at least a methodology, that is the tools, procedures, control times and logistics. If you add that the client is often a public institution with its own high degree of formalism, it is easy to see that the risk of over-extending ourselves is too high.

To move towards a project logic would add about 10% to our profit margins. At the moment we have only one project. What I would really like to do is to document the process of managing a project. Italdata has no operating standards, nor a 'projects completed' file. Even though many of our projects are the same we have never formalized the methodology or process. We simply reinvent the process each time we have a new project. I am embarrassed to admit that in the beginning, when we were small, we had a method. Being only a small firm we benefited from an intense, mutual learning process. Now that we are larger, the solutions are difficult to standardize and we have lost a certain group spirit.

There is also a cultural conflict between the client and us. Many already have a methodology and we are unable to propose our own. I really hope that the Italdata Software subsidiary can help us. They are suppose to be a software factory and will be forced to look for standards.

Techno-commercial co-ordination

Mr Ampia is Commercial Manager, BIS:

How can we interact with the technical people? There are several things that make communication easier. First, the commercial people often have technical backgrounds. A second way is for the commercial people to share their knowledge about client needs and price constraints with the technical people. Another way, more formal, is what we call 'project assurance'. Project assurance is a document prepared and shared by both technical and commercial people. At the very beginning of the project bid the two groups sit down around a table and try to define the best way to serve the customer. The sales people must put on the table all the information they have that can help technical people to define the costs of the project correctly. Then, the two must sign an internal contract, the so-called project assurance. Only after they sign the document will it be sent to top management for approval and be formally offered to the client. Through project assurance sales people and technicians define their mutual responsibilities.

Mr Benvoluti is Commercial Manager, Italdata Public Administration:

We need a lot of co-ordination with the technical people. They give us resources and help us assess projects. It is often hard to negotiate a project assurance agreement with my technical counterpart. My performance is often assessed on my team's total sales but the technical manager's performance is measured by his profitability. He must examine the trade-off between committing his resources to the current offer I propose or waiting for a better, more profitable offer. Usually the technical people do not trust us and refuse to agree to a project assurance agreement because they want to guard their resources for better deals. This is bad for my people since it limits our sales, which directly decreases our pay cheques. You see we have 40% of our pay in action while the technical managers only have 10% of theirs in action. [See Table 4.3.]

Mr Caprese is Commercial Manager, Italdata Public Administration:

There is a lot of psychological tension with the technical people. They say that we under-estimate their needs. We think they just over-estimate the costs. I guess this is natural because once the project assurance agreement has been signed they are fully responsible for it. That is why there are so many tensions between us. We are measured in terms of sales, they in terms of margins, that is, optimization in the use of people. They manage 300 people on average, with the requirement to balance the available size and skills with the customer's demand.

Every good technical manager must determine the best trade-off between optimal use of his people and their development. In order to develop his people correctly he must be oriented to the long-term, so he naturally wants us to provide him with a steady flow of new contracts. But this is impossible and the sales force ends up always pushing the technical staff to help gain or keep a customer. I agree with the technical managers, we have almost no empathy for his problems because we are focusing on ours. We don't help him at all.

Table 4.3 *Italdata's incentives structure*

	Percentage of pay	
Tasks	Fixed	Variable
Sales	60	40
Technical	90	10
Managers	70	30
Top managers	70	30

I see the process as follows. First, we receive a lead for a new contract and we approach the client. We then make a commercial assessment by defining the customer strategy and budget. Third, we try to assess his needs, both alone or following the analysis of the customer. Then, through the marketing support, we try to get more technical information from the client in order to prepare a preliminary offer. Together with the technical manager we negotiate a project assurance agreement and, on that basis, we make our proposal and we start the negotiation with the client. After an order code is opened (by Administration on the project assurance basis), the technical manager assesses his available resources with a Personnel Department Staff Manager who keeps track of available human resources in the company. At about this point the technical area starts the project and we share the job with them; they manage the project, we manage the client. By this I mean we check on the customer's satisfaction and try to enlarge future sales opportunities.

Our weaknesses

Mr Truffucci is Commercial Manager, Italdata Finance:

> First, the relationships with customers. The top management always tries to by-pass us politically. That frustrates me. But also the client is under pressure, because he doesn't understand who he is really dealing with. It is a waste of time. Third, the centralization of a lot of decisions. It reduces the speed, especially in purchasing resources and tools. I expected to be autonomous as a senior manager, but when I have to ask permission from the Purchasing department even to buy a PC I know we are in trouble! I'd like to understand my span of responsibilities. Fourth, I don't see a spirit of co-operation. Co-operation means flexibility. On the contrary, I feel that we are getting more and more rigid. Fifth, I like procedures, standards, programmes . . . they are all necessary. They create a business culture, a company image. But there are no average or standard markets; we must differentiate to survive! And understand why managers try to avoid the rules. Only the weak ones stick to them.

Finale

'Good morning.'

'Good morning.'

'We have a meeting with Mr Marinetti.'

'With Mr Marinetti?'

'Right, we are Angiolini and Talci.'

'Will you please be seated?'

When sitting in the dentist's waiting room, you always know that you will have to read the *Monthly Dental World News* or a magazine describing the secret life in Buckingham Palace, or horror pamphlets on the dangers of smoke, alcohol, sex, driving, tanning, playing tennis or having fun. Waiting for appointments in companies is about the same, except that the armchairs are too low and uncomfortable and the magazines are left over from a golden era when their cost was a small price for the prestige of being 'modern'. The consultant paged through old *Fortune* magazines, circa 1988.

'Good morning.'

'Good morning.'

'We have a meeting with Mr Marinetti.'

'Well, sirs, I'm sorry, he has left the company.'

A short, embarrassing silence followed. Bruno Angiolini, the senior consultant of the team, seemed to absorb the hit with elegance. But even an experienced consultant can sway a little when the man who gave him his job and, more importantly, the one who should sign the final cheque, disappears.

'Well, he wanted to do something on his own, to have a chance as an entrepreneur, I am sure you understand. He has probably opened a bar in Costa Rica.'

'Costa Rica? . . . But we had a meeting with him . . . today . . . at noon . . .'

'We know, Mr Vomero will meet with you instead. Please follow me.'

As the silence deepened in Italdata's boardroom, Angiolini's distress that Marinetti was no longer with the company turned to real fear that he would never be paid by the hard-nosed Vomero. Even Di Marzio seemed distracted and uninterested in what he had heard.

Vomero's voice started again, 'I don't know what Marinetti wanted you guys to do, but it is clear that you know a great deal about our company, maybe even more than we do. We will honour your contract but we want some solutions for this mess, and we want them soon. When can you provide an analysis of your initial findings?'

Professional as he was, Angiolini was visibly relieved, but Di Marzio's voice interrupted his self-congratulations. 'I really appreciate your job. Now, I would like to tell you what worries me for the near future.'

Di Marzio switched the overhead projector on and started to read the points. 'First, we need a new Marinetti. I think he could be someone with substantial expertise in the financial area, but not necessarily an information technology expert. We are prepared to give him a lot of responsibility. Second, something must change in the relationship between the ownership and the management, but I don't know how much responsibility I can delegate given the current level of managerial expertise. Third, we must change the internal structure of the group. We are too heavy but I don't know where to cut. Fourth, we must change our competitive attitude. As far as I can understand the market, we will have more market growth but also more competition, especially in the Public Administration area. Will we be able to survive and exploit this potential? Sixth, I want one Italdata, one homogeneous structure, one brand, one culture. Those are my points. When can you come back with your answers?'

Themes/issues to consider

This case focuses on several intertwined themes, including managerial power, organizational theory and organizational change. It also provides an interesting challenge for students of systems theory, who may use it to trace the diverse elements of organizational problems, including not only the principal elements of the case but also human resource management and sociological issues.

A recurrent fact which every consultant sometimes faces is that companies often seem incapable of changing. Traditionally we are not aware of this because we assume that change is natural and that companies adapt to environmental pressures. But several internal and external sources of inertia inhibit developments. Actors often simply do not see the problems or recognize the solutions. When they do they often fail to estimate the full cost of change, both in cultural and structural terms, which dampens the will to change. Furthermore, internal coalitions want to maintain the *status quo* because the change threatens existing privileges and power.

If one approaches this case from the traditional stimulus–change paradigm, several problems become evident. The complexity of Italdata's interpersonal texture and the compromise of visions and interests appear firmly opposed to the radical restructuring which appears to be necessary from a quick reading of the case. Furthermore, the stimulus–change approach normally requires good information in terms of quality and reliability. In this case, however, the reader can be overloaded with ambiguous and often contradictory data. People talk but do not inform, and their expressed willingness to change often masks personal strategies which have little to do with the company's needs.

At this point, basic questions about change and related concepts should be introduced. What changes? What is the underlying rational of change? Who could contribute to change? How can one integrate problems, solutions and actors? Is there a unique/natural process of change or alternative 'rationality' that should be identified before beginning the change process? What is the role of information in a company? And what really does information mean? Finally, are universalistic models of change useful or is the contingency approach more productive?

Assignments

1. On the basis of the description given by the triad:
   - Depict the current structure of Italdata by creating an organizational chart.
   - Describe the main strengths and weaknesses of such an organizational model.
   - Prepare a report summarizing the results of the preliminary interviews.
2. On the basis of the first few meetings, prepare a convincing (in content and language) preliminary tender for your consultant intervention based on:
   - the main goals of Italdata;
   - the strategic trends of the company;
   - Italdata's philosophy, as drawn from the first meetings.
3. On the basis of the information gathered through the subsequent interviews:
   - List the major problems of the current organization.

- Identify the main levers of change.
- Identify which lever is more suitable for your goals.
- Identify the main strategies for change and development within each identified lever.
- Identify the main tools suitable to support the selected strategies.

Suggested reading

The following books are highly recommended for providing a basic knowledge of organizational design and development.

Galbraith, R. (1977) *Organizational Design*. Reading, MA: Addison Wesley.

Mintzberg, H. (1983) *Structures in Fives: Designing Effective Organizations*. Englewood Cliffs, NJ: Prentice-Hall.

Note

The names of the companies and individuals in this case have been disguised.

5

Joaquín Candel

Rise and fall of an autocratic leader

Carlos Obeso

The Joaquín Candel case is the story of a medium-sized hardware wholesaler. Although the company's customers were, and continue to be, small hardware shops, Candel has been affected by rapid changes in the distribution industry in particular and the globalization of the economy in general.

Founded in the 1950s, the Joaquín Candel company, like so many other small businesses, was set up by an enterprising individual and grew quickly thanks to the fact that the Spanish market was understocked and highly protected. At the same time the political climate favoured autocratic management styles.

The 1980s brought radical changes to the country. Spain's entry to the EC meant that ill-prepared domestic companies had to face highly agressive competition from abroad. Moreover, the return of democracy forced Spanish employers to change their traditional management styles, a change that was not without its problems.

The case examines Ferretería Joaquín Candel's need to reposition itself in order to survive in the new climate of competition. This meant rethinking corporate strategy, making the necessary changes in structure and management style and, last but not least, assessing the corporate management team's ability to act as change agents.

Cultural context

Under the rule of Ferdinand and Isabella, the *Reyes Católicos* or Catholic monarchs, Spain ended an eight-century war against Arab invaders with the conquest of Granada (1492). Spain thereafter became a unified nation, much as it is known nowadays. Arabs who decided to remain were forced to convert to Catholicism, as were members of the Jewish community. Most of them decided to leave and those who remained went into hiding. Very few converted to the Catholic religion.

As a nation of warriors without a war to fight, the Spanish kingdom embarked on a new adventure: the colonization of America. Nevertheless, Spain never took advantage of its four-century rule over that vast continent. The new class of peasant warrior was ill prepared to profit from the situation. At a time when merchants were emerging as Europe's new ruling class, Spain banished its Jewish and Arab communities, the only commercially minded people in the country. So the Castillian feudal system ruled the nation, backed by an ultramontane version of Catholicism. The 'deviants', small clusters of liberals or mercantilists, were persecuted or even sentenced to death. Don Quixote was the symbol of the era, a knight prepared to fight and die for an ideal but terrified by the idea of daily work.

Only the Catalans in the north-east and the Basques in the north were able to avoid the feudal influence. Catalans, with a long tradition of trade in the Mediterranean basin, took advantage of the colonial period to develop a small but strong textile industry. In the wake of the civil war many impoverished immigrants, mainly from the south of Spain, came to Catalonia. Joaquín Candel was one of them.

In the nineteenth century the Basques, an isolated mountain people, developed a heavy industry based on their iron mines. They also attracted immigrants. Only the Catalans and Basques were able to base their industrialization on private enterprise. Industrialization in the rest of the country did not get under way until the 1960s.

By the twentieth century, a number of different forces had emerged and gradually formed a Republican coalition. When they clashed with Spain's traditional powers in the 1930s civil war was inevitable. A 40-year dictatorship followed.

Because the Catalans and Basques had already industrialized, they were able to take advantage of the situation created by the dictatorship, with its low salaries, protection from outside competition, prohibition of trade unions and conservative Catholic ideology. All in all the business community adapted quite well to the new situation and operated within its constraints for many years. It was not until the 1970s that dictatorship was seen as a real hindrance to further development.

Spain, which had long been impervious to outside influences, suddenly began to modernize at the beginning of the 1980s, and by the time it entered the European Community in January 1986 it was one of the most enthusiastically European-minded countries on the continent. The majority of Spaniards hailed EC membership as a collective victory. Entering the European club was seen as synonomous with acceptance as a civilized nation and as a protection against a revival of the Franco ideology. However, it was not long before the less desirable effects of membership became clear.

Foreign companies that set up operations in Spain have definitive competitive advantages over many of their domestic counterparts: economies of scale, executives trained in more aggresive business climates and used to competing internationally with management styles that are appropriate for global markets. Under these circumstances a number of Spanish businesspeople decided to sell out during the boom years. Others, like Joaquín Candel, opted to stand up to the challenge.

Spain's industry consists largely of small and medium-sized family businesses similar to Joaquín Candel's. Their ability to adapt to the new economic situation is limited by many factors: some of which are personal and profusely illustrated in the literature of family businesses; others are financial; and yet others involve these companies' problems in obtaining government grants, market information etc.

Nevertheless, there is no need to exaggerate these problems or conclude that the future of these companies is bleak. The people in charge of these family businesses have accumulated a tremendous amount of experience over the years. What is clear, however, is that the old ways of doing business are now largely obsolete.

In this context, the Joaquín Candel case illustrates a situation which can, within certain limits, be extrapolated to many Spanish firms. Examining the case can help students reflect on, and draw certain general conclusions about, what these companies can do in order to survive in a tremendously competitive business climate.

The history of Candel

To the traveller who arrives by sea, Albacete at first glance appears to be a half-dead city. The sun reflected on the façades of the city's buildings produces a glare that prevents even a glimpse of anything else. And yet, at the vague hour of twilight Albacete turns into an oasis of calm where the greenery and the poplars that line the river banks convert the Mediterranean city of midday into an image that might be almost northerly, if it weren't for the heat.

Years ago, when Joaquín Candel was born, the tall Gothic towers of the cathedral were reflected in the waters of the river. Pollution put an end to that, although some aged poet or other in search of lasting fame still persists in composing odes to past glories:

Ay, torres albaceteñas
que reflejáis in el rio
la esbeltez de las españas
y todo el corazón mio![1]

Throughout his adolescence Joaquín Candel watched the river deteriorate and the city grow. If he ever had any doubts about the wisdom of this, they were soon dispelled by his own enthusiasm for everything modern. It was only when his destiny was no longer linked to the city that he became interested in the river once more, but by then it was too late.

From his grandfather Jacobo, Joaquín inherited a tremendous drive for business and a certain distrust of liberal ideologies (the 'Reds', as they were called then). He also inherited a flourishing hardware store located deep in the heart of the city. The hardware store, famous for its switchblade knives, enabled Joaquín to realize some rather more than generous profits, a situation which his biographer later succinctly immortalized in the following terms: 'the hardware store generated a positive cashflow'.

One day he told his mother, 'I'm going to try my luck in Barcelona.'

To which she replied, 'Be careful of those Catalans.'

Joaquín Candel still vividly remembers his friends waving him off from the station as the train headed towards the endless Manchegan plain, their voices raised in song:

En un barrio de la Habana
se oye a un negro suspirar:
¡ay, señor quién fuera blanco
aunque fuera catalán![2]

He watched them until their figures dwindled in the distance, blending into the landscape he was leaving behind.

His first and only hardware store, located in Barcelona's Gracia district, was every bit as successful as could be expected of a business run by someone as enterprising as Joaquín and in the climate of scarcity caused by the civil war. But he had other ambitions. Unfortunately he was short of capital.

One of Joaquín Candel's favourite sayings was 'Good fortune smiles on those who seek her' and his good fortune took the form of an inheritance. An aunt he had never heard of, Carmina González Candel, popularly known as 'Esmeralda' or 'Tutti Frutti', had enjoyed some fame as an entertainer in her day and certain Central American dictators had bestowed their favours on her.

She is still remembered in the *Pinguin*, a roadhouse of shady repute located on the highway north of Managua, where Tachito Somoza used to end up when he was on one of his notorious binges. The Sandinistas' ascent to power and her advanced age turned Esmeralda into a pious woman determined to repent for her sins while there was still time. So she withdrew to a convent and, despite the desires of the religious community, bequeathed her possessions and the not inconsiderable contents of her bank accounts to her nephew, Joaquín.

Although its name, 'Ferretería Joaquín Candel', translates as hardware store, that is not exactly what the company is that Joaquín founded with his aunt's money. It is actually a wholesaler, buying hardware from various Spanish and foreign manufacturers and subsequently selling it to retailers. There are about 8000 entries in its catalogue (ranging from the tiniest of nails to the latest model power lawnmower), produced by about 600 different suppliers.

Salespeople at the Ferretería Joaquín Candel are in charge of introducing hardware retailers to the newest items on the market and supplying them with familiar products for daily use.

Although retailers could in theory deal directly with the suppliers/manufacturers, the number of products available on the market and the more than abundant choice of possible suppliers exceeds the management capacity of average retailers, which means they have to rely on distributors like Ferretería Joaquín Candel.

For many years, Ferretería Joaquín Candel's best customers were the neighbourhood hardware shops. This type of customer usually ordered whatever they needed by simply specifying something like 'so many screws in such-and-such a size'. However, at the beginning of the 1980s this began to change.

Ramón Areces, a self-made man, had already registered a triumph in the business world with what was to become – and still is – the epitome of Spanish department stores: El Corte Inglés. And, as was only to be expected, the Corte Inglés had a hardware department. So did a number of other shops which, protected by benevolent legislation and encouraged by the prospect of a market consisting of 40 million avid consumers, started opening businesses in Spain.

'Shopkeepers are the backbone of our economy,' Catalonia's president, Jordi Pujol, once said. To which the president of the Hardware Dealers' Association replied, 'renovate or perish', regarding with suspicion the alacrity with which the president and the local bishops (as well as the competent military authorities) accepted invitations to inaugurations of any kind of supermarket, department store or shopping mall, regardless of the nationality of its owners.

Obviously, these large outlets, whether general or specialized as they later became (with the establishment of places like the Bauhaus), were – and continue to be – a lethal danger to small retailers. Not only can they pressure distributors like Ferretería Joaquín Candel into lowering their prices, but they are also large enough to deal directly with manufacturers and suppliers, which means they can offer their customers better terms.

The reaction of the hardware retailers was not long in coming. Some of them banded together in co-operative associations with the stated intention of offering a united front to manufacturers and distributors.

Consumers too were changing their habits or being forced to change them. Even customers of hardware stores were becoming aware of 'brand image', although not to the extent of people shopping for clothing and fashion accessories. In other words, customers were no longer simply asking for 'screws' but beginning to request 'such-and-such a brand of screws', which meant that manufacturers and distributors alike started vying to promote their image and ensure the loyalty of their customers.

Despite the fact that purchasers of hardware goods are not yet generally inclined to buy by brand (with certain well-known exceptions such as Black and Decker drills), it looks as though this will become more frequent in the future. Should this prove to be the case, the comparative advantage of businesses like Ferretería Candel will not be so much, or solely, its broad selection and fast delivery, but also knowing how to sell a particular brand image to its final customers.

It should be mentioned here that there is a steadily increasing tendency for large outlets to stock their own brands. This means they buy items from manufacturers and wholesale dealers and then label them with whatever name they are trying to promote. Should this become a general practice, businesses like Ferretería Joaquín Candel will suffer, because they will no longer be able to make any real distinction between the items they stock and will become no more than middlemen between manufacturers and final customers.

Even the way of selling to hardware retailers is beginning to change (and 'hardware retailers' includes everything from neighbourhood shops to big department stores).Whereas before they were provided with catalogues and they simply ordered the products they wanted, now the trend is to sell them shelving.

Shelving means that certain shelves or other space in a retail outlet are dedicated exclusively to the products of one supplier. In the case of Ferretería Joaquín Candel this involves deciding on the retailer's product mix, arranging displays and restocking merchandise when necessary.

The idea has its advantages for both retailers and wholesalers. The advantage for retailers is that part of their shops are managed by wholesalers, who presumably know more about the market and the right merchandise to offer customers at any given time. If this is really the case, customers will buy more and both retailers and wholesalers will come out ahead.

The advantage to wholesalers like Joaquín Candel is that they obtain exclusive rights to sell their products (or brands as the case may be) in specific outlets without having to bother about their competitors' products (or at least only a limited number of them).

But simple as this arrangement may seem in theory, it is considerably more complicated in practice. First of all, it means the whole idea of selling to retailers has to change (and again, 'retailers' include outlets as large as the Corte Inglés, Pryca, etc.). As mentioned above, it is no longer a matter of selling through the catalogue (although this still accounts for a good share of sales) but of getting the exclusive rights to sell in specific retail outlets. The retailer allows a particular supplier/wholesaler to take over the management of part of his shop, but in doing so he limits his source of supplies and runs the risk of ending up on bad terms with other suppliers.

So the arrangement really only works out if the supplier who has the exclusive rights to a retail space does a good job of managing the shelving. Managing shelving in a particular retail space is not an easy matter. Only German manufacturers and distributors have solid experience in this. The French rank second, although at a considerable distance behind the leaders. And now the practice is spreading to Spain, which means Spanish suppliers have no choice but to climb on the bandwagon.

Among other things, managing shelving involves having a really thorough knowledge of the final customers: where they buy what; what mix of products they usually buy; how they react when they don't find exactly what they are looking for; what products they buy by brand and what products they don't; how the products should be packaged; how many items should be in each package, etc. At first glance it would seem that this is a job that far exceeds the capacities of the typical catalogue salesperson.

Joaquín Candel is not the kind of person who is frightened by danger. His experience as an army officer in Africa in the late 1920s made him particularly adept at adapting to the lie of the land. As so often happens in cases like this, he had profited from his experience on the battlefield, applying it to managing his own business. He liked his employees to call him 'Sergeant', considering that the time which had elapsed since the battle of El Aaiun where, incidentally, the national army had met with utter defeat, entitled him to a promotion. Nobody really cared.

He decided that he needed a broader base of operations in order to resist the threats more effectively. The decisions he made can be briefly summarized below.

He decided to open specialized cash and carry stores. The arrival of large hardware specialists like Bauhaus was a definite threat, because they made it so easy for hardware retailers to make a single trip there and stock up on everything they needed at highly competitive prices. Furthermore, opening cash and carry outlets would help dissuade retailers from setting up their own purchasing groups.

Anticipating an increase in Bauhaus-type outlets, Joaquín Candel opened three cash and carry stores: in Madrid, Barcelona and Albacete. The latter was located on the same, although conveniently enlarged, premises that had once housed his grandfather Jacobo's shop. Although it was definitely the least profitable of his stores, it was still Joaquín's special favourite.

He also set up a 'superstores' division, which he directed personally. He did all the contact work and the actual selling, simply using the division's seven salespeople to distribute the products ordered. He centralized sales to superstores on the grounds that they involved extremely complicated transactions. Superstores are in a particularly strong bargaining position and doing business with them requires a skill in negotiating and making compromises that is beyond the talents of most ordinary salespeople.

Joaquín decided to adopt this strategy while in Albacete for a boring but pleasant family gathering during the Christmas 1985 holidays. Shut in the bedroom that had been his during the years of childhood and adolescence in his still beloved home town, he designed his basic lines of action. The sound of singing reached him clearly from the dining room:

los tranvias de Venecia
los tranvias de Venecia
los tranvias de Venecia
en Venecia no hay tranvias.[3]

Why everyone found this nonsense song so amusing, he would never know. Joaquín reflected that the philosopher J.L. Arangueren was right when he said that men (and women) still belonged more to the animal kingdom than to the human race. What was he doing in a family that was amused by such foolishness? Nevertheless, he kept his opinion to himself.

He had read somewhere that 'structure follows strategy'. Although he wasn't sure if that was true or not, he thought that the time had come anyway to devote some thought to a structure where no substantial changes had taken place in years.

After attending a political meeting on 23 February 1991, he had his first appointment with Antimo Lucea, the renowned consultant and specialist in corporate organization and structure.

Antimo Lucea was deservedly famous as a management consultant, and had a degree from ESADE. His experience in the field of organization included a number of notably successful re-organizations of complex business operations, which indicated that he was the right person to advise about the possible restructuring of Ferretería Joaquín Candel.

What Joaquín Candel told Antimo Lucea

At their first meeting, Joaquín Candel told Antimo Lucea only what he felt the consultant needed to know as an introduction to the company. From the very beginning he made it quite clear that the company's financial situation was not a matter for discussion, but that it was in extremely good shape.

The only figure he was willing to divulge was the 6 billion pesetas in sales the company had registered in 1989. Antimo Lucea accepted that financial information would not be forthcoming and made no protest because, although it was a closely guarded secret, he was absolutely incapable of understanding a balance sheet. He had always considered himself a man of letters and there lay a frustrated novelist hidden deep within his soul.

Table 5.1 *Sales by lines of business*

	1985	1987	1990
Traditional hardware stores	100%	70%	55%
Major outlets	–	15%	20%
Cash and carry	–	15%	25%

The information Joaquín Candel gave the consultant is shown in Table 5.1, Figure 5.1 and the following description of staff and their responsibilities.

Brief description of responsibilities

Chief Executive Officer Joaquín Candel himself. Fifty-seven years old, with a good mind and even a pretty decent body.

Managing Director Ovidio Montllor. Forty-five years old. An industrial engineer, he has been with the company for six years. Tremendously efficient, with an engineer's mind. The following is a direct quote from him: 'Although the company is a collection of individuals, the image we project should be that of a perfectly oiled machine that always performs reliably and efficiently.'

Some of their individual responsibilities are pretty well defined, while in other areas they work together. For instance:

- Joaquín Candel is personally in charge of all dealings with the Board of Directors (all the shares are family owned except for 5% which Joaquín gave to a certain lady by the name of Eloisa). Joaquín's mother has expressly

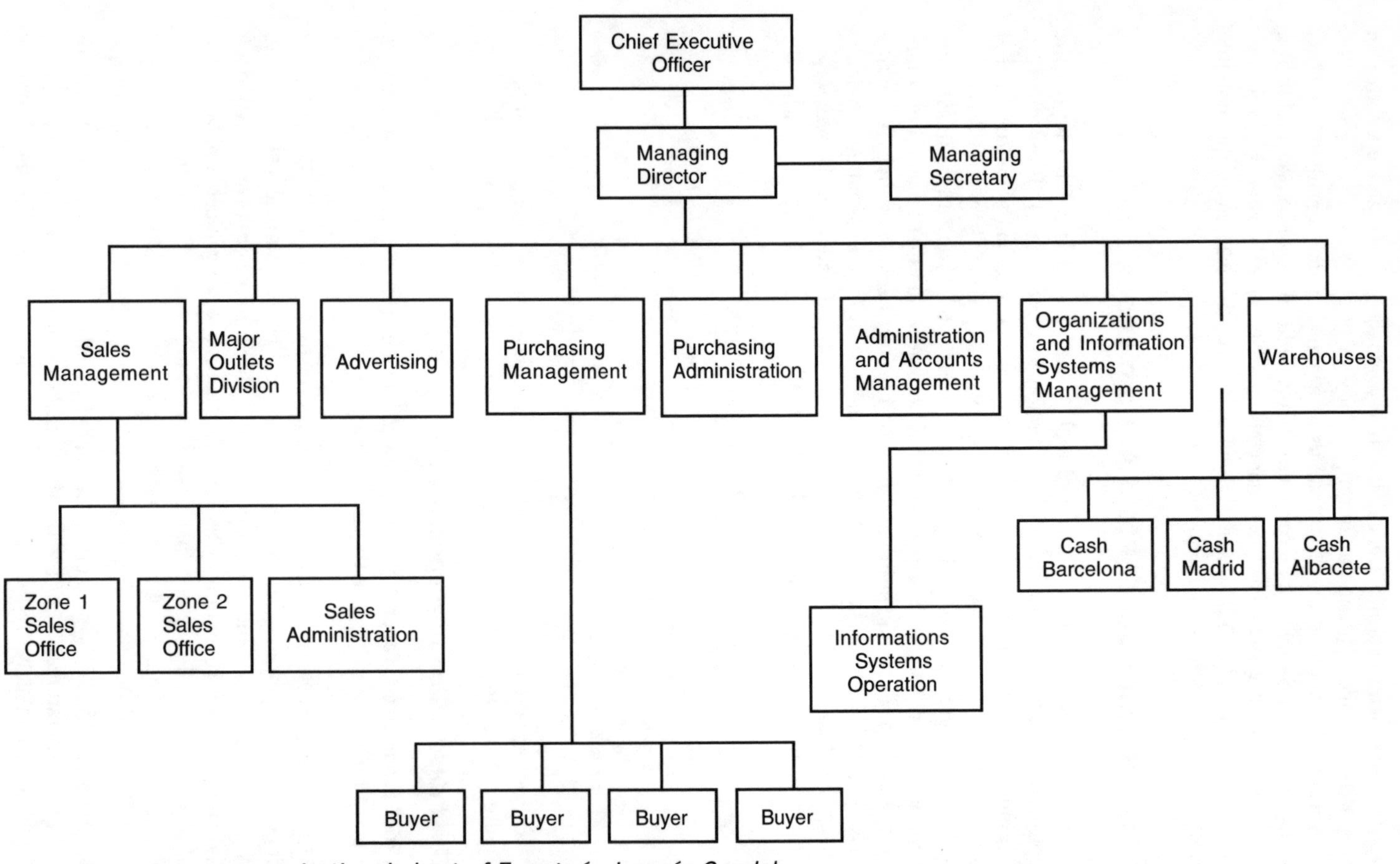

Figure 5.1 *Current organizational chart of Ferretería Joaquín Candel*

forbidden the aforementioned Eloisa to set foot in the boardroom. No one knows exactly why, but they can all imagine.

- Joaquín is also personally responsible for all dealings with banks and other sources of financing, and is the only person who does business with the representatives of superstores.
- Ovidio Montllor is directly responsible for warehouse operations which are a vitally important part of distribution. Fast service and a strict control over stock give the company a major competitive advantage. Ovidio has done a magnificent job managing the warehouse, which compares favourably even with Japanese warehouses.
- Ovidio also acts as Personnel Manager. He probably lacks the proper training for this job, but at least he has a lot of practical experience. At least, that's his own opinion.
- He is also directly responsible for Administration and Accounts, and Organization and Information Systems Management.
- Joaquín Candel and Ovidio Montllor share responsibility for everything else, that is, marketing and sales policies and strategies, operational decisions, etc. Although their opinions may differ on minor details, they usually agree on major decisions and many of the minor ones as well. In addition, they are good friends outside the office.
- Sales Management is divided into two sales territories, each with its own sales office. About 40 salespeople are divided more or less equally between the two offices. Sales Management is in charge of sales to hardware retailers.
- The Superstores Division is Joaquín Candel's personal responsibility. The personnel consists of a middle manager whose title is 'Promotor' and who carries out management's orders and takes charge of administrative procedures, and a salesman who doesn't really sell, but spends most of his time processing orders.
- The Advertising department has only been in existence for the past two years. Advertising is in charge of producing catalogues for the salespeople, taking special care to transmit the right corporate image.
- Purchasing Management is a key department. It consists of a manager and four buyers, each one with his own speciality (nuts and bolts, gardening equipment, etc.). The Purchasing Department decides which products will be added to or dropped from the catalogue. It is therefore extremely important for the buyers to be in close touch with suppliers, either directly or indirectly through trade fairs. To put it simply: the company sells whatever the buyers feel like buying.
- Purchasing is also in charge of placing orders with suppliers, deciding when to buy, etc. Orders and warehouse operations are so closely involved that the Purchasing Department answers to Ovidio Montllor.
- Another of the Purchasing Department's jobs is to contract new suppliers and get rid of those that are no longer desirable. The department also sets prices and decides what discounts, if any, to offer customers. It is directly responsible to Joaquín Candel for all price and discount decisions.

- Purchasing is also in charge of product presentation, including packaging (in terms of both image and quantity). The Purchasing Manager has sole responsiblity for this.
- Senior management feels that the Purchasing Manager is a good buyer and a poor manager. In the opinion of the top executives, purchasing management involves managing the department's personnel (there is a high turnover rate among the buyers) as well as deciding on the product policy, the mix of items to be offered in shelving spaces, presentation, etc.). The company realizes that its current buyers have probably not kept up with the times. Making good buys at good prices is no longer the company's sole differential advantage. Still, this is basically what the buyers know how to do well.
- Purchasing Administration does nothing more than process purchase orders. The department consists of one manager and between three and four clerks.
- Administration and Accounts Management is in charge of accounting in general, credit ratings and arrangements, cash and bank balances, paying commissions, etc. Efforts are currently being made to develop an analytical accounting system. The department consists of one manager and between four and five clerks.
- Organization and Information Systems Management is a newly created department whose primary task is to computerize the warehouse. The department consists of two computer specialists.
- The Cash and Carry outlets are semi-autonomous companies, although they depend entirely on the Purchasing Department for the products they stock. So far at least there has been no talk of making them responsible for stocking their own outlets. Each cash and carry outlet employs approximately eight people.
- The Warehouse employs 35 people who work in two shifts.

When he had absorbed this information, Antimo Lucea asked if there existed a manual describing the company's operational philosophy. With a gesture that an impartial spectator might have described as 'triumphant', Ovidio Montllor handed him a lavender folder, referred to in Antimo Lucea's reports as 'the green file'. For some people colour blindness, like free enterprise, is something you've just got to learn to live with.

Philosophy behind the allocation of responsibilities

The following statements were contained in the area file:

Due to the company's growth, we feel that it is advisable to state on the following pages the responsibilities of each of the departments that make up our company.

Before going on to describe them, we would like to emphasize several points which we consider to be of the utmost importance:

1. As is only logical, allocation of responsibilities implies that the person who is charged with any responsibility is vested with all the authority necessary to carry out the task required. Without authority, there is no responsibility. Authority and responsibility are two inter-related concepts.
2. The person responsible for each department must:
   - define, as clearly as possible, the jobs to be done by each member of his team, remembering to encourage individuals to take the initiative and to create a strong team spirit;
   - verify that the tasks assigned are carried out in a normal way and within the general guidelines established;
   - train his personnel and give them the information necessary and advisable to ensure that communications within the department and with the rest of the company are good;
   - encourage every employee to develop his/her individual skills in order to attain professional advancement and personal satisfaction.
3. The organization chart and job descriptions are not intended to be rigid. On the contrary, the organization should be flexible and able to adapt at all times to market needs and corporate objectives. Although the company is a collection of individuals, the image we project should be that of a perfectly oiled machine that always performs reliably and efficiently.
4. Last but not least, we wish to stress that the attached 'allocation of responsibilities' is by no means exhaustive. Each job no doubt involves many other tasks that are not included in these pages but which are performed logically and in a spirit of collaboration. Nevertheless, this allocation of responsibilities may be enlarged upon and altered as appropriate.

When he had read the document Antimo Lucea asked the following questions:

- *What is the executive turnover rate?* Very high. With only a few exceptions, executives tend to stay with the company for only 3–4 years.
- *Why?* Not because of their salaries, if that's what you were thinking. The truth is, we get rid of them because they aren't professional enough.
- *How do you pick your executives?* We get them through one of the most important headhunters (and one of the most expensive, added Ovidio Montllor).
- *How do you communicate your philosophy and explain the allocation of responsibilities to your executives?* In a meeting where all this is explained in great detail.
- *What kind of executive co-ordination exists?* We have meetings every Monday morning.

- *Is your information system adapted to these decentralized operations that give each executive more responsibility and authority?* This is something that has to be done (although I doubt that the Accounts Manager is equipped to do it, added Ovidio Montllor).
- *How are your executives kept informed about corporate strategies and company performance in general?* In the Monday meetings.
- *What is your general opinion of your executives?* That as a rule they're not very good at managing and they don't have much commercial vision. We were going to have all of them do some courses at ESADE, but we finally decided against it.

At this point a number of comments occurred to Antimo Lucea, the most immediate of which was that he would not like to be in the Accounts Manager's shoes. However, he said nothing and simply went on to review what Ovidio Montllor considered to be the most relevant information about the responsibilities and activities of the various departments.

Sales

Sales management

- Analyses how competitors' articles are distributed at points of sale.
- Analyses market trends in terms of products and quality.
- Proposes commercial policies to management.
- Analyses hardware retailers' preferences.
- Proposes remuneration systems for salespeople.
- Organizes and re-organizes the sales network.
- Decides on campaigns, special offers, etc.

Sales offices

- Gather information from salespeople about the market performance of both company and competitors' products.
- Analyse hardware retailers' preferences with sales management.
- Assign salespeople's territories, set sales goals, decide on the average number of visits salespeople should make, etc.
- Control and supervise salespeople.
- Classroom work: train salespeople in selling.
- Train salespeople in the field.
- Provide sales assistance.
- Hire salespeople.

Salespeople

- Gather and report information about the market performance of both company and competitors' products.
- Make sales.

Purchasing

Purchasing management

- Sets prices.
- Decides what products to buy.
- Decides how products should be presented.
- Decides when and how to create and develop personalized products with their own brands, packaging, etc.

Buyers

- Decide how much to buy.
- Decide when merchandise should be delivered.
- Decide on suppliers.
- Set product specifications.

Advertising

- Designs advertising and corporate image.
- Studies and chooses advertising media.
- Produces catalogues, brochures, etc.
- Prepares advertisements.
- Analyses the impact of advertising.
- Arranges trade fair exhibits.

Lucea's first report

This section outlines Lucea's first report, summing up the meetings he held with Joaquín Candel and Ovidio Montllor of Ferretería Joaquín Candel.

These conclusions and preliminary proposals are obviously based on the consultant's partial knowledge of the company and are therefore intended only to serve as a guide for further discussions aimed at ultimately determining a number of final proposals.

Corporate strengths and weaknesses

The first impression is that the company has a number of strengths and weaknesses, as follows:

Strengths

- Although basic information about the company's market position has not been provided, it appears that this position is good and has actually improved in the past few years.

- It also appears that the company is in good financial shape and would have no problem in carrying out additional investments aimed at making operations more efficient and effective.
- The senior management team, which consists of the CEO and the Managing Director, has a really solid knowledge of the business. This explains the company's expansion and the new initiatives that have been taken.
- There do not appear to be any particular personnel problems and the general atmosphere of the company is adequate.

Weak points

- There is too much turnover at middle management level. This means that both the company structure and culture are fairly weak and leads one to assume that the philosophy of decentralization contained in the first pages of the 'allocation of responsibilities' guide is not really being put into practice.
- As a result, knowledge about the business is likely to be too heavily concentrated in the senior management team. Were this team to leave the company, the organization would be in a particularly vulnerable position.
- There does not appear to be any clear definition of what senior management expects of its middle management team. Senior management's dissatisfaction with the performance of some (not all) of its executives might well be caused by the fact that the role of middle managers has never been clearly defined.
- There does not appear to be a clearly defined long-term strategy. Although under current circumstances defining strategy is a complex task, the impression is that the middle management team is operating on a short- rather than a long-term basis. Long-term strategy appears to be strictly the province of senior management and is not part of the middle management culture.
- Senior management seems to have too many direct responsibilities. This could prevent them from devoting sufficient attention to their strategic management tasks.

There are a number of other strong and weak points, but for the time being we will concentrate solely on those listed above.

Preliminary proposals

I feel that Ferretería Joaquín Candel needs to take the following basic steps in order to strengthen and further improve its market position:

- Further develop its medium- and long-term strategy.
- Promote, structure and rationalize its sales division.
- Build up a stronger middle management team.
- Change some existing operational groups (Accounting and Information Systems) and add some new ones (Personnel).

At the next meeting, Joaquín Candel made it abundantly clear that, although the content of the report appeared to be correct (indicating that he had not actually read it), what he wanted from the consultant was a well-reasoned proposal for restructuring the company.

He specified that if the consultant felt that any new division should be added to the organizational chart its exact responsibilities should be precisely defined. Furthermore, if the consultant felt that any changes should be made in the responsibilities of existing divisions, he should include a full explanation of what these changes would involve. Should he feel that any of the existing departments ought to be realigned or placed under the responsibility of some other division, he should give all the reasons for this opinion.

All the foregoing should be expressed within the framework of a general philosophy about the company's future.

Somehow this made Antimo Lucea feel like a mere employee. Without realizing it, he had abruptly ceased to be a famous management consultant and become a corporate flunky. The boss had made this perfectly clear.

Themes/issues to consider

Environmental adaptation

When we describe the environment of certain organizations as 'stable', 'turbulent', 'complex', etc., we are assuming that environment is 'objective'; something that is identical for all organizations. However, a single environment may be considered stable by one organization and turbulent by another, depending, among other things, on the extent to which the organization is really familiar with its environment. This familiarity is contingent on the organization's capacity to collect relevant information and process it competently. The interesting thing about the Joaquín Candel case is not so much the company's strategic response to the increasing complexity of its operating environment, as the structural response necessary if the company is to enhance its ability to collect and process relevant information.

Leadership

Joaquín Candel's style of leadership can be described in a number of ways: autocratic, dictatorial, etc. This style is partly the legacy of a specific historical era, but even more than that it is an expression of his own personality. We can gamble on the hypothesis that it will be very difficult for Joaquín Candel to change his style. However, the relevant question here is whether he really should change it or if it is a style of leadership that worked at a time when the country was moving away from a 40-year history of dictatorship to a democracy and is perhaps a style that will continue to work in terms of leading the changes the company will inevitably have to make.

There are at least two reasons why the response is not an easy one. First, the existence of a democratic state does not necessarily imply that all its members, or even an important number of them, have deep-rooted democratic values, at least during the early stages of the transition from dictatorship.

The second reason is closely linked to the first. It is a reasonable assumption that no dictatorial government will remain in power for 40 years unless a considerable portion of society either supports it or has at least adjusted to it. This case doesn't contain any information on these subjects, largely because they are too difficult to evaluate. Nevertheless, they force us to consider certain ideas (autocratic leadership, for example) which are negative concepts but which can prove efficient from an organizational point of view. They also force us to consider the conflict that can be caused by a clash between ethical values (what I personally consider acceptable or not acceptable) and functionality (what appears to be most efficient for the organization at a particular moment).

Organizational structure design

In the short term the Ferretería Joaquín Candel does not require major restructuring. The company is profitable and it seems unlikely that this will change in the near future. The challenge facing the company is a medium-term one. The environment is changing to such an extent that we simply cannot ignore the possibility that the company's currently favourable situation may come to an end. Its current competencies may not be enough to face the future. Restructuring should aim to position the company in the immediate future.

Assignments

1. Following the meeting with Antimo Lucea, Joaquín Candel decided to discontinue the relationship with him and invite major consulting firms (groups of students) to consider the problems of Ferretería Joaquín Candel. Joaquín Candel has made all the material available to the new consultants. Your group represents one of these firms.

Naturally you do not want to end up in the same situation as Antimo, so you have asked Joaquín Candel for a meeting where you can ask questions and outline your strategy for a change process at Ferretería Joaquín Candel.

As a preparation for this meeting you should think about the problems that you as a consultant might encounter. These problems might involve Joaquín Candel's personality; the company's business policy and practices, or additional information that you want access to. The whole idea of the meeting is for you to create a 'space' or negotiate a contract with Joaquín Candel that will allow you to work as a professional consultant. Therefore, your asssignment for this first meeting with Joaquín Candel is to find out whether a working relationship can be established, rather than immediately trying to solve the problems of Ferretería Joaquín Candel.

Joaquín Candel has agreed that each consulting company will be allowed 15 minutes to present its strategy and ask questions. He will then probably ask you some additional questions and on the basis of these meetings he will decide which of the consulting firms will be given the assignment to reorganize his company.

It is entirely up to you to choose the format of your presentation, as long as it stays within the stipulated 15 minutes.

2. Following the meetings, Joaquín Candel decided to continue working with your firm. Your assignment now is to make a proposal for possible changes in Ferretería Joaquín Candel.

You should take into consideration the results of the meeting with Joaquín Candel.

You are asked to prepare a presentation of a maximum of 15 minutes for the company's Board of Directors. The report should specify:

- the changes you propose; the means by which you will accomplish them, and your reasons for suggesting them;
- the role of Joaquín Candel in the 'new' organization;
- your role as consultants in the project;
- the change process (that is, the order of the changes suggested and the total amount of time needed to complete the project).

Suggested reading

Daft, Richard L. and Lengel, Robert H. (1986) 'Organizational information requirements, media richness and structural design', *Management Science*, Vol. 32, No. 5, May.

Galbraith, J. (1973) *Designing Complex Organizations*. Reading, Mass: Addison-Wesley.

Morgan, Gareth, (1986) *Images of Organization*. London: Sage.

Notes

1 Roughly translated as: 'Oh, towers of Albacete, whose slender spires are reflected in the river as two Spains and my entire heart!'

2 Rough translation: 'In a native quarter of Havana a black man was heard to sigh, ''Oh, Lord, let me be a white man, even if only a Catalan!'' '

3 'The streetcars of Venice, the streetcars of Venice, the streetcars of Venice ... There are no streetcars in Venice.'

6
Kogen Österreich
Identity lost

Karl Sandner

Kogen Österreich is the third largest grocery retailer in Austria. With more than 1000 outlets it has a market share of about 15%. As a consumer co-operative created in 1856, it has a rich and specifically normative-ideological history. Today, Kogen Österreich is an organization with production units, warehouses, department stores, retail outlets, a staff of 15,000, and some 750,000 members. These members own Kogen Österreich but have more or less no voice. In addition, the original reason for the existence of Kogen Österreich has faded out. A new mission which could carry the organization has not yet been found.

Originally Kogen Österreich was able to accumulate considerable wealth. But during the last 15 years, there have been continuous operational losses in all but one year, amounting to overall operational losses of AS 4.1 billion. In all these years the whole organization (management, workforce, members) and its major stakeholders have found themselves unable to come up with solutions that might solve the economic and the normative-ideological problems of Kogen Österreich.

For an outside consultant with a traditional economic background the situation may look simple: one just had to apply well-known managerial concepts and tools. But that solution, obviously, has not been good enough.

Cultural context

In the nineteenth century, when the first consumer co-operatives in Europe were established, the Austrian Empire covered the major part of central and eastern Europe. Order and direction were provided and controlled by an aristocratic hierarchy and the Catholic church.

After the First World War only a small part (less than 10%) of the old empire remained. That First Republic was confronted with tremendous problems of defining its new identity and at the same time with enormous economic problems. In the 1930s a civil war errupted which was soon contained, but the overall situation remained even worse. With the advent of Nazism (national socialism), many Austrians hoped their problems would be solved.

After the Second World War the country was destroyed. Many people owned just what they could carry in their hands, and a large number of persons had been killed. The questions of national identity and economic survival recurred. Christian Democrats and Socialists, together, started to build the Second Republic. Many of their leading politicians had been imprisoned by the Nazis. These politicians knew that the only chance of a Second Austrian Republic was the building of that republic as a common effort.

That idea of common political effort, of coalition and compromise, was the dominant Austrian political mechanism for the decades to come. One of the first major tests for the new republic occurred when in the early 1950s a Communist revolution was started. Trade union members particularly fought and crushed the Communists in the streets of Vienna and thus prevented Austria from Communist rule, which neighbouring Hungary, Czechoslovakia and others had experienced for decades. Since then the (centrally organized) Austrian trade union acts and is seen as a partner who takes on responsibility for the good of the country.

As the rebuilding of Austria required the efforts of everybody, the major political parties, trade and industry, the farmers and the labour organizations agreed to establish a 'social partnership', and provided that institution with substantial political power. This institutionalized co-operation also meant that no one party could become strong enough to dominate the others. Today, Austria's economic and social status are above the European average and could not have been achieved without the system of social partnership. As an example, the average strike rate is extremely low in Austria: in recent years it was around 60 seconds per working person per year. Today too, the grip of the political parties is much weaker, but – similar to other countries – there are still some 'strongholds' to be found.

These advantages of prosperity and social peace do come with several disadvantages. With the 'social partnership' a class of functionaries developed whose careers in their organizations or companies depended rather on their political 'fit' than on their ability to manage complex economic development. More or less the same people, who had known each other for years, would meet in several committees over and over again, and at the same time would slowly lose touch with their constituencies. Also, owing to the interlocking networks and their interdependencies, rational-economic actions, which should have been taken some time ago, were often delayed or suppressed (for example the closing down of a hopelessly unprofitable steel mill).

A similar system of interlocking powerholders can be found at Kogen Österreich, a large consumer co-operative. Because of its ideological and philosophical background, members, workforce, managers, board of directors and supervisory board were quite often at the same time members or functionaries of the trade union and of the Social Democrat Party. This, of course, as a theoretical aspect, points at the the normative basis of business organizations. But in pragmatic terms it meant that at Kogen Österreich technical-economic rationality would often collide with political rationality, not just in the same enterprise but also for the same person. Obviously, decision making in and for Kogen Österreich was often difficult.

Kogen Österreich is one of the largest enterprises in Austria. In the retail business it holds a market share of around 15%. Because of its size and its close relations with the (centrally organized) Austrian trade union and the Social Democrat Party, it is often called the 'red giant'. On the other hand Raiffeisen, a large farmers' co-operative group called the 'green giant', is closely connected with the Christian Conservative Party.

Co-operatives like Kogen are business organizations. Originally they were established as self-help associations of low income groups (workers, farmers, public servants), and quite a number of them as a consequence of the exploitation of the working class by capitalist firms. Today in Europe they are modern business organizations in the fields of, for example, banking, insurance, trade, production, real estate or farming. Some of these co-ops hold market shares of up to 20% or even 30%, in some niches (such as agriculture) even up to 90%. On the other hand, some of them are fighting for survival.

The goal of a co-operative is to serve its members. It is established to provide its members with (economic) advantages. Profit orientation is not its ultimate goal, but surpluses have to be earned. All co-operatives followed and still follow (at least they pretend to) the following principles:

- open membership: with a rather small initial investment everybody can become a member;
- democratic principle: self-government, one person one vote;
- all major decisions have to be backed by the members (general meeting) or their elected representatives;
- members decide what to do with surpluses (a part of the yearly surplus is reimbursed to the members).

As far as the general business situation is concerned, the retail business for groceries and household products in Austria is one of the toughest in Europe. Competition on the market is dominated by the goal to drive out the competitors. No wonder that Austria had the lowest ratio of citizens per square metre of retail sales area in 1991 (see Table 6.1).

As a consequence, its earnings per square metre of retail sales area were also the lowest. In 1992 an estimated 30% of the turnover was sold as special bargains at cost price to the customers.

Consumer co-operatives: history

In order to understand at least some of the problems which a consumer co-operative faces today, it is necessary to understand the history, that is, the ideological background, of that organizational form.

Based on the idea of self-help, the first consumer co-operative in Austria was

Table 6.1 *Citizens per sq. m. retail sales area, 1991*

Austria	3.12
Switzerland	3.35
Belgium	3.45
Germany	3.50
France	4.48
Spain	4.86
Netherlands	5.41
UK	6.27

established in 1856: workers in a textile plant put their money together to buy some sacks of flour. In the following years the number of co-operatives increased, and by 1910 some 420,000 members were organized in about 1400 consumer co-operatives.

At the beginning of the twentieth century consumer co-operatives were firmly rooted in the working class and found wide acceptance among all low-income groups. For obvious reasons the economic rationale for establishing consumer co-operatives was paralleled by their members' political orientation. The majority of the members of the consumer co-operatives sympathized with the dominant political organizations of the workers, that is, the trade unions and the Social Democrat Party. Often declared Social Democrats were chosen to run a co-operative's business.

Before the beginning of the twentieth century the Social Democrat Party was reluctant to establish relations with the consumer co-operatives. On the one hand, consumer co-operatives were not a sub-organization of the party and thus could not be controlled by the party. On the other hand, many of the co-operatives were managed poorly and again and again encountered substantial economic difficulties. The party did not want to be linked to or even made responsible for poorly run organizations.

In 1903 political strategy and the fact of personal connections between consumer co-operatives, trade unions and the Social Democrat Party led the party to define consumer co-operatives as a 'political instrument in the fight of the working class'. Correspondingly:

- a new central organization for all consumer co-operatives was set up and was soon joined by 70% of all consumer co-operatives;
- a large-scale co-operative purchasing organization was established;
- self-supply (in order to gain independence) was promoted as a political principle. Thus production sites (for example a large bread factory east of Vienna) and department stores (for example for shoes, clothing, linen) were built in major Austrian cities;
- members of the Social Democrat Party were obliged to join a consumer co-operative.

Thus the famous 'three column doctrine' of the political labour movement emerged. The Social Democrat Party, the trade unions and the consumer co-operatives joined as equal partners in the fight for the political goals of the working class. Until today that strategic political alliance has never been abandoned, despite the fact that the way these organizations act and see themselves differs from the old days.

During the next few decades the consumer co-operatives justified their existence: the number of members as well as the number of outlets increased. From 1934 on consumer co-operatives were not allowed to reimburse more than 3% of their surpluses, so hidden reserves accumulated.

After the Civil War and during the time of the Nazi regime consumer co-operatives suffered from political pressure. Their annihilation was prevented by acts of solidarity by the farmers' co-operatives.

In the 1960s the structure of the retail business started to change dramatically: self-service shops, supermarkets, discount shops and chain stores, often backed by foreign capital, entered the market. Fierce competition forced many small retail shops (private and co-operative ones) into closing down.

The rise and the survival of consumer co-operatives was based on their ethical nature: their members were never cheated in the quality or quantity of goods they bought. The original and basic idea of a consumer co-operative was to provide its members with groceries and other products they needed for their everyday life:

- at better prices than private competitors; or
- of a better quality than the competition; or
- at out-of-the-way locations where peole needed a retail shop, but where the demand was not high enough that a private retailer saw sufficient profit.

This idea made a lot of sense – and should receive a lot of praise – in the original context: the situation of low-income groups at the time of industrialization was bad. But by then, in the 1960s, the competition on the market had taken over the former regulatory function of the co-operatives. And more than that, the co-operatives often found themselves unable to offer better prices and/or better quality than their fiercest competitors. They now were just one player in the retail market among others, yet with a different history and ideology.

Non-members in the meantime had also been allowed to shop at co-operative stores. But they, like an increasing number of members, purchased in co-operative stores only when it seemed economically reasonable. Members had one big advantage though, and that counted substantially for the still growing number of memberships of consumer co-operatives: at the end of each year members were reimbursed up to 2% of their yearly purchases.

The structure of a consumer co-operative (Figure 6.1) was based on its members' needs, influence and control. The distance between members and management was small: members were customers and owners at the same time. In addition, members often knew the management personally.

Owing to the competitive market situation between 1968 and 1978, consumer co-operatives had to close more than 400 outlets, because they were far from being able to break even. There was a tendency to merge in order to create larger

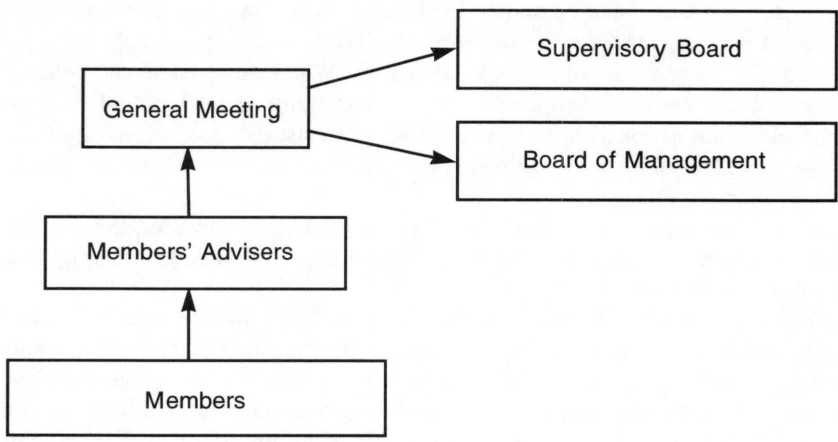

Figure 6.1 *Typical structure of a consumer co-operative in 1978*

Table 6.2 *Consumer co-operatives, 1978 (overall figures)*

Members	738,572
Outlets	1,082
Personnel	19,642
Market share retail	20%

viable units. But overall many consumer co-operatives had no strategy regarding what to do and how to survive in the new context.

So there were some dozen consumer co-operatives of different sizes and in different economic shape with more or less the same history and ideology, who had lost the original legitimation for their existence (see Table 6.2.). They faced fierce competition, and many of them were already in economic trouble.

The creation of Kogen Österreich

In 1978 leading representatives of consumer co-operatives created one central organization: Kogen Österreich.[1] All Austrian consumer co-operatives were invited (some felt pressurized and others felt they were talked into joining) to merge into the new organization: all but 4% did.

Several reasons led to the creation of Kogen Österreich. First, economic considerations. Most of the consumer co-operatives were rather poorly managed, some of them operated at a loss. The necessity to rationalize required concentration. Purchase, production and processing, finance, administration, training, logistics, advertising, etc. were thought to be more effective and more efficient in just one common organization. With one organization instead of many, market share could be transformed into market power. Or as one manager put it, 'It was crucial for survival to become economically powerful.'

Secondly, there were political considerations. When we consider the political history of the consumer co-operatives and the political background of their managers and functionaries, there was no way to resist the idea of having a large powerful organization; an economical powerful organization would be helpful in gaining political power.

Finally, personal stakes may also have contributed. Most of the leading representatives who pushed for the creation of Kogen Österreich formed its new Board of Directors.

Kogen Österreich was now a large enterprise with food processing plants (mills, bakeries, meat processing, winery, coffee roasting), production plants (clothing, packing material, chemical products), warehouses, grocery stores, discount markets, department stores and supermarkets. In addition, Kogen Österreich held an indirect 30.6% share in the Bank für Arbeit und Wirtschaft and an 8.3% share in the Österreichische Nationalbank.

As another result of the merger, Kogen Österreich had to start with a loss carried forward of AS 217 million.

General strategy, marketing and sales

The strategic goals for the years ahead were to rationalize and to grow (higher market share in the retail business) in order to earn surpluses.

One of the reasons for the merger was to take advantage of the potential synergies. It took about four years to get rid of all parallel structures and parallel activities. Purchasing, production, logistics, etc. were then handled centrally.

The second major area where money could be saved was a burden of the old days. It had been a goal of consumer co-operatives to provide their members with nearby retail outlets. Now some outlets were unprofitable because of small size or remote location. The management suggested closing down those outlets where transformation into a profitable self-service market could not be expected. Some members then felt that closing down these outlets was at the same time giving up a part of the old identity. On the other hand, the economic figures required action.

The structural changes in the retail market had led to the economization of the co-operative member relationship among its members; that is, shopping at a Kogen outlet had to have an economic advantage. Indeed, Kogen Österreich members applied the usual criteria for a competitive market: price, quality, availability of parking, attractiveness of the location, etc. In this respect Kogen's position was not bad at all: it had earned a reputation of selling mass products at reasonable prices. As member loyalty slowly declined, the only way to grow was to attract non-members as buyers. So Kogen Österreich had to present itself as politically neutral and get rid of the association with 'poor people'. As a consequence, the original and basic idea of a co-operative, which was to serve its members, had to be changed. The new mission statement was 'to serve as a self-help organization for all consumers'. The problem was that most of the consumers didn't know that, and still considered Kogen Österreich as 'red', as dominated by the trade union and the Social Democrat Party. And this meant that quite a number of the Austrian customers never had and probably never would shop at Kogen Österreich.

Personnel

Because of Kogen Österreich's ideological and political background, a certain normative fit was necessary for an applicant to get a job. In a similar sense, promotions were often dominated by (micro-)political considerations. There was no doubt that all top and middle managers had to be members of Kogen Österreich, members of the trade union, and members of the Social Democrat Party. But working in the labour movement and being politically alert is not necessarily the right training to run a large business organization successfully in a competitive market. The management had a poor professional reputation in the retail business. Policies to improve managerial competencies were discussed.

It is obvious that Kogen Österreich, with its ideological background and its political status, would have comparatively more staff than its competitors, and would pay higher wages than the competition (10–12.5% above the collective agreement). In addition, substantial indirect compensation was granted (end-of-year bonuses, additional holidays). As a consequence, costs for personnel were about 50% higher than those of the competition, based on comparable sales. No explicit policy was developed, but a more performance-oriented compensation system seemed to be advisable.

Members

Theoretically, everybody could be a member. In fact, mainly those with the corresponding political background and those who were looking for the benefits applied for membership. Membership was easy to obtain. One had to subscribe for a share certificate (nominal value in 1978 AS 1000; downpayment 5%, the rest came from the member's future reimbursements). Being a member meant that one:

- was entitled to reimbursements;
- was entitled to special offers; and
- could elect representatives for the general meeting.

In 1978 Kogen Österreich was quite different from what a consumer co-operative had been in the old days. The small or medium-sized co-operative based on the needs of its members was gone; instead there was a large organization, run and dominated by managers and a small group of functionaries. But still, at least nominally, it was the members who owned and controlled the co-operative, and important decisions still had to be brought before the general meeting. For Kogen Österreich there were two major problems connected with its membership. First, apart from reimbursements, what could make membership attractive (considering the problematic financial situation)? Second, in reality it was not a members' co-operative any more but a large organization dominated by its management and personnel.

As a consequence, the content and mode of communication were object specific. On the market Kogen Österreich tried to present itself as neutral and open to all customers as one competitor among others. Internally and at member assemblies the old traditions had to be stressed (for example the democratic basis of co-operatives) and political aspects had to be taken into consideration. In order to take the edge off that contradiction, the new mission statement defined the goal of Kogen Österreich as 'to serve as a self-help organization for all consumers'.

The years of 'consolidation': 1978–88

In the first 10 years reality did not meet the economic expectations connected with the creation of Kogen Österreich.

Turnover

Total turnover, which includes wholesale, rose from AS 17.9 billion in 1978 to AS 32.6 billion in 1988 (see Table 6.3). This is an increase of 82% (average of 6.2% per year). Retail sales rose from AS 17.4 billion in 1978 to AS 26.6 billion in 1988. This is an increase of 53% (average of 4.3% per year).

If we take into account the price index, that is, the inflation rate, retail sales only increased by 0.4% per year on average.

In 1988, when Kogen Österreich increased its retail sales by 0.8%, the total retail sales market in Austria increased by 5%.

Results

Between 1978 and 1988 surpluses seemed to have been earned in all years but three, the total of losses exceeding the total of surpluses by AS 73 million (see Table 6.4).

The specific figures for each year do not mean very much because extensive – legal – balance-sheet cosmetics were applied. If we remove the extraordinary

Table 6.3 *Turnover (in AS billion)*

Year	Total turnover	Retail sales	Production, wholesale	Outlets
1978	17.9	17.4		
1979	19.0	18.8		
1980	20.4	20.2		
1981	26.1	21.3	4.8	
1982	27.1	22.1	5.0	
1983	28.0	22.9	5.1	
1984	30.7	25.0	5.7	
1985	31.6	25.7	5.9	
1986	32.1	26.1	6.0	1032
1987	32.5	26.4	6.1	1010
1988	32.6	26.6	6.0	1025

Table 6.4 *Annual results (in AS million)*

Year	Result before tax	Result after adjustment for extraordinary items[1]
1978	+0.8	–132.8
1979	+26.4	–342.8
1980	–110.9	–202.9
1981	–79.1	–315.4
1982	+16.5	278.9
1983	+93.0	+105.6
1984	+8.8	–88.9
1985	+5.8	–273.5
1986	+1.3	–240.2
1987	–31.2	–377.3
1988	+22.7	–413.2

[1] Differences before and after adjustment of results stem from, for example, selling property and leasing it back.

earnings and the extraordinary expenditures from the balance sheet, then all years but one show substantial losses, for example AS 413 million in 1988. Thus the ordinary results beween 1978 and 1988 amounted to losses of AS 2.56 billion.

Profitability

Low profitability was owing to two main reasons: stagnation in turnover and cost structure (especially personnel costs, interest on borrowed capital, logistics).

Kogen Österreich still operated mainly in the lower end of the mass product retail business, where competition was fierce and margins were small. When the very low end of the market (discount shops) was considered strategically important, discount outlets were launched in 1986. To enter the up-market business, two locations were remodelled to fancy department stores (Graz in 1986, Vienna in 1988). Yet their turnover did not meet expectations, so they too produced losses.

The second major problem was the personnel cost structure. As could have been expected some 10 years earlier, nothing had happened to change that. Personnel was still around 19,500, more or less the same as in 1978 (see Table 6.5). In 1984 the number of personnel had peaked at 20,700 and since then slowly decreased. Personnel costs were 50% above those of Billa (the main competitor). Compared to its competitors Kogen Österreich was overstaffed and its personnel overcompensated. In addition, not even the reimbursements to members had been earned.

In 1988 Kogen Österreich was still by far the largest retailer in Austria. Its original function as a price regulator had been lost to the competitive mechanism in the market. Kogen Österreich was obviously in substantial trouble. The old internal slogan, loaded with underdog emotions – 'Wir vom Kogen bringen alle

Table 6.5 *Staffing levels*

Year	Number of personnel
1978	19,642
1979	20,109
1980	20,588
1981	20,057
1982	19,442
1983	20,706
1984	20,737
1985	20,401
1986	20,120
1987	19,705
1988	19,148

Table 6.6 *Retail market share*

Year	Kogen	Billa
1985	20.6%	
1986	20.4%	12.1%
1987	20.3%	
1988	20.0%	15.0%

Table 6.7 *Members*

Year	Number of members
1978	738,572
1982	812,560
1985	810,430
1986	814,236
1987	812,430
1988	786,361

um' ('we will kill them all') was not heard any more. The years to come would be the years when they had to fight for survival.

The concept 'Kogen 2000' (1988)

Messages and strategies

In 1988 the concept 'Kogen 2000' was presented by the Vice-Chairman (Gerner). He would be elected Chairman of the Board of Management in 1990 when the old Chairman retired. The economic disaster of the previous decade

Table 6.8 *Reimbursements*

Year	Reimbursements in AS millions
1978	201.7
1979	237.4
1980	261.9
1981	277.0
1982	284.0
1983	292.5
1984	291.0
1985	297.0
1986	288.0
1987	289.1
1988	138.9[1]

[1] In 1988 reimbursements were cut from up to 2.5% to 1%.

had forced Kogen Österreich to define existing positions and to develop new strategies. Thus the concept 'Kogen 2000' contained several messages and strategies.

A warning The staff, hard core members and political allies were warned implicitly: 'We are in trouble. We have to act. Just talking about acting, like in the years before, won't do!'

An ideological message Not by coincidence does the concept contain a strong formal oath of allegiance to the co-operative idea: 'We are a co-operative and we serve our members.' The purpose was to reassure: 'We may have to act like every other competitor in the market; and if there are no differences any more – in our hearts we remain a co-operative.'

But then the re-definition of the constituency followed: 'We also serve the general public.' That re-definition of the 'common interest' was accompanied by commitments:

- to strive for above average customer satisfaction;
- to co-operate with organizations which serve consumer interests;
- to protect the environment and to preserve natural resources.

A marketing strategy In order to increase the number of customers (members and non-members) and to increase purchases per customer, Kogen Österreich should primarily:

1. Stop the diversity of shops and concentrate on fewer shop types (see also Figure 6.2):
    - grocery outlets ('The Fresh Kogen'): between 250 and 400 sq.m. sales area;
    - supermarkets: between 400 and 1000 sq.m. sales area;
    - hypermarkets: above 1000 sq.m. sales area;
    - department stores.

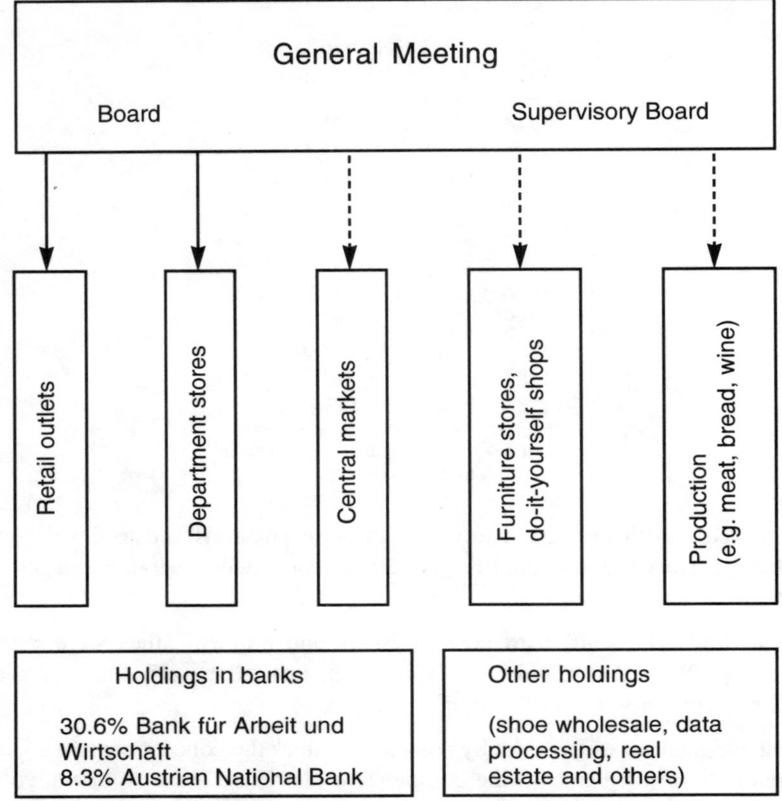

Figure 6.2 *Group structure of Kogen Österreich in 1990*

2. Work on the profile:
   - acquire a strong image for freshness and quality of products;
   - redesign the exterior and interior appearance first of the grocery outlets, then of the supermarkets;
   - stress that a co-operative identifies itself with the goals of its members and customers and thus can be trusted.
3. Reduce the share of self-produced articles in favour of brand names.

A message to personnel Two intentions, which should help improve productivity, were announced:

- to increase the share of part-time workers; and
- to change the compensation system towards performance-related pay.

The meta-message was: 'We know it and you know it, something has to be done. We will try not to hurt anybody.'

Yet the management already knew that reality would be different.

No substantial message to the members The concept briefly mentioned the members in the traditional way (reimbursements, special offers, democratic structure). No new ideas were presented.

In 1989 the general meeting agreed on the concept 'Kogen 2000'.

Problems

In order to understand some of the difficulties Kogen Österreich faced, the major influencing factors have to be illustrated.

Contradictions In the old days and even quite some years after the Second World War, the original idea of a consumer co-operative, self-help, made sense. But by the end of the 1980s the retail market had changed substantially.

Advertising In the beginning a consumer co-operative would not advertise in the way a profit-oriented organization did, it just wanted to inform its members/customers about the products they might choose to buy. For a long time advertising was thought to be expensive and to tempt people into decadent luxury. That led to the situation that the advertising activities of Kogen Österreich were – seen from a competitive market view – just mediocre.

Packaging and display A similar example is the packaging of their own products. In the old days of co-operatives you didn't want to have fancy packaging and you didn't sell images with your products – you wanted to sell what was needed. No wonder that the presentation and the display of most of the goods they produced themselves was rather simple and sometimes even looked poor.

Design and architecture The same was true of the exterior and interior design of the grocery outlets and of the central markets. When the reason for your existence is to provide your members with groceries and other products at a reasonable price and quality, then the purchase of these products does not have to be a 'shopping adventure'. As a consequence, the exterior and interior design of most of the grocery outlets and central markets looked cheap, because it was cheap.

Careers The way careers were made in Kogen Österreich can be illustrated by taking the example of H. Gerner, who was elected Chairman in 1990. Gerner was born into a carpenter's family of six children. Politically the family followed a strong Social Democrat orientation. When he became an apprentice Gerner joined the trade union and was soon head of its local youth branch. Later he worked as an employee of a labour protection organization. When comparatively old he earned his BA and some years later his doctorate in law. Gerner started at Kogen as a member counsellor. He became head of the regional consumer co-operative, and with the merger in 1978 he promoted himself to the Board of Management of the new organization. After being the Vice-Chairman he became Chairman in 1990, when his predecessor retired.

Interference From a strictly economic point of view it was clear that quite a number of outlets were not profitable and could not be saved. They had to be closed down. Then economic rationality met local stakeholders. Mayors, representatives of the union and members intervened. Often the closure was delayed by years or even made impossible.

Kogen Österreich and the trade union

At the general meeting in 1990, when the new Chairman was to be elected, the head of the Supervisory Board also retired. That person was probably one of Austria's three most powerful men in the previous decades. He was also head of the trade union, and for some years President of the Austrian parliament. In 1990, when Kogen Österreich was desperately trying to attract new consumer groups, he talked at the general meeting about the trinity of the Social Democrat Party, trade union and Kogen Österreich for the working class. It is easy to assume that at Kogen Österreich economic rationality would repeatedly not win over political rationality.

Personnel and Works Council

Kogen Österreich was over-staffed and its personnel over-compensated. Labour costs were still 50% higher than those of the competition. Retail personnel were paid 10% and administrative personnel 12.5% above the collective agreement. Retired personnel were paid an extra bonus to their pensions. A positive correlation between salary and work attitude could not be found, however. Customers had the impression that Kogen Österreich's retail personnel were probably some of the least motivated in the whole retail business. Overall, additional payments and other voluntary contributions amounted to AS 750 million in 1990.

When it became obvious that labour costs had to be decreased, the Works Council opposed this. The head of the Works Council made her position clear in public: 'We will not give up one Schilling, and the percentage of part-time workers will not rise!'

Owing to the system of a centralized trade union in Austria and the overlapping networks of trade union, Works Council, workforce, members, and even the board of Kogen Österreich, at the shop level the trade union supported the Works Council but never fought in the front line. It would have been somehow paradoxical if the trade union had fought against a management of an organization which was at least partly controlled by the trade union itself.

Management

It should by now be clear that the context in which Kogen Österreich had to be managed was different in some ways.

It took 12 years of continuous and substantial operational losses until a Chairman dared to talk about the necessity of putting Kogen Österreich back on its feet in the general meeting (1990). In addition, and somehow paradoxically for a consumer co-operative, information concerning the problematic economic status was given neither to the media nor to the members.

In addition to all the stakes, the decision-making process in a consumer co-operative, which, on the formal level, was based on being a self-governing and democratic organization, was slow and complicated. On the one hand, members, member advisers and regional advisers held up to 2500 meetings per year. The management often had the impression that lower-level member representatives either did not understand and/or delayed necessary decisions. On the other hand, outside observers had the impression that the management seemed to be paralysed by the stakeholders and often acted rather like administrators. This should not be a surprise: most of them had worked for Kogen and/or a workers' organization for their entire lives. Most of them had never worked in a private enterprise, and had not experienced the job-hopping quite normal in the private retail business. When Gerner became Chairman, outside observers felt that he was the best choice Kogen Österreich had; they also felt he wouldn't match the tasks the organization faced.

And now Gerner and his management team had to take action regarding the substantial economic problems and they had to take care of the management of meaning: there was a large organization, with 750,000 members and 15,000 personnel, that had lost its old identity.

Members

A co-operative is owned by its members and based on the will of its members. At Kogen Österreich the gap between the management and the workforce on the one side and the members on the other side slowly widened. The members' influence on their co-operative more or less dissolved. Of course, in the general meeting and on other official occasions the importance of the members was stressed. In reality, members were seen rather as a problem one didn't know what to do with. No concept to change that situation was developed.

The members themselves felt ignored and, as a result, just 10% on average showed up to elect their representatives.

Can 'red' turn into 'green'?

During the 1980s it became clear that Kogen Österreich was confronted with the problem of its ideological identity. On a competitive market there was no need for the price-regulatory function of a (former) self-help organization.

At the end of the decade two events happened to coincide. The designated Chairman presented his concept, 'Kogen 2000', which, of course, had to have a strong impact on marketing. At the same time the public awareness and discussion about environmental protection and the preservation of natural resources reached a level where most enterprises realized that they would soon be confronted with this problem in one way or another.

It is probably impossible to say to what extent the marketing strategy influenced the discussion about Kogen Österreich's identity and vice versa (yet the marketing people think they know). But the goals of environmental protection and preservation of natural resources were considered to be important. Marketing took a strong turn towards green, fresh, healthy, light ('Der frische Kogen', 'bewußt leben' – 'the fresh Kogen', 'live consciously'), which was put into effect with the products themselves, in their presentation, in advertising, and in the exterior and interior design of the outlets. And marketing also took advantage of Kogen Österreich's sometimes quite remarkable 'green' activities.

As early as 1988 Kogen Österreich acted as a 'gatekeeper':

- In November 1988 it stopped selling certain types of tunafish.
- Sprays that contained aerosols were banned from the shelves long before they were prohibited by law.
- From July 1989 Kogen Österreich did not sell any detergents which contained phosphates (two months before, detergents containing phosphates had made up about 50% of all detergents sold at Kogen Österreich).
- Its own industry was ordered not to use PVC-wrappings after July 1990, and external suppliers were urged to do the same.
- In 1992 neon lamps were delisted.

In 1991, following legal decrees, the Austrian retail business had to find ways to do something with the immense amount of waste it generated (wrapping material, cans, bottles, etc.). As far as beverages were concerned, the majority of retailers and suppliers agreed to collect empty bottles and cans and to have the customer pay for this by charging higher retail prices. Kogen Österreich opposed that plan. They felt that this system would not help to avoid waste, but would merely subsidize its collection. In consequence of Kogen's opposition, beginning with September 1991 major suppliers of beverages (such as Coca-Cola) boycotted Kogen Österreich. The ban was lifted when in April 1992 Kogen Österreich, the other retailers and suppliers agreed to work out another method of waste avoidance. Since that time Kogen Österreich has again been able to sell beverages in non-recyclable bottles or cans, but it still would not promote such products in advertising.

In accordance with its new 'green' stand, Kogen Österreich has also started to work on the political level by providing suggestions and comments to the legislative authorities.

In terms of publicity and public awareness the 'green' policy was successful. Today Kogen Österreich is considered to have been the pioneer in the field, and competitors were forced to follow. But today it is also clear that at Kogen Österreich 'green' as a new ideological basis never really had a chance. The pragmatics of finance and marketing soon prevailed.

The years after 1990

Members

In 1991 the general meeting voted for some changes in the statute. The central mission was defined as 'to benefit the members, all customers, and the general public'. Environmental protection and the protection of natural resources also found their way into the new statute, and another major change concerned the democratic structure of the co-operative (Figure 6.3).

The decision-making structure was shifted to reduce member influence. Now members meet less often, once every five years (unless the management or a set number of members calls for an extraordinary meeting) and the general meeting only has 100 member representatives instead of the previous 1200. This does not give the members much of a voice (bearing in mind that it is the members who own Kogen). Another action that put more distance between the management and the members was disbanding the Kogen's women's association. This

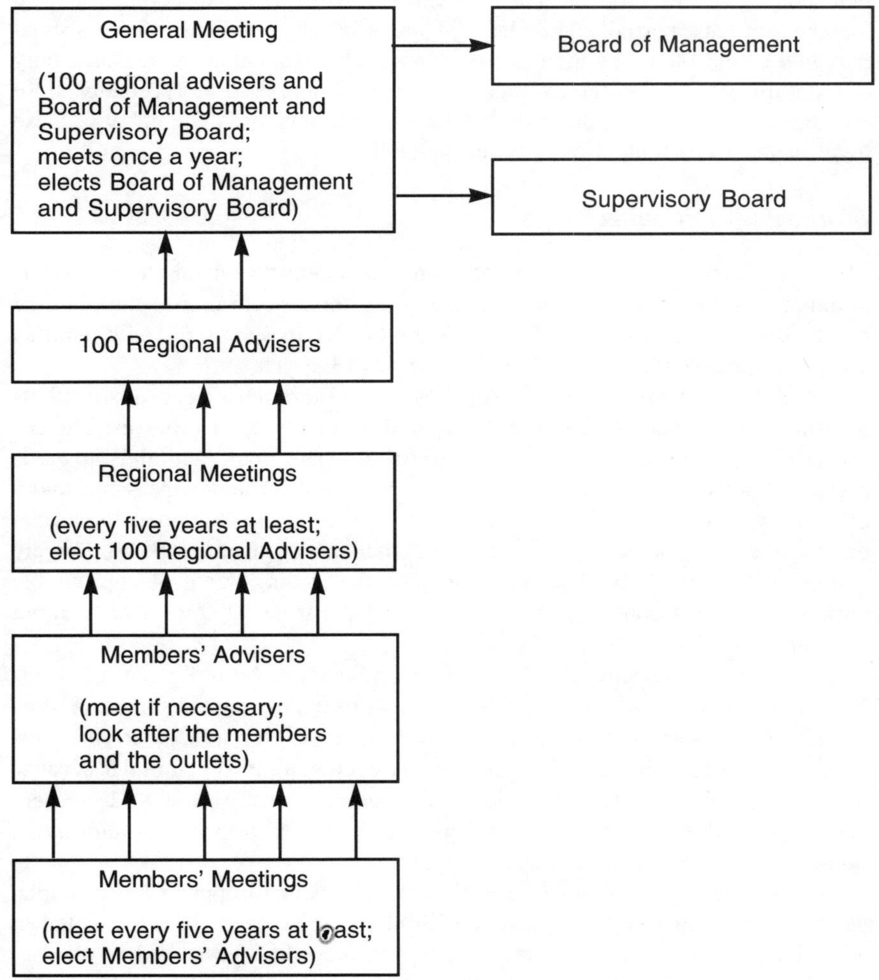

Figure 6.3 *Democratic structure of Kogen Österreich (put into effect 1991)*

women's association had never been extraordinarily brimming with life. But still it was the women who by shopping had the closest contact with the organization. Now their forum was gone. The discontinuation of the company magazine helped to cut down costs, but it also resulted in less member information.

Overall, the management seemed to have gained some additional independence from the members. On the other hand, when we take into account that the Board of Directors and the Supervisory Board always met and decided together, then not much of a control structure seems to be left: the Supervisory Board operated on the same level as the Board of Directors.

The total number of members (731,344 in 1992) continued to decline at a yearly rate of 2%. Because of the operational losses the reimbursement percentage had already been cut to 1% in 1988. In 1991, to compensate the members at least partially, the OKAY-Club was set up, which offered special bargains to the members three times a year. Through unknown reasons, only every third member on the average asked for reimbursements (probably those members who had higher purchases). The goal is to increase the number of these loyal members/customers from about 270,000 to 400,000.

Marketing and sales

The retail business in Austria remains tough. Competition on the market is dominated by the goal to drive out the competitors. According to the plans of two of Kogen's main competitors (Billa and Löwa), these two intend to gain an additional market share of 15% within the next 3–5 years.

In 1990 after years of heavy losses Kogen Österreich closed down all its discount outlets. They had 'earned' losses of around 10% of turnover. The co-operative with its ideological bias towards its personnel (and thus towards higher labour costs) was unable to run discount outlets under the same tough conditions as its competitors. Some of the outlets were upgraded to normal outlets, and the remainder (57) were sold to the main competitor (Billa). Largely owing to the sale of the discount shops and the closing down of unprofitable outlets, turnover dropped by 9% in the three years from 1990 to 1992 (without counting the inflation rate).

As laid out in the concept 'Kogen 2000' and assisted by its 'green' activites, Kogen Österreich gained some profile in terms of quality and freshness. A slow increase of non-member customers could be noticed. But still, older Austrians with a conservative background would never even enter a Kogen outlet because of its 'red' history. At the same time, member loyalty slowly decreased: confronted with the alternative of 'being part of an idea' or price consciousness, often economic considerations were applied.

In 1992 most of the bold 'green' activities were dropped: for example, delisting of products was stopped, soft drinks in cans were again promoted in advertising. The 'green adventure' during the preceding years had resulted in estimated losses of AS 600 million. For Kogen Österreich 'green' thinking as an ideological alternative had lost its battle on the capitalist market: it just couldn't afford 'green' activities based on normative considerations any more. From then on they were adopted according to their usefulness within the marketing strategy.

Personnel and Works Council

Beginning in 1991, the Works Council refrained from action because of the serious situation. Lay-offs were not opposed any more, at least not seriously. The percentage of part-time workers (retail) rose from about 27% in 1989 to 43.3% in 1992, and is forecast to reach about 50%. At the competition up to 80% of sales personnel are part-time workers.

Owing to the situation the old doctrine of recruiting managers only from inside had to be given up. In 1991, in first and second level management (20 people altogether) seven were from outside.

The concept 'Kogen 2000' also contained a message about the use of typical human resource management tools such as performance appraisal, performance-based pay systems, career planning or management development. These do not yet exist as organization-wide concepts. If a manager uses such tools, which of course happens now and then, it is his or her personal decision to do so.

Management

Business journals, as well as former Kogen managers and experts in the co-operative business, voiced increasingly critical opinions on the activities and the abilites of Kogen Österreich's management. For example:

- the selection of new locations and the investments required were accompanied by too many failures;
- marketing activities (based on the concept 'Kogen 2000') came far too late (for example modernization of outlets) and were insufficiently realized (drop own products in favour of well-known brand names);
- the ratio of borrowed capital was too high;
- management still seemed unable to enforce important decisions against the will of the Works Council;
- the depoliticization (trade union, Social Democrat Party) of the organization and its re-orientation towards a modern consumer-oriented structure came late and took place too slowly;
- the identity and role of a consumer co-operative in the 1990s was still unclear.

Without any doubt Kogen Österreich used to be very successful – quite some time ago. As some sort of excuse the management refers to other European consumer co-operatives, which are in a similar situation to Kogen Österreich. The management claims that a consumer co-operative has to have some 'room' to survive. In a highly competitive market, they claim, survival would be difficult or impossible.

Marketing experts and at least one example (Migros Switzerland) tell differently. Competition will still be influenced by market prices, but price competition will partly be replaced by competition on ideas and innovation.

In 1992 managers thought they were able to announce a small success. According to their own calculations the productivity of Kogen Österreich retail sales personnel was already above the average of the retail market. It had reached a per head turnover of AS 2 million. At the same time, Billa had a per head turnover of AS 2.7 million. (See Tables 6.9–6.14.)

A new future ahead?

In 1992 the management had to announce they had been looking for a strong partner for quite some time. Raiffeisen Österreich (a farmers' co-operative

Table 6.9 *Turnover (in AS billion)*

Year	Total turnover	Retail sales	Production, wholesale	Outlets
1989	33.6	27.1	6.5	1047
1990	33.4	27.6	5.8	1025
1991	33.0	26.1	6.9	1004
1992	31.5	25.1	6.4	995

Table 6.10 *Annual results (in AS million)*

Year	Result before tax	Result after adjustment for extraordinary items[1]
1989	+30.3	–481.7
1990	+45.8	–480.0
1991	+20.0	–528.1
1992	+17.1	–37.8

[1] Differences before and after adjustment of results stem from, for example, selling property and leasing it back.

Table 6.11 *Staffing levels*

Year	Number of personnel	Part-time workers (retail)
1989	18,978	27.0%
1990	17,821	31.7%
1991	16,498	38.2%
1992	15,318	43.3%

Table 6.12 *Retail market share*

Year	Kogen	Billa
1988	20.0%	15.0%
1991	16.6%	
1992	15.4%	19.0%

Table 6.13 *Members*

Year	Number of members
1989	775,330
1990	759,384
1991	744,085
1992	731,344

Table 6.14 *Reimbursements*

Year	Reimbursements in AS million
1989	139.3
1990	128.7
1991	126.3
1992	114.1

group) and the main competitor, Billa, had already turned down Kogen Österreich's advances. Finally Migros, the large Swiss consumer co-operative group, had been found. Initially Migros was to take over the western Austrian Kogen outlets and work together with Kogen Österreich in a newly established organization, which would be responsible for Kogen Österreich's purchasing, logistics and marketing.

Migros is the largest consumer co-operative and also the largest grocery retailer in Switzerland. It holds a market share of about 30%. Migros claims to work on the basis of 'social capitalism' which, among other things, has meant that it has earned substantial annual profits up to now. It also means that its management interacts with its workforce in a very pragmatic and performance-oriented way. Its salaries are above the market average, as are its profits. Its ideological background can be described as calvinistic and social-liberal, with some puritan aspects (it does not sell tobacco products and alcohol). As a consumer co-operative it is strongly oriented towards the quality of its products and towards consumer information. Migros is also engaged in 'green' activities.

On 1 October 1993, after very protracted negotiations, the contract between Migros and Kogen Österreich was signed. Critics fear that, owing to the fierce competition on the Austrian retail market, Migros has made a mistake. Like two other Swiss retailers before (Denner, Jelmoli), they might not succeed in Austria.

Themes/issues to consider

This case centres on a simple fact that Cyert and March told us some 35 years ago: firms are normative organizations within a normative context.

Traditionally we are not aware of that (especially in business schools), because 'business as usual' relies on a pre-defined and given context. But think of for example the rise of the ecological movement during the last few years. In essence this movement tries to redefine the terms of doing business. Thus we have come to realize that the context of doing business is a very political one, and each *status quo* is just a specific normative expression. This is neither good nor bad, but it helps us to understand why organizations and people in organizations act in specific ways.

If one approaches this case in a traditional 'business as usual' manner, one will find several problem areas which have to be solved: marketing (for example customer loyalty, exterior and interior design of outlets, advertising), finance (for example the ratio of own capital to borrowed capital, interest on borrowed capital), human resource management (for example professional qualifications, indirect compensation), organizational structure (for example decision making), and so on. At this point basic questions about 'change' and related concepts have to be addressed: What does 'change' in that context mean? By which rationality should it be governed? Why? Who would benefit?

These problem areas have been known at Kogen Österreich for years. Nevertheless, most of them have not been solved. The next step in the analysis of this case then leads to questions about power, stakeholders and interests, coalitions and networks: organizations as mixed interest games. Usually these concepts are used to understand dynamic processes – in this case they may explain paralysis.

Finally, questions of organizational identity and culture, legitimacy, and the management of meaning should be addressed. At this level of interpretation one could try to use different perspectives to 'see' the case, for example along the stakeholder concept. Moving then to the next level, to constructed realities and negotiated orders, we may come to realize that there are no 'correct' answers anyway, that our answers are just logical consequences of our questions.

If one sees all these problem areas and then wonders why so little has been done in all these years, we have to come back to the Cyert and March statement. From here, as always, there are several possible directions one might choose. The 'business as usual' approach obviously won't work, papers and discussions didn't change anything. On the other hand, a bottom-up redefinition of the mission, and as a consequence a change of functional policies via organizational development processes, will be problematic. It may easily happen that Kogen Österreich disappears from the market before such a process shows reasonable results. And if one chooses a radical approach (such as transformation into a stock corporation), one might be able to solve some of the economic problems. But at the same time one has eliminated Kogen Österreich. As a specific organization, with its own background, history and identity, it wouldn't exist any more.

The analysis of this case may also raise a discussion about the abilities of organizations, dominated by or related to the Social Democrats, to run a business in a competitive market. Cheap prejudices should be avoided – Kogen Österreich merely serves as an example of the normativity of all (business) organizations.

Assignments

For the assignments please see yourself in the position of an external consultant.

1. Assume that you have to assess the situation of Kogen. Why won't it be sufficient to analyse the situation at Kogen in a traditional 'business as usual' manner, that is, from an economic point of view? Why is it necessary to use different perspectives, and which problem areas come into your analysis by doing so?
2. A rather easy solution is that something has to change. What should be changed? Who should be involved in the goal-setting process? Who will benefit from which changes? How do you justify the differing advantages and disadvantages which will result from the change process for the stakeholders?
3. Try to see Kogen as a 'mixed interest game'. Who pursues which interests? How much power do the specific stakeholders have? In the previous assignment concerning change you probably had a new power structure in mind: how do you legitimize this new (better?) power structure?
4. This is the once-in-a-lifetime chance most managers dream of. There is a large organization which:
   - is in economic trouble but can be saved;
   - has lost the original reason for its existence and its ideological background has slowly faded;
   - definitely needs a 'mission' for the years to come.

Your task is to work out a 'mission' which could carry Kogen Österreich into the future. To do this you will have to assess Kogen's organizational culture and identity, and you will have to address the possibilities of the 'management of meaning'.

Suggested reading

Brazda, J. and Schediwy, R. (eds) (1989) *Consumer Co-operatives in a Changing World, Vols I and II*. Geneva: International Co-operative Alliance. In an international overview (e.g. Germany, France, Italy, Japan, Sweden) the general situation of consumer co-operatives is explained. This allows the specific situation of the Kogen case to be related to similar developments in other countries.

Crozier, M. and Friedberg, E. (1979) *Macht und Organisation, Teil 1*, Königstein: Athenäum. (original (1977) *L'acteur et le Système*. Paris: Editions du Seuil). The 'game' metaphor illustrates the possiblities and limits of action in structured fields of action.

Dülfer, E. (ed.) (1994) *International Handbook of Co-operative Organizations*. Göttingen: V&R. This handbook offers a good introduction to the field and the problems of co-operatives.

Meyer, J. and Rowan, B. (1977) 'Institutionalized organizations: formal structure as myth and ceremony', *American Journal of Sociology*, 83 (2): 340–63. The authors argue that the formal structure of many organizations often reflects the myths of their institutional environments instead of the demands of their work activities.

Mintzberg, H. (1983) *Power In and Around Organizations*. Englewood Cliffs, NJ: Prentice-Hall. pp. 31–109. The main external stakeholders of organizations are presented, and their means and strategies discussed.

Note

1 There exists no organization with the name of 'Kogen' in Austria. But there *is* an Austrian consumer co-operative which in many respects is very similar to the one portrayed in the case. All data used in the case are 'real' and they stem from many different sources. The case was written in such a way that none of these data can be considered as 'protected' or 'secret' – all data are also publicly available in business sections of newspapers, trade journals etc.

7

Rhine and Rhone Transport

From strong cultural fit to weak results

Hugo Letiche

This case highlights a series of managerial problems and paradoxes: if a company's cultural fit (that is, its adaptation to national norms and values) is exceptionally strong, this can be a source of rigidity and ineffectiveness; if a company sells itself exceptionally well in the financial markets this can lead to a severe loss of strategic control; if decentralization leads to fragmentation, restructuring can become unmanageable.

The RRT case is based on extensive research into Dutch haulage companies; the description of RRT is a composite picture drawn from many companies emphasizing processes which have been repeatedly witnessed. Thus the enterprise described is a Dutch transport company which grew with its market into being a significant international player. While the company began with haulage (dominant activity in the 1960s), by the early 1970s the switch had been made to expedition (arranging transport for clients mostly not with one's own equipment).

RRT is an ex-family company which via mergers and acquisitions has grown into a major incorporated firm. The case focuses on issues of decision making, (transnational) strategy and organizational culture. The trends and problems discussed were identified through the use of interviews with company and industry insiders. It is important to clarify that all persons and situations portrayed are fictional.

Cultural context

The Netherlands is one of strongest supporters of European integration. It is not mere coincidence that it was under Dutch chairmanship that new initiatives for the EU were launched via the Maastricht Treaty. The Dutch willingness to be

European is not merely philosophical but economic as well. The Dutch balance of payments (normally) displays a strong surplus in relationship to its EU partners. Thanks primarily to EU regulations, the Dutch can more or less sell their products, and make their investments, in the UK, Germany, France and the other EU countries on the same terms as do nationals.

On the one hand, Dutch society is divided into the so-called four pillars: Protestant, Catholic, Socialist, Liberal. Everything from political parties to amateur soccer teams, from broadcasting networks to schools and hospitals, is divided along the lines of these four pillars. But on the other hand, the diverse groups constantly negotiate agreements with each other on almost every level. The Netherlands is diversified along regional, ideological and cultural lines and integrated by collective legislation and other agreements. There is little or no drive for hegemony in the Dutch tradition. The government is always a coalition; labour–management–government relations are based on the principle of negotiated compromise. Companies as well try – to a high degree – to co-ordinate their policies and to co-operate.

The renunciation of hegemony produces the typically Dutch tradition of tolerance. The Dutch do not really accept difference, but since no group ever expects to predominate, no one can legislate generally applicable norms or mores. Everyone has had to learn to live together with other groups with which they are in disagreement. Just as long as 'otherness' – different, and potentially alternative, life styles, values or norms – does not butt its way into another sub-group's world, it is accepted that the great variety of sub-groups can all go their own way. This tolerance is not based on acceptance, but on a fairly benevolent process of ignoring one another.

In his cultural history of the Dutch Golden Age, Simon Schama stresses the economic advantages of the relative openness of Holland as a factor for its development into a trading and banking society. The culture evolved with a pride in its materialist achievements and identifying the aesthetic quality of clothes, goods, surroundings with the person's spiritual merit.

The ability to tolerate difference continues to have its commercial advantages. International trade demands insight into difference and skill in negotiation. But the Dutch economy knows very few other areas of international strength. Some fairly large sectors are clearly under threat: light and heavy machine industry, steel production and chemical companies. Economies of scale have not been achieved in the production of autos (DAF-Volvo), trucks (DAF-Leyland) or aeroplanes (Fokker). Machine tool production is still often labour intensive and not state of the art, and is heavily dependent on the German market. The Dutch electronics industry (Philips) has survived longer than many others, but certainly has not prevailed (that is, consistently retained market leadership and/or high profitability). The Netherlands is not a leader in software production, tele-communications or biotechnology. It is, however, strong in the food sector (packaging, distributing, retailing and processing of food), the provision of transport services (logistics on a European level), and import/export (including financial services). Successful multi-national companies such as Unilever and Shell are, in reality, more international than they are Dutch.

Dutch management tends to ignore classical management principles. Unity of command is rare as employees often refer to several 'bosses' in the organizing of their work. The division between staff and line authority is vague. Centralization, leading to managerial control, is often blocked by job descriptions which make virtual 'free agents' of employees. If employees must do something more than what is explicitly required by their job descriptions, then management has to cajole and persuade them to make an exception or try something new. Employees have become virtually unmanageable as management has not retained a right to demand change.

Furthermore, a spirit of shared responsibility which severely limits centralization is often demanded by employees. This leads to problems as the balance between authority and responsibility is often vague. On the level of espoused values it is not managerial control and authority (discipline) but shared commitment which is championed.

In practice it is often impossible to locate decision making. A process of discussion and interaction does seem to lead to consensus and to a shared sense of responsibility for action. Decision making takes a long time but implementation can be swift. Organizations assume a high level of homogeneous responsibility because many employees are expected to share in the active pursuit of organizational goals. Not top-down authority but shared commitment is the crucial managerial principle. Many foreign managers working in The Netherlands feel that Dutch society lacks individuality and is excessively collectivized, but many Dutch see their own society as democratic and based (as far as possible) on win–win relationships.

The tradition of collective leadership makes it possible for an organization to be close to its clients (the client speaks to someone 'in authority') and ensures that strong personal commitment is deeply anchored in the organization. But corporate-level management relinquishes hereby almost all control, making it difficult to reach strategic choices.

Some societies pride themselves on their success stories. The Dutch tradition is much more 'pessimistic'. Throughout the eighteenth and nineteenth centuries The Netherlands was in economic decline. Since the Second World War economic growth has replaced past poverty, but not the tradition of self-doubt. Dutch literature portrays the individual as relatively powerless and in the hands of often destructive forces. The past, one's social and religious origins, historical and economic powers, as well as fate, all prevail over individual destiny. The leading Dutch novelists of the second half of the twentieth century, Harry Mullisch and W.F. Hermans, both illustrate this trend. Dutch managers reflect this cultural tradition by being highly self-critical. Their successes should not be dwelt on, while dangers or weaknesses should be discussed at length. There is more attention, in the Dutch media, to what has gone (or threatens to go) wrong, than to the idealization of leaders and 'their' successes. In The Netherlands authority and leadership are, in general, poorly accepted. Shared responsibility and common cultural mores are championed.

While the Dutch often claim to be ill at ease with the phenomenon of old boy networks, membership of clubs (Rotary, Lions), participation in exclusive sports (especially golf and tennis) and university training (membership in student societies) actually all play an important role in business. Top management often maintains its business contacts via 'élite' social networking by going to the same restaurants, vacation spots and social events. While there is much talk about 'social levelling' (denial of social differences), there is in practice a strong hierarchical pattern in the social networks. Senior managers who play significant roles in obtaining finance and investment capital use these networks heavily. Mergers and acquisitions are also often prepared through such networks.

The Netherlands is a highly 'legislated' society. Firms are confronted by rules for work and health conditions, for the level of pay increases, for the costs of the high-quality social services. The firm is not free to hire and fire as it wishes, nor to take fundamental strategic decisions without consulting its workforce via the required Workers' Councils. The labour laws severely limit the firm's freedom; for instance, downsizing is often only possible after having argued one's case in court. On the other hand, there are few strikes as conflict is institutionalized in the legislated process of negotiation. There are managers who complain about their loss of autonomy to the legislators, but there is widespread acceptance of consultation and negotiation as a way of life.

Managerial values stress continuity and stability more than fast profits and opportunism. Although financial management and marketing are now more valued than in the 1960s, production has been able to regain much of the status it lost in the 1980s. The efficient and effective production of high-value-added products is seen to be crucial to success. Traditionally Dutch managers are engineers and lawyers, although university courses in management have become more popular. Human resource management is seen to be 'soft' and is often less valued. Both engineers and lawyers often favour quantifiable evidence rather than unsubstantiated claims. Nonetheless, management consulting and training are very highly developed in The Netherlands.

The negotiation process has to be protected since if it threatens to break down (which happens often these days) external experts are needed to repair the damage. The company's own human resource staff is almost always considered to be a part of the organizational pattern and thus, as stakeholders, unable to tackle critical organizational problems. Changes in organizational culture and/or design are decided by senior management and are carried out with the help of external advisers. When 'normality' returns, the customary negotiation process begins again without the external advisers.

The cultural fit of Rhine and Rhone Transport (RRT) to its surroundings is very strong. One can characterize Dutch society as a series of jealous villages, where life in one resembles life in any other. The villagers are very aware of each other's failures and successes. If one village has better crops than the others, everyone wants to know why. The comparative focus is not only economic. Dutch Calvinist villagers believe that richer villages are not only economically successful but also ethically superior. Wealth is assumed to be teleologically determined; that is, success comes to those who deserve to have success. Therefore everyone tries to study everyone else in order to learn their secrets of success.

RRT: an opening metaphor

The basic activity of each RRT Unit (village) is expediting; if anyone is exceptionally successful, the others will immediately ferret out the principle of success and copy it. The units are therefore competitive and dynamic. But they are focused on the very small, relatively closed world of RRT. The units are much less outwardly directed to the broad business environment (commercial practices, applications of technology, economic and trade patterns) than inwardly directed towards inter-unit competition. Thus the business units of RRT form tightly knit, very independent sub-organizations whose identity is defined in relationship to the other units. If one's profitability grows faster than the others, one is a success. If one lags behind in service levels one has to catch up. If one brings in more new customers one creates jealousy. The question is, however, does this corporate culture which metaphorically resembles small village rivalries function economically?

Company profile 1989–90

Rhine and Rhone Transport (RRT) is a major Dutch road transport company. Although it is one of the five largest Dutch transport companies, the largest is approximately 10 times its size. The largest company is much more intensively involved in other sectors of transport (by boat, parcel delivery, air freight, etc.) than is RRT. RRT was created by merging the original family-owned company with a number of smaller companies (mainly outside The Netherlands, creating a network of agents throughout Europe) and by adding one major acquisition, RoDo (Rotterdam Dordrecht Transport). A key strategic concern of RRT is to achieve appropriate economies of scale. This means that efficient trucking and client attention must operate on a small scale, but a larger scale is required for warehousing and information system management.

Transport is traditionally considered to be a strong sector within the Dutch economy. Dutch hauliers transport far more goods within the EU than the Netherlands' percentage of the European gross national product would lead one to expect. The harbour of Rotterdam is a factor facilitating this leading role, but a reputation for rapid and accurate service probably plays an even greater part. Dutch transport is not cheap but it is effective (deadlines are met) and efficient (it has good information systems, accurate billing systems, up-to-date vehicles). Not only are the Dutch strong in road transport, they have a very strong maritime tradition and the national airline is considered one of Europe's most successful. The combination of a trade-based economy, strong banking sector, good language skills and an international orientation form a strong cultural basis for proficiency in the transport sector. Also the very strong entrepreneurial tradiion among Dutch small companies provides the large transport corporations with very vigorous sub-contractors who, in fact, do most of the actual trucking.

RRT began as a small family business in 1890 transporting vegetables. The company is now active in:

- international expediting (accepting responsiblity for arranging transport);
- transport (actually trucking the cargo);
- warehousing (storage of cargo) and distribution;
- development and operation of logistic systems.

International haulage encompasses arranging a client's movement of goods from any single point to any other. The actual movement of goods can be sub-contracted to any appropriate combination of carriers and can include all sorts of transport. The product sold is a service: the knowledge of how best to move goods from any one spot to any other. Obviously many different definitions of 'best' are available: the safest, the fastest, the cheapest, etc.

Working for RRT are some 15 'expediters', each of whom is specialized in specific regions and/or types of transport. They are the key actors in the transport process, as they assign the loads to the truckers who work directly for RRT or who are sub-contracters. A senior expediter can earn a substantial income, approximately Dfl 75,000 annually. The job is normally a salaried position with annual bonuses being the industry practice. Innovativeness is rewarded in prestige and in salary rates. Expediter cleverness is a key determinant of profitability – a shipment of metal will quickly reach the maximum permitted tonnage but leave a huge unfilled space inside a closed truck. The clever expediter will then add a cargo which is very light (such as plastic coffee cups) to maximize profits.

The organization is formed around the expediters. Expediters are divided into two categories, senior and apprentice. A typical RRT office is organized with expediters in the centre and the secretaries, accountants, telephonists and customs experts surrounding them. Each senior expediter has an apprentice to assist him or her as training is on the job. Thus they are literally the centre of attention. Some 90% of successful managers in the industry are ex-expediters. Expediters work long and irregular hours for which they are well paid; have high social status in the organization and are on a privileged path toward management careers.

Until the opening up of borders in 1992, one very profitable aspect to haulage was the arranging of import and export documentation for customs procedures at the European borders. RRT had a chain of border offices which completed these tasks at considerable profit to the company. Transport itself is far less profitable than expediting. For one thing transport is very sensitive to economic conditions. During periods of economic growth the flow of international trade increases and there is strong demand for trucking capacity. Many drivers leave their employers to start their own small (3–5 trucks) companies.

As long as economic growth continues the small operators can repay their bank loans and make a living. But the danger of over-capacity, when competition leads to falling freight tariffs, is large. When a recession comes, over-capacity is inevitable and price wars often ensue. Operators have to accept loads at (or even under) cost price to keep repaying their bank loans. In good periods bonuses, paid 'on the black economy', are common, making actual earnings quite a bit larger than those which are visible to tax officials. But during a recession these earnings also dry up, making economic hardship all the more severe.

For a large corporation such as RRT, actual truck transport is a fairly unattractive activity. The small operators can undercut RRT's prices, since they have far fewer overheads and can operate on the black market with less risk. Having little advantage in maintaining high-risk, fixed assets such as trucks the large companies generally limit their equipment to trailers. RRT has just enough trucks and employed truck drivers to meet emergencies. This permits the company to meet its obligations if something goes wrong somewhere with one of its sub-contractors. Thus trucks and drivers are maintained as part of a defensive strategy and not as a source of profit. This also limits excessive dependence on sub-contractors. At best RRT hopes to break even with its direct trucking activity.

Warehousing (that is, storage of material) and distribution are growing areas of business. Large multi-national clients are increasingly outsourcing all their haulage needs. For instance, a producer of white goods in the UK (refrigerators, cookers, etc.) has decided to entrust all its continental logistics to RRT. This means that RRT has to pick up the goods at the factory, transport them across the Channel and warehouse them (duty free) until they need to be distributed to national sales organizations. RRT therefore must build and operate warehouses to meet these demands. In order not to have to make large capital investments, RRT found an investor to finance the construction of the warehouse, which RRT then leased from the investor.

Effective warehousing and distribution depend on having a state-of-art computer system to keep track of all goods movements. Manufacturers demand that their logistics partners know exactly where all goods are at all moments. Obviously the quality of one's expediters determines how cost-effectively one is able to provide distribution from the warehouse to the local destinations. Goods are regrouped at the warehouse and shipped to their final destinations. Logistics systems provide the services just described, that is the information and forwarding services entailed in a system of transport, warehousing and distribution. A company may define the design, production and marketing of household appliances as its core business and divest itself of its logistics activity; RRT can then offer to manage these logistic systems. In comparison to trucking, logistics services demand much more precision and expert skill.

Just-in-time (JIT) strategies have affected logistics systems because they reduce inventories. But it makes production very sensitive to logistical error, therefore increasing the demand for high quality logistics systems. Logistical failures can have enormous cost implications if, for example, a parts shortage makes a factory idle or products cannot reach retailers during high-turnover sales periods. RTT's key customers have demanded logistics services, forcing the company to enter this market. The investment in people (training) and information technology is substantial.

RRT's profitability came from having few fixed assets. Impressive office facilities are not necessary since it is the skills of the expediters which are being sold. Capital investment risks are shifted onto the shoulders of the small truckers to whom work is sub-contracted. But RRT's major clients are also following this strategy of capital risk transfer, leaving the firm to assume the risk of maintaining warehouse and logistics services. RRT's solution is to lease warehouse capacity and computer hardware, but investment in the human resources necessary to use modern information technology effectively is unavoidable. Also the terms of the warehouse leases limit RRT's flexibility and increase corporate risk.

RRT has 115 offices in 15 countries, including The Netherlands, UK, Germany, Belgium, Italy, France, Norway, Austria, Ireland, Denmark, Sweden, Switzerland, Spain and Portugal. The chief activity of these offices is to receive freight orders and to feed these back to one of the corporate hubs in The Netherlands where the expediters plan freight movements. In its less developed markets the sales office and trucking services are often integrated because RRT has purchased small trucking companies. In larger markets, such as in the Lyon region of France, the RRT office uses local sub-contractors.

Until 1987, RRT was solely owned by Mr Jan van Rijn. A strongly driven entrepreneur with a very forceful personality, he has been characterized as a 'charismatic leader'. He was very knowledgeable about the transport sector and had a 'feeling' for his business. He intuitively made decisions about where to invest and did not shrink from taking risks. Jan van Rijn knew what he wanted, made strategic decisions single handed, and relied on the rest of the organization to carry out his orders. When he decided to develop his business in the UK (especially the south) he sent a trusted employee to England with the message to get on with it and 'if you need money, borrow it from the bank'. Van Rijn retired in 1986 at the age of 63. He thought that RRT would have to develop in the direction of providing business logistics and that this would demand computer and systems expertise which he lacked, as well as large investments which he did not want to make at his age.

Under van Rijn RRT had evolved from a trucking firm to an expediter. Profits came from organizing transport for customers; the operating core provided the service of arranging transport of anything, to anywhere, for a client. The client would have his or her contact (customer agent) within RRT, an expediter who serviced the account. As mentioned earlier, the expediter keeps track of the goods from the moment of pick-up to moment of delivery (while the goods will often be transferred twice or more from carrier to carrier). The added value of the expediter is in the total management of the process of moving goods from factory to sales point and knowing exactly where the goods are at any moment.

Being in the middle of the process the expediter must therefore maintain very effective control of sub-contractors while at the same time developing strong, trust-based relations with major clients. The expediter operates independently, on an operational level, with clients and sub-contractors and negotiates transport daily with major clients.

New service contracts are generally won by senior management intervention. In the past major multi-nationals spoke directly with van Rijn, while smaller clients met with RRT's regional directors. At present top corporate and/or regional management are responsible for RRT's marketing. The expediters interact with the client's logistics departments. Thus the operating core of RRT has always been split from its marketing activity. Large contracts occur on the basis of reputation and trust between senior managers (on both sides), while the expediters/logistics managers have to realize the agreements in practice. Price competitiveness is sharper for large contracts than for small ones. Expediters charge very different tariffs to small users than to major contractors. The trailers and few trucks which RRT owns are mainly used to react to emergency needs of large contractors.

Throughout, the profits are made via the services rendered. The expediters do not offer total logistics services; a special division has been created to do this. Because a total logistics service involves a broad range of services, normally spread throughout Europe, a special team has been formed to maintain and offer the necessary helicopter vision. At a minimum, a total logistics service entails picking up goods as soon as they are produced (imported) and storing them until they have to be delivered. At a maximum, raw materials are transported as well as goods. The added costs of total logistics services are those of the information system which maintains up-to-the-minute inventories (and the personnel costs involved), those of the warehouses (and warehouse services) and potentially those of the planning services which program the contracting company's logistics processes. Expediters generally do not have all these skills. They are specialized in the transport of certain types of goods (perishables, chemicals, clothing, bulk goods, etc.) along specific routes (UK–Continent, The Netherlands–Scandinavia, Germany–Spain).

On van Rijn's retirement the company 'went public' and 3,500,000 shares were sold with a nominal value of Dfl 10 per share (the actual share price was Dfl 35 per share). Two new directors were appointed, one as CEO, Mr de Groot, and the other as Operational Director, Mr Klein. The bank which supervized the share offering played (via the Board) a major role in the selection of the directors. De Groot was RRT's senior Corporate Controller. It was believed that RRT, in the new incorporated situation, would need tight financial control. Likewise, Klein had a financial management background in the transport sector, but not in RRT.

On assuming office de Groot and Klein made the following analysis of RRT's position:

- RRT was a potential candidate for a takeover. The economies of scale in transport determined that RRT would have to grow quickly to remain independent. Thus, the goal should be to become one of Europe's 10 largest expediters.
- RRT's financial situation was such that new capital investment was desperately needed. In order to grow by acquisitions RRT required investment

capital. The decision was made that de Groot's primary task would be to develop a positive stock market image for RRT, to make future stock offerings successful.

- The decentralized organizational model would be continued. The four, rather independent divisions would have the responsibility and authority needed to function effectively.
- They also defined the following corporate mission statement: 'RRT has as its goal to become one of the 10 largest European transport companies. In order to offer an integrated network throughout Europe acquisitions will be made to cover all relevant markets.'

RRT initially divided into four divisions: Expediter/Transport (which dominated everything), Air–Sea Transport, Border Customs Procedures and Business Logistics. Two specialized transport activities answered directly to corporate headquarters (one in The Netherlands specialized in flowers, the other in Germany specialized in clothing). As long as these fairly small operations remained profitable, they were left free to go their own way.

The Expediter/Transport division was split into three regional offices, each of which answered to a Regional Director. Since the CEO had set a policy of direction at a distance, the Regional Directors were *de facto* in charge of their own operations. Under van Rijn the Regional Directors had been 'Yes men' who did what he wanted. Now they had to become leaders of semi-independent profit centres with real managerial responsibility. While they all welcomed the change, most of them quickly failed at the new, expanded task. On van Rijn's retirement Road Transport (the expediter/transport service) was divided into three units (South Netherlands, North Netherlands, West Netherlands). The percentage of gross earnings per division was South 40%, North 20%, West 40%. Corporate headquarters was in the same city as the Southern division, but there was little or no link between the two. The two Corporate Directors and the three Unit Directors only met a few times per year. The Unit Directors did everything possible after van Rijn's retirement to champion their new found freedom.

Each unit offered the same sort of services as the other two, but with an emphasis on different 'lines.' A 'line' is a service offered on a regular basis (for example, South Netherlands to Austria four times a week). Thus RRT guarantees its customers that it can deliver merchandise within two working days to Austria. The 'lines' work in a feeder/hub structure. All the freight for Austria is brought together at the warehouse in Southern Holland, put onto the 'line' service and unloaded on arrival in Vienna. It is then redistributed to wherever in Austria it has to go. Each unit maintains a certain number of 'lines'. Reporting to each unit are a number of foreign offices. Thus there is a line Southern Netherlands–Switzerland which has an office in Basel answering to the Southern Netherlands division. There is also a line North Netherlands–Switzerland with a local office in Zurich. In general North specializes in freight to Scandinavia and North Germany; South services Germany, Austria and Switzerland; and West deals with UK, Belgium, France, Spain and Portugal. But there are many exceptions to these rules; for instance, West does almost all the chemical transport.

Several multi-nationals have contracted RRT to provide total business logistics for their European operations. RRT guarantees that it can deliver any item it has in storage within four working days to anywhere in Europe. Foreign multinationals can therefore avoid maintaining storage or logistics facilities of their own within the EU. Their 'logistics partner' takes care of everything. No one unit office found it acceptable that such a contract would be co-ordinated by another unit (inter-unit jealousy is strengthened by the practice of comparing unit profitability as a means of determining unit success). A special division (called Business Logistics) had to be created to negotiate with the previously existing units to achieve the necessary service provision. For this Business Logistics division, negotiating price and conditions of carriage via the three unit offices is a full-time job. The customs/border procedure service had offices at all major international border crossing points which took care of RRT cargo paperwork, and contracted this same service to third parties. This service was very profitable.

Growth strategy implemented

In 1989 RRT's acquisition policy was successful. After two failed negotiations with other potential takeover objects, RRT was able to acquire a medium-sized transport company called RoDo (Rotterdam–Dordrecht Transport) based in West Netherlands. All predictors for the transport sector were very positive. Eventual European integration would reduce border procedures and encourage trade. Increased industrial/commercial integration would cause a growth market for goods transport. Thus potential targets for acquisition demanded a price which took the optimistic market predictions into account.

De Groot and Klein were not willing to pay too much, but their reputation as dynamic managers was in danger. The business press was claiming that their translation of the mission statement into reality was bogged down. Thus they were relieved when a deal was possible with RoDo. RoDo's operations were some 20 km from RRT's West Netherlands office. RoDo was a family business whose owner/director (Mr Jansen) sought a guarantee for the continuity of his company. He had most of his money in RoDo and wanted to regain control over his assets to undertake other investments and to ensure the financial security of his family.

Furthermore, RoDo was too large to function as a mere sub-contractor to a larger company and too small to make the sort of investment that an effective entry into the business logistics market demands. It did not really fit the economies of scale which were beginning to emerge in the road transport sector. The industry literature claimed that there was one market for small companies with a few (up to five) trucks and some trailers, and one for very large companies who offer haulage services (with a few trucks and a significant number of trailers). The large companies offer logistics expertise more than trucks and trailers. Their profits come from organizing the movement of freight, thus from their expediter expertise. RoDo was not large enough to maintain a worldwide expediting service (although it had offices throughout Europe, one in the US and one in the Far East) and to develop business logistics (full service from producer to warehouse to consumer, all in the hands of the haulage company).

However, RoDo was very well placed in several important markets (The Netherlands to and from: Switzerland, Northern UK, Belgium, Scandinavia), and it knew the ins-and-outs of several markets very well (such as the import of new autos into the EU). Its expediters were excellent, but its information system lagged behind. Billing was computerized but expediting was not. The expediters claimed that the costs involved in creating an expediting information system far outweighed the potential savings. The computerized holding of warehouse inventories was not yet in use. RoDo had not really entered the business logistics market – neither the investment in warehousing (even via leasing) nor information technology had been made.

RoDo had an office in Chicago which RRT did not take over. De Groot claimed that RRT should 'stick to its knitting' in Europe. Jansen retained ownership of the Chicago operation, and RRT negotiated that he would stay on at RoDo as adviser for two years.

Between 1986 and 1990 RRT's share price rose from Dfl 35 to Dfl 120. Initially the strategy of developing a positive press had been very successful. But another factor had also played a key role. A large American shipping corporation invested in a small freight airline serving a Dutch regional airport. The threat of an integrated foreign air–road freight operation, operating on Dutch soil, seemed imminent. The European airlines were very concerned at the idea of such competition in their own backyard. They believed that safe home markets were absolutely necessary to their continued survival. Thus 35% of RRT's shares were purchased by an airline consortium so that a competing integrated road–air freight system could be realized if necessary. This investment was essentially a defensive strategy: the airlines had no proactive plan to create an integrated freight system. Despite announcements to the contrary in the financial press, the airlines made no moves to integrate their computer systems and those of the freight operator.

While de Groot and Klein were very pleased to have the airlines' investment (the high share price protected them from any unwanted takeover), they had no real operational plan for what to do with the link. The units were too small to co-operate with the airlines, and the Business Logistics division was finding it difficult enough to get its own job done without entertaining a much higher level of complexity inherent in operational co-operation with the airlines. The share price remained high because the market expected a merger of some sort between the airlines and RRT. Earnings per share did not justify the share price. The organizations involved took no real steps to create an integrated air freight/road transport network; in fact there was no proof that any such network created by these organizations would be effective. No strategic or marketing research had been done by RRT into the concept, and the airlines' long-term motives were unknown to RRT.

A strategic report commissioned by RRT identified the following issues: Are the information technologies of the airlines and RRT compatible? Did RRT have the marketing expertise needed to make a combined land–air freight network effective? What partnerships did they have (need) outside Europe to deliver freight to Asian or American destinations? Were the corporate cultures compatible? How would RRT expediters co-operate with airline staff? How would price structures be determined and profits divided? How would RRT relate to the airlines' other strategic partners in and outside Europe?

Via acquisition RRT had grown from 500 employees in 1980 to 1800 in 1987 and 4000 in 1990. While RoDo was the most important acquisition, many smaller ones took place. For instance, the West Netherlands unit purchased a small Northern Portuguese trucker (Porto). However a journalist on a Dutch financial magazine noted that acquisitions had not brought RRT improved profitability. The relationship of share price to dividend had deteriorated dramatically from 11% (1986) to 2% (1989). Thus he claimed that the share price was too high in relation to earnings. His conclusion: 'One can better put one's money in the bank than buy RRT shares, if one is looking to one's return.' Only anticipated further growth in share price, he believed, justified holding the shares. In addition, he pointed out that while in 1987 gross sales per employee was Dfl 725,000, it was only Dfl 550,000 in 1989–90. Thus more employees were now needed to generate the same results. Furthermore the employee net sales and net profit ratios revealed the same trend. The high gross sales in relationship to net sales reflected the strategy of outsourcing much of the trucking. Profit on (net) sales had remained a rather unimpressive, approximate 3%. For a service organization, he thought it was an unimpressive track record.

Overview of RRT's financial position

The role of the Dutch home market has radically changed for RRT. While in 1985 60% of all revenue was earned in The Netherlands, in 1990 70% of revenue was earned outside. It is worth noting, however, that +/– 60% of the business still originates in, or passes through, The Netherlands. The financial results are presented in Table 7.1. (The number of shares increased during the acquisition process from 3,500,000 to 4,500,000.)

Table 7.1 *RRT financial results (milllion ECUs)*

	1989	1988	1987	1986
Gross sales	1124.5	811.5	659.5	597
Net sales	427	307	262	237
Cash flow	24	19	15	14
Net profit	12.3	9	7	6.5
Own equity	49	38	30.5	26
Profit per share (ECU)	2.7	2.3	1.9	1.7
Dividend (ECU)	1.1	0.9	0.7	0.7

According to Klein RRT has been successful in transcending the culture of the family company. When van Rijn retired the unit directors all felt themselves to be independent entrepreneurs. Establishing a strategic leadership role for corporate management was a problem. This was attempted by setting up an Organizational Business Committee in 1987 which was divided into four sub-committees each dealing with a critical issue. One group dealt with questions such as how to share loads and network services (each unit was a separate profit centre); how profits from shared loads should be allocated; how should common overheads, such as information technology, be shared between units. Another dealt with the problem of improving shared logistics. The current separate Business Logistics division was a less than ideal solution to the necessity for co-operation. The third group concerned itself with the need for further special-ization. This was required to respond to increasing environmental legislation regarding chemical and dangerous material transport, as well as live animal transport. Finally, RRT needed further general strategic planning to meet a changing environment and the new challenges of providing combined air–land service and realizing strategic partnerships.

Corporate management wanted to gain more control over the units by setting up the joint business committees. More commitment to corporate-level planning needed to be gained from the unit managers and they could be drawn into corporate-level issues. Furthermore, interdependence between the units was to be fostered by facilitating joint planning and action. But the unit managers preferred to stay encapsulated in their own sub-organizations than to come out into the open and directly confront each other.

The tasks of the unit managers included negotiating with clients (marketing and pricing), direct control of the RRT truckers working for the unit, motivating and supervising expediters, general unit office management. Thus their activity was fairly concrete and directly linked to transport. Unit managers are not especially at home with broader logistic, automation and strategic issues. They are (mostly) ex-expediters who see their task as the management of an expediting organization. Direct hands-on work appeals to them, so they abhor long discussions and detailed meetings.

Thus the co-operative planning model was stillborn. Most of the committees never met and no suggestions or reports were recorded. The unit managers were too jealous of their autonomy to risk open discussion or deliberation. While they all realized that joint action was necessary for corporate level profitability, they found it unattractive for their local positions. Rather than being confronted with the overwhelming rational arguments for co-operation, the unit managers stayed at home and maintained deaf ears to general issues and problems.

De Groot and Klein believed that the Business Logistics division was a bad solution to the synergy question, but Joint Business Committees did not appear to be a viable platform for discussing reform. A separate division ought not to be necessary to meet contractual obligations which transcend any one unit's ability to deliver service. Furthermore, the introduction of new services was being severely retarded by the regionalized model. No product champion could effectively work from one unit and reach the others. The development of new value-added services was blocked. Investment in new information technologies was slowed down (because unit managers always tried to avoid having to pay for them). The principal power which de Groot and Klein had was to divide and rule when unit managers wanted money to invest; only on a corporate level could funding be obtained for new initiatives. But the unit managers, to avoid having to relinquish autonomy, made fewer and fewer demands for large investments. Thus the unit model was creating defensiveness and policy inertia.

Integration of RoDo

The integration of RoDo into RRT posed a series of problems. RoDo had an office in Lyon literally next to that of RRT North, yet both remained separate and independent. Some RoDo 'lines' were profitable while parallel RRT 'lines' were not, and vice versa. But any plan to redistribute 'lines' met with violent unit suspicion and opposition. Unit performance was measured by comparing year-to-year results. If 'lines' were to be redistributed there would be no automatic criteria for judging performance. It was feared that this would invite questions and comparisons and ultimately would threaten unit autonomy.

But having acquired RoDo it would have to be integrated into RRT in some way. In the short run RoDo complicated inter-unit politics by replicating many 'lines' found elsewhere in the company. When an expediter received a request from a client which he could only partially meet, or couldn't meet at all, he had to find an alternative provider of transport. Thus RRT West would contract with RRT North for goods to go to Scandinavia. If RRT West was not satisfied by the price offered by RRT North it would look elsewhere for transport. Once RoDo joined the company, expediters could often choose between working with RoDo or working with another unit. For instance, RRT West virtually stopped making use of RRT North 'lines' and bought these services exclusively from RoDo. Half-full loads, longer delivery times, misunderstandings with clients and extra office work all resulted. Corporate-level profits were hurt by this inter-unit bickering. But de Groot and Klein seemed incapable of doing anything about it.

In 1990 the necessary fusion of RoDo into RRT was taken as a platform to create a new organizational structure. Division-level management would be strengthened, and each division would gain a Divisional Director. Road transport would retain the three original units plus gain RoDo as a fourth. But a new Divisional Director would have overall responsibility for division performance. The unit directors would no longer answer directly to de Groot and Klein, but to the Divisional Director. The four Divisional Directors would all become non-voting members of the corporate Board. In addition, the position of the Area Managers would be strengthened. Area Managers (Benelux, Iberia, UK/Ireland, Scandinavia, Germany/Austria/Switzerland, etc.) would co-ordinate the offices in the regions more independently, providing senior managerial positions to non-Dutch natives.

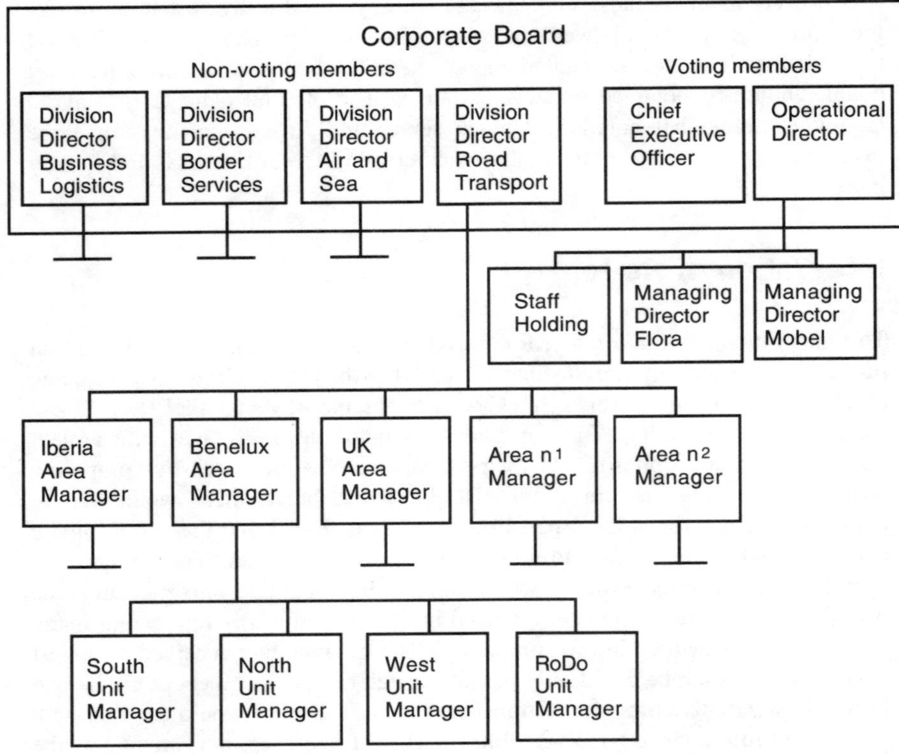

Figure 7.1 *RRT organizational structure*

Previously, all management positions had been staffed by Dutch nationals. Even the more senior middle management positions (such as UK Manager) were occupied by Dutch nationals. Increasingly, marketing and operations in the field were becoming crucial to profitability. Thus more aggressive senior field managers were needed to sell services effectively. In this new model the unit managers lost much of their power because they had little direct access to the Board. They would answer to the Area Manager Benelux, who would in turn answer to the Road Transport Divisional Director. The Unit Manager's counterparts in the field would gain power. Instead of the three traditional Unit Managers running the show, there would be three units plus RoDo, plus at least seven Area Managers, plus a Divisional Director.

Although the proposed new managerial model was announced to the press, it was never operationalized. First, the proposed profusion in managerial positions would have cost several million guilders. Corporate profitability did not permit such luxury. Thus what happened, to save face, was that existing managers were appointed to several positions so that the new managerial model was carried out on paper. Jansen (from RoDo) became interim Head of Road Transport (Divisional Director) and Benelux Area Manager. The other Divisional Managers (Air and Sea, Border Services, Business Logistics) became Divisional Directors. The only change was that the four so-called Divisional Directors became non-voting members of the Board. The reorganization meant that Jansen was *de facto* responsible for road transport management and that de Groot and Klein withdrew from that responsibility. But Jansen only had a two-year contract. Leadership over the Road Transport division became ambiguous. While the original RRT Unit Managers may not have liked Jansen's key position, they were in no real position to oppose him. The head of the Northern region had reached retirement age, and the head of the Southern region was forced out of his job because of poor performance.

Jansen approached his new found power with considerable ambivalence. He was willing to commit himself fully to RRT only if he was made a full voting member of the Board and had a profit-sharing contract as did Klein and de Groot. But no permanent position had been offered, no profit sharing discussed, no board voting rights hinted at. Jansen realized that his power rested on the lack of operational expertise in transport among the top corporate players. De Groot and Klein remained financial managers who had little real feeling for the operational side of transport. They could not, and knew they could not, give the necessary leadership to the core activity of RRT. Jansen decided to try to rationalize RRT by bringing the expediters together in one centre and by streamlining as many field offices and 'lines' as possible. He correctly estimated that internal opposition would be weak because two of the three old RRT Unit Managers were gone, and the new RoDo Manager had never tasted feudal power. Klein and de Groot clearly wanted more centralization, because unit performance was proving unpredictable and unit behaviour erratic. The Divisional Manager for Business Logistics desperately needed more centralism to make the information technologies he wanted to introduce practical.

A history of examination

Many people have examined the problems of RRT, ranging from an MSc student's research to professional consultancy reports. The principal conclusions are summarized below for two time periods.

Key issues, 1989–90

A business student, majoring in OB, writing his thesis on RRT concluded:

> Just as the initial attempt to achieve networked co-operation failed [the Business Committees], Jansen's decision to centralize is disputable. The decentralized units provide close company–client interaction via the expediters. Furthermore the unit managers are rough-and-tumble trucking types who can keep the sub-contracting

> truckers in line. If RRT centralizes there is a chance that the needed control over subcontractors will deteriorate and lead to poorer service. The units are an adequate solution for the span of control problem. Centralization may be dangerous. The subcontractors cannot be held in line via bureaucratic controls and contractual arrangements. One needs direct contact and forceful persuasion to maintain standards. RRT as well as RoDo have always been up-market transporters. Their prices are +/– 10% higher than 'cowboy' hauliers. Clients buy transport from RRT/RoDo because they are sure of on-time delivery and a minimum of damage/loss. Client loyalty on an operational level depends on expediter/client contact. If this link is disrupted loyalty will be endangered. Company-to-company contact is between unit managers and local companies and/or between Board members and large clients. Jansen could never fulfil all these obligations. Who will do so? Would an alternative be as effective as the *status quo*?

An institutional shareholder commissioned a consultant to analyse RRT Board-level options. He concluded:

> Present RRT organizational design puts Jansen in a key power position. Should the Board fear his power? If he leaves RRT after two years could he take many key clients with him? Of course there is a clause in his contract forbidding him to start up a new transport company within three years of his contract termination. But is such a clause really watertight? Jansen is a crucial resource, a man who understands the core business. What do you do when you lack that ability? Do you fire Jansen to get rid of a potential threat, or try and incorporate him into the Board to make use of his abilities? Or do you try and find another practical figure so you can 'divide and rule'? Are Jansen's (potential) conflicts of interest so critical that depending on him is irresponsible?
>
> Would a management buy-out led by Jansen be the best solution? Has perhaps the usefulness of Klein and de Groot passed? After all, the no takeover policy via a high share price has become a liability. Eventually either RRT will be integrated into the airlines (policy of defending independence fails) or the share price will fall to a level sustainable by the level of earnings. At which point RRT becomes a takeover prospect all over again. Because RRT's equity is minimal it remains a potential takeover object for more production-oriented corporations. The Board's best policy might well be to try and sell RRT to a larger transporter. The organizational risks facing RRT are so great that bailing out, while the company is profitable, seems the best solution. If logistic management really takes off, a very difficult process of centralization will be necessary. If local client contact remains crucial RRT will have to rebuild its unit-level management which has virtually collapsed. Either way, RRT is in for a difficult period of self-redefinition. Furthermore, RoDo will have to gain a logical place within the entirety.

De Groot commissioned a consulting firm to investigate the pace at which information technologies should be introduced. They reported:

> The Business Logistics Division favoured rapid change. But ... the line management, in general, opposed it. They did not believe that the expediters needed or wanted an 'Expert System' to do their work. They think that the development costs of such a system would be far too high and that the risks of failures far too significant. We propose that RRT adopt a strategic position of 'close follower'. Let others innovate and take the risks. If the technology proves itself then one can invest in it once it is foolproof. The risk of alienating clients via technological experimentation is far too

> great. A simple inventory system for warehousing, added to the automated billing system, suffices in the short term.

But other consultants had argued to de Groot and Klein that their only hope at controlling the firm was to install modern information technologies which would break their dependence on the craft skills of the expediters and Jansen. They argued that since knowledge is power, the Board members had better centre it much more on themselves.

A young MBA was hired by the Business Logistics division to work on strategic planning. He left to a larger competitor after 18 months. His questions and comments were:

> Does RRT/RoDo possess sufficient managerial commitment? Does it need a matrix organization in order to gain more committed management behaviour? Was the fault of the Business Committees not that they went too far, but that they did not go far enough? Should management shift away from the growth by acquisition policy and centre all attention on creating a strong consistent company-wide culture? RRT needs to be transformed into a coherent organization by rationalization and the development of a matrix structure. Creating additional layers of management will not help to create an effective organization. De Groot and Klein have to abandon their 'management at a distance' and get directly involved in running RRT. RRT needs to become a large integrated enterprise and not a family of warring feudal islands.

A business professor jotting notes in the margin of his field study wrote:

> How important is it really to rationalize RRT? Since the quality of customer service is the crucial selling point, what counts is remaining near to the customer's needs. Centralization may well create distance between the company and the client and be counterproductive. Since there is virtually no expensive equipment involved, there are next to no savings to be gained by increasing the scale of operation. Warehousing and inventory control does need to be centralized, but these services are separate from the expediter's. Jansen will try and centralize the expediting service to gain control over the core business. Only if he centralizes the expediters can he supervise them and follow their actions. But is this a sufficient justification for change? The corporate centre has not had real power because the company has been a loose federation of three units. Only the charisma of the previous owner, Mr van Rijn, prevented this unstable structure from collapsing.

Postscript, 1993–4

Almost none of the crucial dilemmas has been solved. Jansen is still a non-voting member of the Board, although he has been asked to become a full member. He has requested six months to think about it. RRT is no longer profitable. Instead of producing enormous growth in trade, the opening up of European borders in 1992 brought about a glut in transport capacity. Under the old system trucks spent some 20% of their time standing on borders waiting for border procedures to be completed. Once the procedures were abolished, there was a *de facto* growth of 20% in trucking capacity. This started an industry-wide price war. Furthermore recession set in, first in the UK, then later elsewhere. RRT and RoDo both had large cross-Channel operations as well as UK domestic ones, which were hard hit by the UK recession.

More examinations of the company followed. The judgement of one external financial analyst was:

> RRT has not adequately analysed its profit structure. It does know which units are profitable, but it has not realized what the divisional structure means for its future. Post-1992 the Border Formalities division, more or less, closed down. The employees were integrated into the Road Transport division. The loss of profits from the Border Offices caused by the 1992 EU single market reforms, which made this service redundant between EU countries, coupled to the recession, has tilted RRT into the red. Top management had not realized how important the border services had been to profitability. The Business Logistics division continues to run at a significant loss; projected warehouse and inventory service usage have turned out to be wildly exaggerated. Not wanting to lose key multinational clients, RRT has been forced to provide logistics services at a loss.

Another commentary by a marketing specialist suggested:

> RRT quality control is suffering from a lack of effective hands-on management and the negative influence of centralization (administration and expediters). Clients find RRT increasingly impersonal and at a distance. Instead of reaching the same person every time they call, they complain that they get someone else each time who often doesn't know them. The worsening financial position has forced RRT to rationalize functions as much as possible. But this same rationalization is alienating clients and worsening company reputation.

An insider from RRT UK observes:

> The crisis in power and authority has not been tackled. Mangers in the field have not gained more influence. The non-Dutch managers continue to see RRT as a 'Dutch Mafia' wherein there are no real career possibilities for them. Thus the best foreign managers quit RRT when they can, taking clients with them.

A consultant hired to study corporate efficiency concluded:

> The lack of central control which allowed for strong client–company contact in the past has become a liability in the recession situation. RRT is over-staffed. Far too much bureaucracy has crept into operations. But no one is empowered to reorganize it. Jansen clearly realizes that a cut in administrative personnel is needed (the Billing Office needs to shed at least 40% of its personnel); but isn't willing to take unpopular decisions, opening the way for de Groot and Klein to get rid of him once he's done the dirty work. De Groot and Klein are increasingly preoccupied by the airlines' plans. They either have to integrate RRT into their freight service or unload their shares. Neither option is very attractive. If investors knew the airlines were withdrawing, share price would plummet; but integration would end operational independence. Furthermore, it is not clear if RRT, integrated into a large bureaucratized air freight operation, could be successful.

A Dutch journalist from the financial press recounted:

> The limits to RRT's mission statement are becoming painfully obvious. Size in itself is not a goal. RRT has no operational identity. Its product is not clear (expediter services meeting immediate client needs; business logistics offering rationalized JIT support services; ground transport delivery within a multi-national (air) freight system;

or something else). The demands inherent to the different potential identities are contradictory; RRT has been avoiding self-definition and decision making far too long.

A sociologist who studied RRT reported:

> The typical Dutch system of management by consensus threatens to destroy this company. Management has not been able to impose a definition of RRT's future. In fact they do not really have any such definition. The corporate culture is in limbo. Management wants to lead by negotiation and consensus. When everyone agrees, then the organization will move forward. This need for discussion and agreement is counterproductive in a rapidly changing business environment where, if management does not get things right fast, RRT could disappear. Top management is very isolated. Contact between decision makers and operational functions is ineffective.

In a frank analysis, Jansen confided:

> I have partially withdrawn from RRT, refusing to take ultimate responsibility unless I am granted the matching authority. De Groot and Klein are victims of their own mindset. They are not entrepreneurial leaders, but bureaucrats who rely on others to do the work for them. In a matrix model or in a professional service model (with the expediters as the key professionals) de Groot and Klein could function effectively. But at present RRT is dominated by organizational chaos and a leaderless drift. Enforced managerial control (via MBO or some such thing) might fail hopelessly, but the *status quo* can only lead to disaster. The problem is not that strict managerial control is by definition necessary, but weak managers can only function when there is a critical mass of empowered stakeholders who are willing to make decisions. De Groot and Klein remain controllers who formally have retained classical managerial clout but do not know what to do with it. At no moment have they shown an ability or willingness to let key stakeholders make things happen. They are clearly ineffective and will be replaced.

The conclusions of a high potential manager who has left RRT were:

> New leadership will have to initiate a relevant and realistic managerial policy. No more acquisitions for acquisitions sake will be wanted (or possible). The growing irrationality caused by the contradictions in goals will have to be solved. Over-staffing and the accompanying lack of responsibility on lower levels will have to be checked. RRT will have to struggle to regain its reputation of being a responsive expediter, which clients can feel close to and feel safe with. Performance criteria for administrative staff and sub-contractors will have to be set and stuck to. Attention to meeting market needs has to replace internally oriented self-absorption.

And finally the climax

After very disappointing fourth-quarter figures (1993), the board had to decide whether to dismiss de Groot and to appoint an interim manager. In his defence, de Groot argued that RRT's problems were caused by the general recession. He claimed that as soon as the economy improves the company will recover, and pointed out that the worst loss makers within RRT had been reorganized. He had assigned direct line responsibility to Klein for one subsidiary (not discussed in the case) which was doing very badly; Klein fired 60 of the 120 employees and ensured that no further losses occurred. Management buy-outs of several small subsidiaries had been arranged. RRT, de Groot argued, was successfully refocusing itself on its core business. De Groot asserted that current management is loyal to him and Klein. RRT, he claimed, will emerge 'lean and mean' from the recession.

But the Board knows that Dr S.J. Snel, a well-known Dutch interim manager with an excellent track record as turn-about manager, is available and wants the job of saving RRT. As de Groot left the boardroom the members turned to one another and asked, de Groot or Snel?

Themes/issues to consider

The RRT case has described the fortunes of a corporation with a seemingly optimal cultural fit, with the company's decentralized, individualistic and consensus-based way of operating closely matching Dutch cultural norms. But this strong cultural fit left RRT paralysed because necessary diversity which is often a source of adaptation and innovation was lacking. Although RRT operates in a sector of traditional Dutch strength, the organization does not currently seem able to stay one step ahead of events. In the past entrepreneurial and employee flexibility combined to produce high-quality, dependable and cost-effective service. But the implementation of information technology has forced Dutch hauliers to seek efficiencies of scale which up to now have appeared achievable only via mergers and acquisitions. Small-scale flexibility as a principle of competitive advantage is threatened. Alternative organizational principles, such as virtual organization and/or outsourcing state-of-the-art knowledge work (that is, business logistics), have not really been considered.

The mechanisms of the social market economy, which have led to few or no strikes, employee commitment, slow decision making but effective implementation, are all evident in the case. At issue is whether this model is adaptable to current circumstances. Would RRT be more effective if the power of the unit managers were broken? Does the organization need the reassertion of some sort of strong central control? Or is fragmentation a good thing in principle, allowing each business unit to maximize efficiency? Is there too much or too little flexibility in RRT? Would RRT have been destabilized and brought into crisis without the influence of the company-level holding and its financially driven growth strategy? Is the push to centralization, required by the market demand for instant information attainable by centralized information systems, really inevitable? Have key make or buy decisions (in-house computerization versus purchased services) been made well? The flirt with high technology seems to be a cost without a corresponding benefit to the firm. Will information technology help the organization to fulfil its goals better or disempower it until it becomes unrecognizable?

The case invites discussion of the relative strengths (and/or weaknesses) of analysis via perspectivism (that is, a situationalist focus). Since Gareth Morgan put imaginization (reading or interpreting situations, for instance by means of metaphors, to produce multiple understandings and alternative patterns of action) on the map, there has been deep unease about the possibility that social constructionism has gone mad. Has organizational knowledge being abandoned to relativism and nominalism? Does RRT support all and any description? Is there any one point of view which is more valid than the others? When readers are confronted with a series of differing readings, do they accept polyphony (so many observers, so many points of view) or do they think that some form of totalization or reduction is required?

Assignments

The case is divided into two sections. The first is written from the perspective of 1989–90 and the second (a postscript) from 1993–94. The data presented, including that of the consultant analyses, were readily available in the organizations studied. All information included in the initial description of RRT is of the sort which is typically made available to researchers. There are no key 'company secrets' or 'analytical tricks' involved. Readers need constantly to question the data and to ask themselves what these 'facts' mean in practice. The case could be approached from the perspective of a potential corporate cultural change agent who asks what change strategy is possible, at what cost and with what chance of success. This is not a 'didactic case' in the sense that there is one right answer which ought to be discovered. There is simply a series of problems and dilemmas.

The case assumes background knowledge on the level of Stewart Clegg's *Modern Organizations* and Gareth Morgan's *Images of Organization*. Clegg's discussion of 'embeddedness' and Morgan's 'perspectivism' need to be understood to cope at ease with the case. The human resource development questions at the end may be understood by using a text such as Mike Pedler's *Action Learning in Practice* for insight.

1. Would you dismiss de Groot and replace him with Snel? What are your reasons? Do you think that the real Board would do what you think to be the 'right' thing. Why?

2. Assume that the Board has dismissed de Groot and hired Snel; Snel has ordered three reports. The first is a financial overview to clarify which activities are profit making and which loss producing. The second is a market report revealing likely trends for the next 12 months in the transport sector. And the third is an internal analysis of RRT with the goal of stimulating RRT's entrepreneurial potential.

You are responsible for the (third) internal analysis. The crucial questions posed to you are: How can RRT management and staff be empowered to be more effective? What sources of organizational strength can you identify and how do you think they could be made more manifest? What skills are present in RRT (even if latent) and how can they be developed quickly?

What will you do with the trade-offs between organizational process and structure generated in RRT by the tension between decentralization and centralization? How will you behave towards the conflict between corporate-level control and business unit autonomy? Will you be able to achieve synergy within RRT and its strategic partnerships (alliances)?

How will you approach the role of corporate culture? Would you continue to want to have a strong mission statement? What will be your attitude to the role of technological control versus the uses of professional bureaucracy? Will you encourage alternative leadership styles? Will organizational learning have a high priority? How will you deal with the cultural tensions between consensus thinkers and those whose desire is for hierarchy? Will you favour the proponents of hands-on management or those of management at a distance? Will you support the arguments for meritocracy championing the need for more managerial professionalism?

3. Review and assess RRT's strategic decision making. Evaluate its successes and failures. What were the strengths and weaknesses of the strategic choices made? What options were (probably) not chosen? Define at least two alternative strategies for RRT from 1989 to 1993. What organizational changes would your strategies have demanded? What would have been their effect on RRT's organizational design? Would stakeholder power have had to be differently distributed for your alternatives to have been implemented? What effect on the organizational culture could alternative strategies have had? How could the necessary changes in organizational culture have been implemented? Describe the most appropriate process, in your opinion, for setting a mission statement for RRT in 1989/90, and what you think would have been a desirable result.

4. Instead of keeping or replacing de Groot, an alternative solution is proposed to the Board. It is recommended that RRT be dismantled. The regions will be offered for management buy-outs or, if that fails, put up for sale. It is proposed that logistics services not be developed independently by RRT, but in the future be purchased from a (much larger) competitor. RRT is to return to delivering quality transport solutions mainly for medium sized companies. Instead of seeking safety in size, each business unit is to go it alone. The ills of RRT are attributed to too much growth, too many pretensions, not enough attention to basics. RRT new style will continue to exist as a loose confederation of networked independent units. What is your analysis of this plan? Would you commit yourself to it? Why or why not?

Suggested reading

Clegg, Stewart (1990) *Modern Organizations*. London: Sage. An examination of the cultural factor. Much less focused than Linstead et al., but the ideas are better worked out than in Morgan's chapter on the 'cultural metaphor'. The descriptive material is very approachable (see Chapter 5) and of interest.

Hermans, William F. (1958) *De donkere kamer van Damokles*. Amsterdam: van Oorschot.
Hermans, William F. (1962) *La chambre noir de Damocles*. Paris: Seuil.
Hermans, William F. (1966) *Nooit Meer Slapen*. Amsterdam: De Bezige Bij. A novelist who portrays the powerlessness and even metaphysical desperation of a humanity faced with a fate which it cannot control. The first book is a classic in Dutch literature of the effort to work through the Second World War. The second wrestles with issues of individual ethics and science; in a society which tries so hard to be 'rational' and 'scientific', what do these values really mean? The third provides insight into the restraints and limits of Dutch culture.
d'Iribarne, Philippe (1989) *La logique de l'honneur*. Paris: Seuil.This book describes the Dutch consensus society in comparison with French and American illustrations. It is especially interesting for readers who want (are able) to compare the cultural background of French management to that of the US/Netherlands. The description of Dutch attitudes and in-company practice largely confirms the ideas presented in this case.
Linstead, Stephen, Jeffcutt, Paul and Grafton Small, Robert (eds) (in press) *Understanding Management*. London: Sage. A collection of perspectives on studying the organizing process with an eye to organizational and corporate cultural issues. A serious effort to bring some depth to the examination of cultural factors. Few answers, but many important questions.
Morgan, Gareth (1986) *Images of Organization*. London: Sage. While some management schools swear by this well-known textbook, it remains anathema for others. In the battle between contingency theory (however mediated or revised) and process thinking (in a post-modern, emancipatory and/or critical, ethno-methodological or symbolic internationalist mode), this book remains an important stepping-stone to the latter positions. It is easy enough to skim through the metaphors, but it is difficult to really work through what perspectivism means in practice.
Mullisch, Harry (1982) *De Anslag*. Amsterdam: de Bezige Bij.
Mullisch, Harry (1986) *The Assault*. London: Pantheon.
Mullisch, Harry (1993) *L'attentat*. Paris: Babel.Three editions of a book which introduces the reader to the darker, less free side of the Dutch culture's strong tendency toward continuity. Memory and the past pursue the person in the tightly knit intimacy of Dutch society. The traumatic quality of the Second World War is clearly depicted.
Pedler, Mike (1991) *Action Learning in Practice*. London: Gower. This case demands inter-disciplinary co-operation to handle its many aspects. It is written from an action learning perspective which expects rich problems to lead to valuable learning without ever providing 'right answers'.
Schama, Simon (1987) *The Embarrassment of Riches*. London: William Collins. This richly illustrated and very well-written cultural history of the Golden Age links Dutch seventeenth-century creativity and prosperity to attitudes of tolerance and materialism. An excellent book for seeing the strength of cultural continuity.
Schwartzman, Helen (1993) *Ethnography in Organizations*. London: Sage. A long essay which introduces the reader to ethnography. Its point of departure, the Hawthorne study, positions the book more than other (anthropological) manuscripts within the focus of attention of the management student.

Note

The author would like to acknowledge the CEMS Organizational Behaviour Inter-faculty group and particularly Peter Dachler (Hochschule St Gallen) for their comments and suggestions. He would also like to thank his many student assistants who conducted field interviews for the case.

8

SR-Bank

From regulated shelter to deregulated storm

Martin Gjelsvik and Odd Nordhaug

This case is about a savings bank which was suddenly confronted with a crucial turnaround challenge caused by profound changes in its external environment. These changes were induced by the authorities' deregulation and liberalization of financial markets that swiftly and radically altered the competitive conditions and rules of the game in the banking industry. In order to cope with this challenge, a comprehensive organizational development project was introduced in order to create a learning-based turnaround of the way of doing banking business. The chief goal of the project was to transform the bank's employees and work teams from being passive 'order takers' to becoming active 'sales people'.

It is hence a story of having to leave the shelter of strict, predictable government regulation and cartel-based non-competition to face the storms caused by deregulation. This is a story that today repeats itself in many industries throughout Europe and other parts of the Western world, and like all other businesses exposed to such a dramatic change the bank had to learn how to compete more or less from scratch. Such a major organizational challenge required a profound and rapid redevelopment of human resources.

The bank that has been selected for this case, SR-Bank, is one of the largest Norwegian regional savings banks and maintains a strong position in its local market. Still, on an international scale this is a small bank organization. It was founded in 1839, but appeared in its 'modern' form in the mid-1970s when 22 savings banks agreed to merge and form a new, larger bank. After the merger, the previously independent regional savings banks maintained a substantial degree of autonomy, through the existence of local boards of directors, local control committees and local management with considerable autonomy. Owing to dramatic changes in its external environment and competitive conditions, the bank had to pursue a comprehensive organizational development programme that could make it capable of coping with the altered demands.

In addition to the description of the organizational development project, attention will be paid to the thoughts and reservations of the management and employees of the bank during the planning and implementation stages of the project. The chief goal of the project was to transform the bank's employees from being relatively passive 'order takers' to becoming active 'sales people'. Expressed differently, this is a story of having to move out of the shelter of strict, predictable government regulation and cartel-based non-competition to face the storms caused by deregulation of financial markets. The bank, just like most others, had to learn how to compete more or less from scratch, which is a tremendously comprehensive organizational challenge. How could this be accomplished?

Cultural context

In this section, a few elements of the particular cultural context in which the bank is embedded are introduced. The presentation is limited solely to elements that are especially relevant to the case.

Traditionally, Norway is a country characterized by strong egalitarian values. It has for a long time been predominantly a society of farmers, fishermen, craftsmen and workers. Unlike most other European nations, there has never been an aristocracy to speak of and the political position of the farmers has remained powerful. Moreover, in a larger European context, the position of the urban bourgeoisie has been comparatively weak.

During the period after the Second World War, Norway has to a large degree been ruled by social democrat governments through the Labour Party (Arbeiderpartiet) which, together with most other parties represented in the Storting (parliament) has strongly advocated social equality as an over-arching value. Even the Conservative Party (Høyre) has, when viewed against the dominant European scene, pursued a policy which has not been unaffected by mainstream egalitarian values.

The emphasis on equality, or more precisely the absence of great inequality, has gone hand in hand with a very high unionization and powerful local and national unions that have played, and still play, active parts on the political arena. In the public service as well as in many large companies, particularly the banks and insurance companies, the principle of job security has until the last few years been regarded as sacred. Hence, downsizing by firing employees has not been seen as necessary and the banks have been obliged to find other solutions when changing their business strategies and when having to cut costs during economic recessions.

Owing to these egalitarian values, wage differentials have stayed relatively small and Norwegian managers are among the lowest paid in the Western world. In addition, employees and unions in many industries have resented individual performance assessments and compensation has to a substantial degree been determined through collective bargaining.

Norwegian banks have in general been among the most conservative work organizations in the country. This is partly because they were for a long time sheltered from real competition through cartel agreements that determined the interest rates. The cartel arrangements were given the blessings of most politicians and public authorities and were not considered illegitimate in any sense by most people.

Norwegian savings banks

Norwegian savings banks have their roots in the local communities where they were established in the 1800s intended to deal primarily with local matters. Norway's first regional savings bank was established in 1976 when 22 savings banks merged to become Sparebanken Rogaland, SR-Bank. This provided the bank with a good start with regard to the competition for customers when the domestic financial market was liberalized in the mid-1980s.

In 1977 a new Savings Banks Act was implemented. Now savings banks were given basically the same competitive conditions as the commercial banks. Yet the ownership structure remained very different, and the savings banks were not obliged to keep fixed capital ratios. There was no need for such a requirement since losses were virtually non-existent. Furthermore there were no troublesome profit requirements in the markets where the banks operated and, consequently, no systems for analysing or measuring credit risk were in place. The financial industry was therefore largely unprepared for the important changes which the subsequent deregulation would bring about.

The new Savings Banks Act lay the foundation for a strong expansion in savings banks' operations. The product range was substantially widened, and savings banks became full service banks for businesses as well as for individual clients. The largest of them developed specialist skills, while the smaller ones gained access to these skills through co-operation. Compared to the rest of Western Europe, Norwegian savings banks have a unique position with regard to both their range of products and services and their market shares. This is indicated by the overview given in Table 8.1 of the distribution of domestic (that

Table 8.1 *Distribution of loans 1980 and 1991*

Type of finance institution	Proportion of loans (%)	
	1980	1991
Savings banks	18.5	23.1
Commercial banks	22.0	25.7
Government banks	39.4	24.3
Financing companies	2.2	2.7
Private credit companies	10.1	15.0
Insurance companies	7.8	9.2

Source: The Norwegian Savings Banks Association

is, within Norway) loans to the general public, including companies, households and public institutions.

If we limit the perspective to individual clients, that is, exclude corporate customers, the savings banks are the most important type of lending institution, followed by the commercial banks and the government-owned 'Postal Bank'.

Deregulation

The deregulation of financial markets in Norway was given increasing political priority during the early 1980s, similar to most of Western Europe and the United States. The process culminated in 1985, when the following changes had been completed:

- the banks' silent, cartel-type 'interest rate agreement' was abolished;
- volume restrictions on lending were eliminated;
- the obligation to invest in gilts (government bonds) was terminated;
- restrictions on the right to issue bonds were removed;
- legislation widened the range of assets that could be mortgaged to firms' inventories;
- the right of virtually unrestricted establishment of banks and bank branches was introduced.

In retrospect, it is easy to see that deregulation was pursued at an inappropriate time. Liberal tax rules combined with high inflation rates resulted in negative real interest rates after taxation. Private clients considered house ownership to be a golden investment. Investments in real estate were regarded as almost totally risk free, since the value of houses had increased steadily throughout the post-war period. A public financial policy based on expansion goals further stimulated the willingness to invest. The previous regulation of the banks' volumes of loans led to loan applicants being channelled first to the private financing companies and credit companies which were not subject to strict regulation. In this period, regulation of the banks generated a very strong growth potential for these institutions. Correspondingly, they experienced very large loan volumes but later even more sizeable credit losses.

The Savings Banks Association concluded as follows in its Annual Report for 1991:

> The authorities were too late in developing faith in the market mechanism as a means of controlling the development of the deregulated Norwegian market, and came too late with solvency requirements and credit loss regulations which were in accordance with actual market conditions. The authorities' responsibility for creating the necessary framework for a market-oriented financial industry was ignored by the authorities themselves. The fact that, in a deregulated economy, the interest rates were still fixed by the government, triggered an unprecedented demand for credit which was facilitated by funds from the Central Bank. It is this, among other things, which is a distinctively Norwegian element in the current financial crisis.

'This is SR-Bank'

In its annual report for 1989, the bank presents itself in these words:

> The SR-Bank's organization, technology and distribution network have all been adapted to the requirements of our clients. Our products and services are characterized by high quality. There is a short distance, organizationally speaking, between our customers and the decision makers at our bank.
>
> Personal service and counselling constitute an integral part of the financial services available to our customers, being of crucial importance in order to achieve our overall targets. Our high quality standards are met through careful and well planned recruitment and personnel development, high performance expectations and by remunerating our employees based on effort and actual results. In this structured manner the SR-Bank will be able to strengthen our position as the largest supplier of financial services in south-western Norway.
>
> There is an obvious need for high quality products, and indeed for profitability, both from the point of view of our customers and our distribution network. Operating profits of the SR-Bank should produce a markedly higher return on equity capital than the ratio earned on ordinary lending. Our minimum interest rate requirements in respect of equity and subordinated loan capital are intended to provide us with the necessary freedom of choice and a wider range of options, and also to create confidence in our bank in the markets.
>
> Against this background of a well defined business concept and a self-imposed standard of unimpeachable business ethics, the SR-Bank will become known as an important, effective and profitable district bank, which is prepared to adopt a very responsible and caring attitude towards all our retail and corporate customers, trying to help solve their problems and meet their requirements, and at the same time being aware of the part our bank has to play in the local communities.

At the end of 1989, SR-Bank's total staff numbered 831, of whom 624 worked on a full-time basis and 207 on a part-time basis. This was the equivalent of 757 people-years, down from 770 a year earlier.

The bank's organization chart is shown in Figure 8.1. In Table 8.2, a survey of the bank's profit and loss account covering 1985–9 is presented.

Strategic change

As indicated above, the deregulation of the Norwegian banking industry in the mid-1980s created many new challenges for the industry in general, and the particular savings bank studied here represented no exception. One of the most salient features of this changing picture was the largely increased number of options available to managerial discretion. The market, which had previously been stable, uniform and relatively undemanding, became increasingly turbulent, multi-faceted and complex to handle.

In a market of the above type, it is meaningful to engage in strategy projects aimed at defining an organization's course, its markets, and increasing competitive advantages by developing unique capabilities. In a homogeneous, institutional, government-directed market, however, such activities are not particularly meaningful as the competitive options are virtually non-existent.

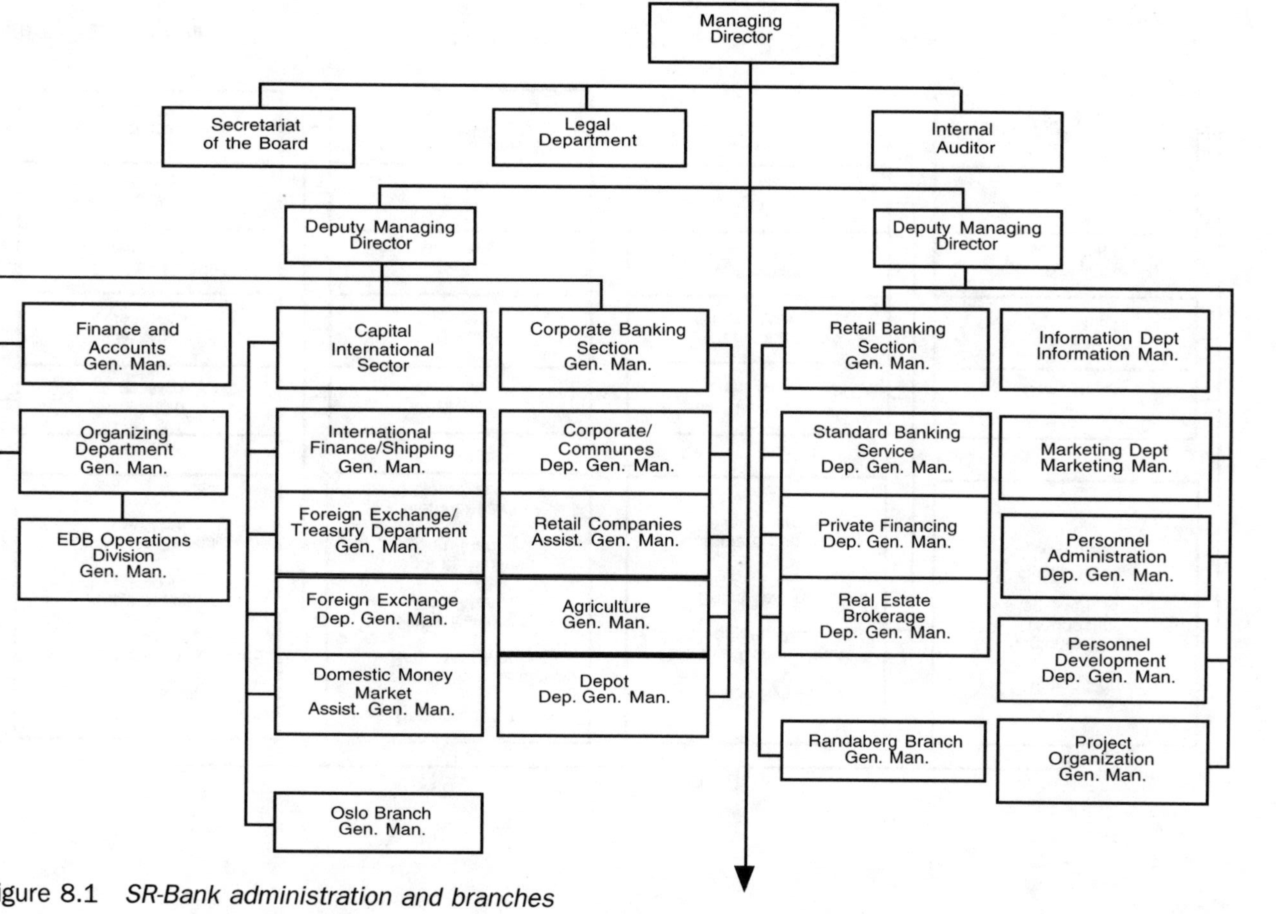

Figure 8.1 *SR-Bank administration and branches*

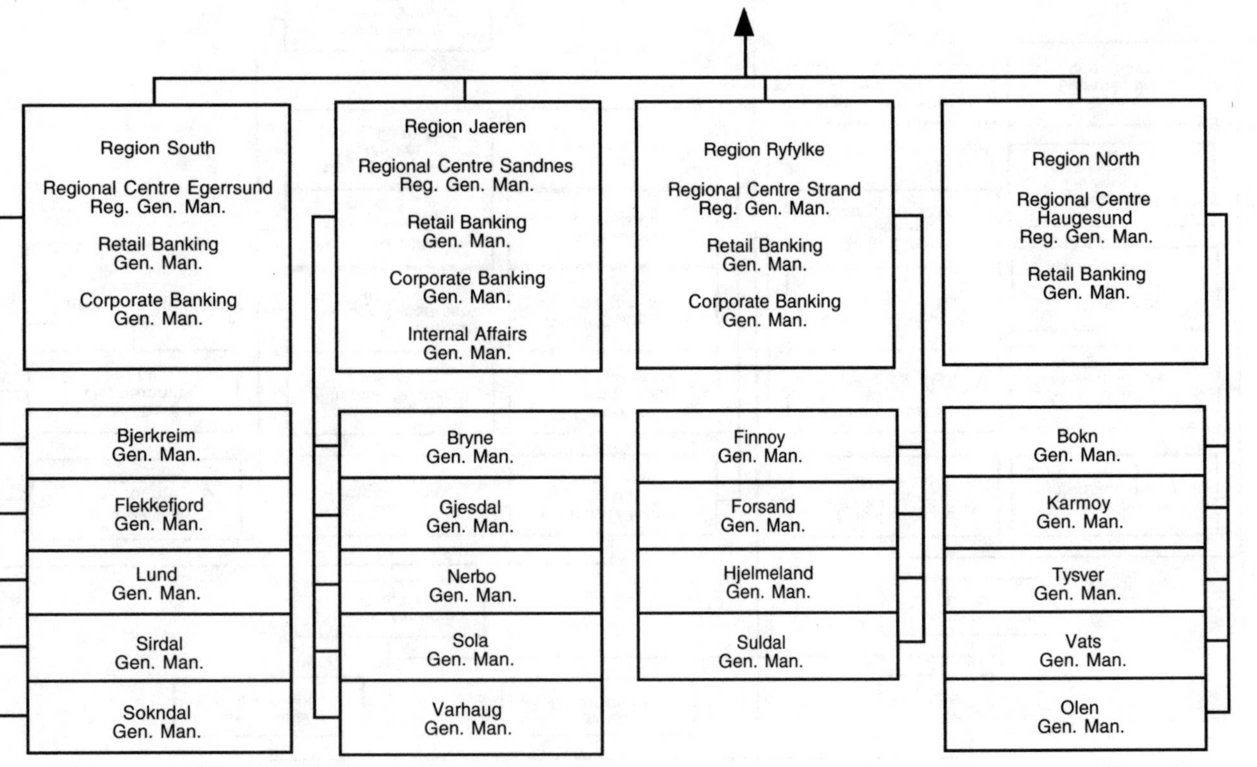

Figure 8.1 *continued*

Until the end of the 1970s, bank products were virtually identically designed, and the so called 'interest rate understanding', a silent cartel-type agreement between the banks, regulated interest rates. Furthermore, a large percentage of banks' liquid assets were tied up in government or local public authority bonds, as banks were required by law to invest 30% of their deposit growth in such bonds. Payment transfer was also free of charge. Thus, before 1978–9 there was no competition on either price, product or quality.

Table 8.2 *SR-Bank profit and loss account, 1985–9 (NOK million)*

	1985	1986	1987	1988	1989
Interest and credit income	1,047	1,414	1,809	2,016	2,008
Debit interest	752	1,091	1,366	1,529	1,396
Net interest	295	323	443	487	612
Other commission income	65	97	61	72	86
Net rate gain on securities	2	6	0	5	11
Net rate gain on foreign exchange	7	9	11	19	37
Other receivable	7	6	0	7	–
Sum of other income	81	118	82	103	200
Wages and other staff expenses	138	162	181	201	214
Other operating expenses	109	139	167	187	193
Ordinary depreciation	17	25	28	36	47
Depreciation of shares in subsidiaries	–	–	–	–	102
Sum of other operating expenses	264	326	376	424	556
Operating result before losses	112	115	149	166	256
Losses and provisions for losses	62	89	106	123	242
Operating result after losses	50	26	43	43	14
Balance sheet					
Short term receivable	2,767	3,580	3,528	4,048	2,945
Net loans	6,394	8,685	9,970	11,560	11,785
Fixed assets	299	510	634	679	622
Sum of assets	9,460	12,775	14,132	16,287	15,352
Deposits from banks and customers	8,589	11,800	12,562	14,467	13,290
Other debt	352	439	802	1,050	1,230
Subordinated loan capital	0	0	193	182	171
Tax free equity capital	68	78	93	107	146
Equity capital	451	458	482	481	515
Sum of equity capital	519	536	768	770	832
Total liabilities and equity capital	9,460	12,775	14,132	16,287	15,352
Average total assets	8,620	10,520	13,170	15,518	16,187

Table 8.2 *continued*

	1985	1986	1987	1988	1989
Key figures (% of average total assets)					
Interest income	12.15	13.45	13.73	12.99	12.41
Interest expenses	8.72	10.37	10.37	9.85	8.63
Net interest	3.43	3.08	3.36	3.14	3.78
Sum of other operating income	0.94	1.12	0.63	0.66	1.24
Sum operating expenses	3.07	3.10	2.86	2.73	3.43
Operating result before losses	1.30	1.10	1.13	1.07	1.59
Losses and provisions for losses	0.72	0.85	0.81	0.79	1.50
Operating result	0.58	0.25	0.32	0.28	0.09
Losses in percentage of loans	1.0	1.0	1.1	1.1	2.1
Provision for bad loans in percent	2.9	2.8	2.5	2.2	2.2
Equity capital in percentage	5.5	4.2	5.4	4.7	5.4

Source: SR-Bank 1989 Annual Report

When the deregulation came, numerous challenges were suddenly facing the bank, both internally and not least in respect to the bank's relation to the market. Internationally, it became clear that the organization itself was not suitable for the new state of affairs. A highly decentralized organization was difficult to manoeuvre in relation to an exceedingly volatile market. The banks were managed by local boards, the members of which were recruited from outside the banks. In general, they possessed insufficient knowledge about the new market forces and their consequences for profitability and customer demands. Their way of reasoning was very much traditional and 'path dependent'. Customers, with a good deal of help from the authorities, became more demanding. It was therefore obvious that the bank had to become more market oriented, and three main markets were identified: retail, the corporate and institutional, and capital.

The development of a strategic plan was not aimed exclusively at positioning the bank in rapidly expanding markets. The internal function was equally important, in that the plan functioned as a rallying point for organizational units and employees. Thus, in the introduction to the written strategic plan, the Managing Director made this written statement:

> You and I and all the employees in this organization have a need for a common ground on which to base the many thousands of decisions that we make every day in this bank. We have therefore developed a strategic plan which will ensure that we all want the same things and that we all are working towards the same goals. This is necessary in order for us to succeed. It is therefore crucial that we feel that this plan is our own, that we feel it is a part of us.

The previously decentralized organization had to be unified and integrated, and to be perceived in the market as an effective and powerful unit. Local knowledge was to be combined with shared strengths. As a co-ordinating mechanism, direct control from the Joint Board or the Managing Director was out of the question, given the existence of individual Boards of Directors representing the local banks. Common goals, basic values and attitudes had to be developed.

Such a process takes a long time, and can only be implemented if all organizational levels participate. A broadly based, participative strategy-development process was initiated, with participation from all of the branch banks. There was a far larger proportion of employee representatives involved than intended by law. We may therefore say that this process reflected the resilient political traditions of the savings banks.

The process was as important as the contents. Given such broad participation, in which consensus and team spirit were paramount, it was necessary to arrive at compromises and relatively general policy statements. The development of the plan, and later revisions of it, were primarily administrative processes run by the top management team. Both the Joint Board of Directors and the local Boards actually had only peripheral roles. On the other hand, the local bank managers were all represented. This representation was aimed at creating greater loyalty and commitment to the common goals as such, as well as to the top management. For the bank's top management, the approved plan was an important tool of creating legitimacy. In accounting for their actions to the bank's governing bodies, that is, the Joint Board and the Superior Committee, the management wanted to be able to document full support from the whole bank for the strategic choices which were proposed. It became increasingly difficult for local boards to oppose central plans. Their spokesperson to the bank's headquarters, the local bank manager, was himself involved in developing the plan. Even though some bank managers felt themselves pulled in opposite directions, this was more the exception than the rule. Furthermore, under such circumstances the Managing Director of the bank or one of his closest associates was ready to step in as a sort of missionary (an expression which was actually used in a couple of instances).

The plan was to be implemented through local plans of action. The local bank manager was given a relatively large degree of freedom, but local plans were to be formally approved by the Managing Director. Local adaptations were also emphasized in the introduction to the plan: 'This plan has been developed in the form of a handbook, with space provided for your own comments. It should be read with the aim of extracting the specific consequences it will have for you and your job.'

The internal orientation and function of the plan were illustrated by its contents: out of 20 pages, a total of 14 dealt with the internal life and activities of the bank in paragraphs such as 'Human Resources Management', 'The Bank's Organization', 'Technology', 'Internal Control and Quality Assurance', 'Security', 'Subsidiaries', 'The Bank Structure', 'Information and Communication' and 'Ability to Change'.

Retail market division

In the following, the focus is on the bank's largest division, the Retail Market division, in which two-thirds of the bank's staff are employed. As a part of the market orientation process in the mid-1980s, a separate division was established under the name *Personkunde-markedet* (Retail Market division). This division gradually developed into a separate profit centre and had its own management and General Manager who was on the bank's top executive team. Thus, the co-ordination of the three market areas was the responsibility of the bank's top management.

The change in the bank's priorities was reflected in the various editions of the Strategic Plan. In the first edition in 1983, the three market segments were barely mentioned, and the part of the plan pertaining to the retail market was limited to half a page. Five years later, in the 1988 edition, the description of this market filled three pages.

In order better to describe the bank's goals and priorities in the Strategic Plan, the actual contents of the 1988 edition are quoted below.

Strategic plan (1988)

The Bank maintains a strong position in the retail market. We possess the most comprehensive sales network and cover a very broad range of services. These competitive advantages will be exploited in order to increase sales in the retail market and to augment the market share in this area. This is to be accomplished by:

- Creating lasting customer relationships by satisfying the changing financial services needs of the private customer.
- Providing good products and services with high quality customer service and availability, aiming at high profitability in operations.

As a full service bank, our goal is to turn our profitable customers into all-round customers. We must develop new ways of maintaining customer loyalty. We must offer products and services which the customer needs in various situations and stages in life.

The Bank is to provide a complete range of financial services for all individual customers in the retail market, with varying systems for service provision based on the differing needs of the various customer groups. The process of segmentation and specialization which we have begun shall continue. The customers who are not profitable to the bank today shall be turned into profitable ones through sensible pricing and increased efficiency in banking routines.

Individual customers within the retail market must be divided into groups on the basis of similar needs, such that they may be provided with the proper products and services at reasonable distribution costs. The division into the three sections, Standard Services, Tailored Services and Senior Service, is an expression of this view of the customer group.

We are interested in long-term customer relations. A long-term relationship provides a solid basis for sales of additional services/products, and ensures stability in operations. Such customer relations are contingent on our ability to provide services throughout the customer's life.

Standard Services

The Standard Services Section is designed to cater to the customers' need for daily bank services, that is payment transfer, deposit and loan facilities, insurance, and other services which are easily standardized. Such services should be simple and readily available to the customer. The confidence of the market is won through correct execution of tasks and highly qualified, service-minded employees. Self-service and automation are prerequisites for profitability in payment transfer. An additional aim is to provide more products to each customer.

Tailored Services

The Tailored Services Section shall provide for the customers' needs in regard to personal advisory services and sales of special financial services. The aim of such services is to help the customer achieve the best possible arrangement of his/her personal finances. The needs of the customer are to be met partially through the bank's own services and partially through sales of others' products, primarily those of subsidiaries. Emphasis shall be placed on training and recruitment of employees with the necessary knowledge and skills in investor services, taxation issues, computer models. It is also important that employees are encouraged to become more sales oriented. Quality and creativity form the essence of competitiveness.

Senior Services

The Bank shall develop and provide services for target groups over 60 years of age. A separate sales system to ensure the necessary quality and profitability is to be created.

The sales network

The Bank has a very well-developed distribution network. This network represents a significant leverage on our competitors and shall be effectively exploited. New technology has made an ever increasing number of services immediately available on a self-service basis. Increased customer demands have resulted in a greater degree of specialization. At the same time, increasing costs in distribution have made provision of financial services increasingly expensive. These developments and the need for increased profitability at every level have made an evaluation of the bank's sales network necessary. This evaluation is to be conducted according to the following guidelines:

- Branch offices which primarily provide simple, immediate services shall be replaced with automated offices or closed.

- Branch offices which provide all immediate services as well as regular finance services shall be improved aiming at increased sales of profitable bank services, using current staff.
- Some branch offices shall be expanded to provide a complete tailored services concept aimed at attracting new customer groups as well as offering current customers a complete range of financial services.

Real life

In real life, there is frequently a substantial discrepancy between policy statements and the implementation of the policy. In certain cases, the implementation of strategy precedes its actual formulation, so that what is expressed in formal written plans serves as an *ex post* legitimation and normalization of existing administrative decisions and priorities. The segregation between the three market segments had, in fact, partly been carried out before the plan was approved. For example, several Standard Services offices and one Senior Service centre had already been established.

The question of the sales or distribution network (including a significant number of branch offices) was the subject of a heated debate. The branch network tied up considerable resources and incurred a major part of the fixed costs. An advanced and well-functioning ATM (automatic teller machines) network together with an electronic payment transfer system significantly reduced customers' needs to visit the bank in person. Consequently, there were several good reasons for downsizing the branch network. In this discussion, two contradictory points of view were present:

- The bank needs to cut costs. Since the branch network incurs large costs, it must be reduced as much as possible. The basis for this line of reasoning was thus purely cost oriented and statistical. Branch employees' contribution to revenues was not taken into consideration.
- The branch network, including both the physical and human resources it comprises, represents a unique competitive advantage. In this respect, we differ significantly from our competitors. Such an advantage must be developed and exploited, not destroyed.
- Furthermore, we are responsible for our employees and their jobs. The challenge is: How can we use these strategic resources more efficiently than we have been doing in the past?

Ultimately, the former point of view was defeated by the latter. However, as indicated by the above comments, the sales network had to become market oriented and hence faced the imperative of specializing in order to cater to three very different markets. This process turned out to be quite laborious. Many people failed to recognize the necessity of change. The ideals of improving the knowledge and competence of employees as well as providing high quality were easily agreed, but the process of translating these ideas into practical action gave rise to considerable differences of opinion. For example, there was great disagreement regarding the need for change in recruitment policy, career procedures and reward system.

In determining the salary of employees working with the retail market, earlier practice involved relating salary to the amount of loans the employee was authorized to grant. Lending was 'good', it meant more authority and power *vis-à-vis* the customer, it provided status within the organization, and it meant more pay at the end of the month. However, the distinction between Standard Services and Tailored Services implied that the division of labour had to be based on different criteria. It was obvious that the biggest and most complex loans had to be allocated to the Tailored Services section. Standard loans, such as car loans and student loans, were to be granted by the Standard Services section. Employees in the latter unit were thus allowed less authority to lend than had earlier been the case. The main rule was that personnel should not be authorized to lend more than they had a real need to in their daily work. A good number of employees, and not least their union representatives, hence feared a decrease in compensation. A more real fear was that major and minor leagues of players would develop, based on the old criteria specifying what was 'desirable'. Therefore it was necessary to create a new basis for status-giving work, in addition to the processing of loan applications. The magic word became 'sales'.

From order taking to sales

By choosing to concentrate on the branch network as a strategic resource, the bank had decided on continued high fixed costs. The challenge thus became to generate higher revenues, which was far more easy to desire than to accomplish. Bank employees were not primarily sales people; on the contrary the most prevalent motive for seeking a job in a bank had traditionally been a wish to obtain a stable income and a secure job.

A common, in-a-nutshell description of bank employees engaged in work with private customers was 'order takers'. This kind of reactive work behaviour was relevant and adequate as long as there was no reason for a customer to frequent more than one bank; as long as the customer, regardless of the service required, *had to go* to the bank. As previously described, the market and the demands it placed on the bank had changed radically. The main questions were now these: How could a sales-oriented culture be developed? How could prevalent attitudes and work behaviour be changed?

For several years the bank's management had preached, 'We must get better at selling' and 'We must become better at understanding customers' needs.' There was no end to what bank employees had to 'get better' at. But can anyone be expected to improve without having the relevant tools or instructions indicating *how* this is to come about?

The first step chosen to cope with the altered competitive conditions and environment was to stake out a path by formulating a special strategy for the retail market. This was outlined by the division's management:

1. We shall turn profitable customers into all-round customers by:

- providing a full range of financial services;
- offering products and services adapted to different situations and phases of the life cycle;
- being an active problem solver for the customer;
- developing customer loyalty through cross-selling.

2. We shall develop our customer orientation through:
   - increased professional skills;
   - higher quality of service;
   - needs-oriented sales;
   - specifically focused market communication.
3. We shall ensure quick and efficient customer service through:
   - simplicity;
   - easy availability;
   - self-service.
4. We shall develop profitable customer segments through:
   - pricing;
   - needs orientation;
   - automation and standardization of mass-market products.

Of course, this strategy was inspired by the Strategic Plan and signalled new specific measures, particularly in the area of customer orientation. The notion of 'needs-oriented sales' was introduced to distance staff from the common perception of an aggressive insurance salesperson; a salesperson more interested in his or her own bonuses than in the customer's needs. 'Soft sell' was the buzzword, the starting point was always to be the customer's actual needs. People had to be convinced that 'over-selling' would backfire in the form of complaints about poor and sloppy financial advice.

The Human Resource Management department assumed responsibility for arranging sales courses. These courses were typically one-day or weekend courses aimed at teaching employees various sales techniques. However, this approach was not successful, and there were many reasons behind the failure. The courses were not specifically directed at sales in banks: the ideals and techniques were taken from traditional retail businesses. The concepts of 'soft sell' and the establishment of long-term customer relations were not at the forefront. Moreover, it had to be acknowledged that courses which were not part of a larger organizational context would easily result in the creation – at best – of only short-term enthusiasm among the participants. The need for structural changes which could allow such learning to have a lasting effect on the organization in the form of new attitudes, new routines and revised computer programs became increasingly evident. The instructor's job was completed when the course was completed: he or she had no responsibility for either the use, implementation or follow-up of the individual learning that had taken place.

Coincidentally, at this time the management came across a sales training programme which seemed suitable for its purposes. The general manager of the

Retail Market division was on a business trip to the US with a group of colleagues from other banks:

> The purpose of the trip to the US was to look into a number of new business ideas, including telephone sales and direct marketing. In one of the most important American marketing organizations, we were introduced to someone who turned out to have been a previous colleague. He was now self-employed not too far from where we were, in Nashville, Tennessee. In an extremely persuasive and entertaining 45 minutes, he presented his programme. This programme turned out to be just what we needed! It was precisely what we had been looking for during the past two years.

After having returned to the bank in Norway, an attempt was made to spread the enthusiasm. Needless to say, this turned out to be quite difficult. Comments such as 'this will be expensive' and 'the United States is not Norway' were indications of a profound scepticism. On the other hand, the programme was tailor-made for banks: it had been used extensively and had been tested in a number of American banks. It had gradually evolved through practical experience. Thus this was not 'theory', a well-known taboo in the banking business; it was practice. Not only was it practice, it was banking practice. Hence, there were very convincing arguments in favour of the programme.

After a year's tug-of-war within the organization, the bank signed the agreement. By that time the programme's American creator had visited SR-Bank twice, and through a continuous process of alliance building within the bank (the Marketing Director and the Director of Personnel Development were early converts) the bank's top management was finally persuaded. One of the conditions was that the programme was to be 'Norwegianized' and adapted as much as possible to the bank's own culture and language.

The development programme

A brief description of the project, a fairly comprehensive organizational development (OD) programme, is provided below. The target group included all staff members working in the bank's Retail Market division. All employees in this division were involved, including managers at all levels. Over 500 employees thus took part at various stages.

The primary objective was to learn to understand and utilize the process of communication between the customer and the bank employee providing services to the customer. The aim was to develop the capability to determine the customer's current and future needs and, furthermore, to endeavour to satisfy these needs through the bank's products and services.

The sales and organizational development project was labelled SESAM, which is the Norwegian acronym for ***S***alg ***Er SAM***_arbeid_, 'sales is co-operation'. The reason for placing so much emphasis on the co-operative aspect was related to customers' perception of the bank. Market research had shown that customers tended to perceive the bank as one organization. Most customers expect the bank to 'recognize' them regardless of who they approach in the bank. Therefore, it became crucial to stress the significance of intra-organiza-

Table 8.3 *The nine steps in the SESAM project*

1. Create commitment.
2. Define the task.
3. Improve management skills in sales management and training.
4. Generate service and sales skills.
5. Create product knowledge.
6. Set goals and measure performance.
7. Create motivation, rewards and recognition.
8. Remove sales barriers.
9. Prepare the sales team.

tional co-operation, also across sub-unit boundaries. For example, information about the customer must be exchanged and made available to all customer service and support personnel. Even though the bank was divided into specialized functions, the customers usually anticipated experiencing the bank as one entity.

The nine steps in the SESAM project are illustrated in Table 8.3.

The SESAM project had a long-term perspective. The organization was to be transformed from an 'order-taking station' into a 'proactive sales train'. At the same time, in the course of the project, it was realized that *none* of the bank's employees had joined the bank because of an interest in sales. This did not make the challenge less demanding.

It was considered crucial that a project of this nature needed to be harnessed with legitimacy and support from the organization's top management. The first requirement for success was therefore that the Managing Director and his closest associates demonstrated a visible, sustained and serious commitment to the programme. Research within the bank (see Table 8.4) had revealed several reasons why the employees were not performing as expected.[1]

To delineate what was expected, the tasks of each individual employee (refer to point 2 in Table 8.3) were clearly defined through so-called *winning plays*. Such plays were developed for tellers, customer service personnel, support staff and managers at all levels. General quality norms were introduced under the following concepts: Competence, Courtesy and Consideration. Even the actual process of communicating with the customer was outlined in detail in 'The Five Fs' (in Norwegian): (1) discover the customer's problems, needs and opportunities, (2) determine the customer's awareness and interest, (3) decide on the best

Table 8.4 *Reasons why employees did not perform*

1. Don't know what is expected.
2. Don't know how to do it.
3. Don't want to do it.
4. Can't do it.
5. Don't know why to do it.

service, (4) discuss your service suggestions with the customer, (5) develop the business. (Separate concepts for emphasizing the new element of the situation and for providing the programme with an efficient pedagogical element were also created.)

The 'how' aspect was dealt with in points 3–5 in Table 8.3. Sales managers were taught modern sales management and trained in developing sales teams at their work locations (branches/offices/divisions). Training of the remainder of the personnel had a dual focus: it consisted partly of training in service and sales skills, and partly of transmitting and perfecting employees' knowledge of the bank's products and services.

The motivational aspect had to be given considerable attention. Performance evaluation and continuous feedback were important new elements. Performance measurement occurred locally at each workplace (for example, branch or office) in order to establish a direct link between each individual's and team's efforts on the one hand and the results achieved on the other. Reward and recognition systems based on documented degrees of goal attainment were then developed. Local reports of results were given on a weekly basis, and aggregate reports for the whole bank were prepared every month. The aggregated reports covering the whole bank included rankings of the various sales offices and suggested rewards designated for those who had been most successful in reaching the sales targets. Furthermore, separate 'sales barriers teams', consisting of employees and representatives from different professional groups, were created and given the tasks of identifying, reporting and removing sales barriers.

In spite of hard training and efforts to create motivation, there were still a few employees who did not master the skills required of them. Attempts to solve this problem involved changing the division of labour at the local workplace or transferring the employee to another part of the bank.

Point 5 in Table 8.4 ('don't know why') is an indication of notable cultural differences between Norwegian and American business. It is interesting to note that this point had to be added to the original American version of the programme. American businesses, not least in the banking industry, are characterized by a higher degree of management by directive than are businesses based on the more egalitarian, profoundly participative Scandinavian model. Therefore, bank employees in the USA typically have less autonomous jobs than their Norwegian counterparts. Employee behaviour is directed more through extremely detailed manuals than through development-oriented, co-operative educational projects. This is illustrated by the fact that the bank's management in Norway was a far more active and visible participant at all stages of the project than was the management in the USA. The top managers not only took part symbolically in the project but also required reports on results and acted upon them. They became actively engaged in training programmes, used and disseminated the 'new language' and discussed further development of the project in the top management team.

We have also indicated, indirectly, one of the most important reservations regarding this project. In the programme, the means of achieving behavioural change were built on purely behaviouristic theory and assumptions. Given employees who are relatively submissive to authority, this provides considerable opportunity for managerial manipulation of employees. In this context, conflicts could be eliminated with a reference to SESAM. Somewhat incidentally, the management came into contact with a renowned organizational psychologist and asked him to consider the ethical implications of the project. His advice was that the programme was ethically sound given that the bank's employees were informed ahead of time about the objectives of the measures taken, as well as about the means which were to be used.

Implementation of SESAM

The aim of the SESAM programme was to establish lasting changes in the organization: failure to do so would make it worthless. Considerable investments were made both in terms of financial and human resources. Learning processes to transfer knowledge from the individual to the organization level had to be created. Ideally, these processes would eventually become self-sustaining, so that the need for further financial support and other external resources would be minimal. One of the conditions of the project was, as mentioned earlier, that it had been 'Norwegianized', adapted to the specific, local Norwegian context. It was therefore clear that most of the instruction had to be carried out by the bank's own personnel.

Winning plays

Each individual employee's role was defined through the use of so-called winning plays. These plays were used for tellers, customer service representatives and support personnel. Furthermore, all levels of management were equipped with winning plays, from the first-line managers to the Managing Director. A hierarchical system was also developed to 'capture' all management levels and relevant categories of employees at the operational level. The sales manager of a particular bank outlet (for instance, the local branch manager) was familiar with his subordinates' winning plays. Conversely, employees also knew their superior's winning play. Thus the two could check each other, and measures were generated through which the individual could continuously perfect his or her role performance.

Two examples of winning plays are provided here in order to illustrate their substance.

Winning play for tellers

1. Greeting and presentation

- Greet the customer politely so that he or she feels important and welcome.
- Look up, smile, establish eye contact.

- Even if you are busy with something else, greet the customer by saying something, nodding or waving.
- Ask how you may be of assistance.

2. Carry out the customer's wishes

- Deal with the customer's requests in a competent and polite fashion.
- Use your knowledge to deal with requests, be precise and effective.
- Address the customer by name – if you don't know it you can often find it in the papers in front of you.
- Speak calmly, clearly and politely.
- Try to smile and maintain eye contact throughout the transaction stage.
- Draw the customer into conversation – establish contact.

3. Uncover needs

- Discover what PBMs[2] a customer may have, show interest and consideration.
- Comment as you serve the customer.
- Listen for sales opportunities in what the customer says.

4. Give recommendations

- Find out which service best suits the customer and recommend it.
- Explain the solution using PINs and one-liners.[3]
- Use brochures actively.
- Recommend that the customer talk with a member of the customer service personnel.

5. Refer the customer to relevant colleagues

- Use a customer presentation card (CPC).
- Write the customer's name, the services you've suggested and your name on the card.
- Enclose your business card and any other relevant documents.
- Refer the customer to the right person.
- If possible, escort the customer and introduce him or her. Give your colleague the customer presentation card.
- If you are unable to escort the customer, explain who he or she is to see and give the customer the customer presentation card.

6. Conclusion

- Thank the customer politely, using his or her name.
- If possible, shake hands.
- Welcome the customer back again and offer your help in the future.

This winning play covers point 2 in Table 8.3, 'define the task'. If we disregard the obvious for a moment, the winning play revealed a very important and previously controversial point for tellers. The tellers themselves were not asked to cross-sell, they were asked to refer the customer to a customer service representative if an opportunity for cross-selling arose. However, the tellers had previously reacted negatively to any suggestions that they assume a more proactive attitude towards sales. They claimed that sales activity would 'only lead to long lines at the counters'. The management had previously been unable to provide any specific suggestions as to how these two seemingly conflicting demands, that is, prompt service and active cross-selling, could be met simultaneously. The solution had been detected, and the tellers' attitudes towards sales immediately became more positive.

The second example of a winning play was designed for the general manager of the Retail Market division.

Winning Play for the division General Manager

1. Define and communicate the results you expect from each manager

- Establish 'Winning plays for sales managers'[4] as a standard for sales management and training.
- Set targets together with the managers.
- Gain acceptance for expected actions and set targets, both for superiors and subordinates, so that the desired behaviour is measurable.

2. Be a good example

- Practise what you preach.
- Be optimistic and enthusiastic.
- Practice the three Cs (Competence, Courtesy, Consideration).
- Use PINs and one-liners.
- Demonstrate correct customer service when you are involved in sales yourself.
- Use the winning play.
- Be consistent.

3. Empower your employees

- Share information.
- Arrange monthly follow-up meetings with your managers.
- Give your managers opportunities for individual development.
- Delegate authority and responsibility.
- Remove sales barriers.
- LISTEN! LISTEN! LISTEN!

4. Build team spirit

- Set goals for the region.
- Communicate goals and results.

- Map progress in the region.
- Don't forget the humorous side of things.

5. Check on your expectations

- Execute hands-on management by visiting the local banks in your region.
- Review the local bank's results monthly with each manager, using the sales reports.
- Ask the customers if they are satisfied with the bank.
- Go through customer messages, letters, etc.

6. Reward and recognize

- At your monthly meetings, reward and recognize those who have achieved good results.
- Reward and recognize both individual employees and teams.
- Express your approval for a well-done job on a daily basis.
- Catch your employees doing a good job.

Considerable emphasis was placed on measurable behaviour. Behavioural change was to be observed and reinforced through various forms of rewards: attention, praise and prizes. Reinforcing positive behaviour was a priority. In the earliest phase of the project, during the first year, managers were not 'allowed' to punish those who did not succeed, including employees at any level, operational or managerial. Since it was realized that the project would lead to considerable changes in behaviour in some cases, the first year was designated to be a trial-and-error period. Employees who were not able to adjust during this period were helped to overcome their problems in their current position or were transferred to another position.

'Catch your employees doing a good job' was the slogan which expressed the positive team spirit the bank sought to nurture – and a particularly heavy responsibility was placed on managers.

Slightly simplified, the job levels involved can be summarized as shown in Table 8.5.

In a hierarchical bank organization, this was of course nothing new. Budget and accounts reporting were carried out along the same lines. However, whereas previously the demands from management had been diffuse and ambiguous – and had created uncertainty and insecurity among many of the employees – clear instructions about *what* was expected and *how* it was to be accomplished were now provided. Demands were now made concrete, clear and precise.

Table 8.5 *Job levels involved*

1. Managing Director
2. Regional Bank Manager
3. General Manager – Retail Market
4. Sales Manager
5. Customer Service Representatives
6. Tellers/Support Personnel

Earlier, employees in direct contact with customers had been under considerable pressure to cross-sell. Increasingly, demanding customers had an insatiable appetite for greater flexibility, better service and exceptions from general price lists. This put a higher pressure on the 'back stage' or support personnel who had to juggle conflicting requirements to handle a fluctuating work load and at the same time deliver products and services just-in-time. The internal administrative support teams carried out a good deal of the follow-up work on customer service cases, yet without having direct contact with the customer. The management's cries for increased revenues, effective utilization of resources and higher sales grew even louder. Yet, with the SESAM system, all of these groups could agree on *common* expectations, centred around a core point: the customer.

Formal training

Responsibility for the training of tellers, customer service personnel and support staff (all of whom were employed at the operational level, in all about 500 employees) was allocated to these employees' immediate superior, the sales manager. The sales managers, of whom there were approximately 60, were trained by an external consultant who was also in charge of training 20 bank employees to act as on-the-job instructors. These instructors assisted the sales managers in their training of their personnel. A new position as co-ordinator for the entire programme was established on a contract basis.

The co-ordinator, the outside consultant and the General Manager in charge of the Retail Market division completed an intensive two-week training session in Nashville. It was at this time that the project was 'Norwegianized'. The entire programme was reviewed and scrutinized in great detail, and the two representatives from the bank were in charge of adapting the programme to allow for local Norwegian conditions. The main task of the consultant was to become familiar with the programme and to receive a few pointers on pedagogical matters.

Initially, on-the-job instructors and sales managers completed a five-day course with the consultant, the co-ordinator functioning as his second. At the operational level, a course spanning 2–3 days, depending on the specific employee category, was implemented. It was only at this initial stage that the training took place off site. At later stages all groups had one-day sessions once every six months. These sessions functioned partly as a forum for mutual exchange of information, partly as a corrective to activities which had been put into effect, and partly as an introduction to new activities.

Over time, these sessions assumed various forms. The first gathering, after six months of experience, was characterized by a very optimistic tone. Comments such as 'this is hard work, but it's fun' were indicative of the mood. Immediate results were achieved in the form of surprised and satisfied customers, sales figures moved upwards, and personnel felt more secure and able to face new challenges. New creative measures were carried out at many workplaces in order to increase the level and quality of service. Only a very small minority felt that they could not cope. The sessions were very participant oriented, with role playing being an important ingredient. At the initial sessions, the participants assumed the role of bank customers and visited competing banks. These 'simulation shopping trips' had an enormous pedagogical effect. For the first time, bank employees put themselves in the customer's position. Many actually felt they had received lousy customer service, and on the whole, these generally critical judges gave the competitors low marks. This activity contributed to the establishment of realistic views of competitors. It became evident to employees that there was considerable room for improvement, and that they themselves could make their own workplace come out on the top. The motivation for active participation and acquisition of knowledge and skills was at this point very high.

By the second gathering however, the tune had switched to a minor key. The behavioural change progress had levelled off. It was less exciting to keep on working at improvement. The trainer kept saying, 'We need something new and creative, the battery needs recharging.' The disappointment was considerable when the course instructor's message became clear: that there was a long way to go before the ordinary, everyday things were being done well enough. He reinforced this message by saying, 'It is by doing what we're doing now with fewer mistakes, and with more cheerfulness and greater enthusiasm that we'll get results.' Employees began returning to their 'old' arrogant attitudes from the days when the organization had a near monopoly. Apparently, the level of knowledge was not high enough, and performance could still be greatly improved. Adjusting expectations was a very difficult process.

Weekly meetings

The most important learning process occurred in the local banks and branches. The sales managers were responsible for arranging weekly personnel meetings. These meetings were held in the morning before the bank opened and usually did not last much longer than half an hour. The meetings followed a fixed pattern in one-month periods. Two meetings were designated for service improvement, one meeting for product knowledge, and one for presentation and discussion of sales targets. The cycle was repeated every month. This responsibility was a new challenge for the sales managers, and the quality and results of the meetings varied greatly. Some attempts were made to avoid the meetings on the basis of various practical excuses, but no deviation from the plan was allowed.

The weekly meetings were one of the measures aimed at institutionalizing the learning process, which was an important tool for the transition from project to organization, from experiment to routine. The weekly meetings were always based on local experiences. Employees were encouraged to present good or bad examples of customer service or responses. These examples served as the basis for a discussion of improvements, changes, needs for new system solutions and advertising material. Staff members also participated in preparing meeting agendas, for instance they could take turns being in charge of product presentations.

This learning process was also important for political and ethical reasons. Local learning based on the group's own experience could serve as an important counterbalance to the more centralized and behaviourist learning model on which the project was originally founded. This local learning, which became increasingly significant, led to a 'democratization' of the organizational development which took place, and successful agendas for weekly meetings were exchanged among sales managers.

Product manual

The fact that individual learning and knowledge became visible in formal standard operating procedures was another indication of the transition from learning at the individual level to learning at the organizational level. The product manual was developed in conjunction with, and as an integral part of the SESAM programme. It was written in the language of SESAM, with an emphasis on the PINs and one-liners mentioned earlier.

Another important point was to translate the facts about the product into benefits. As counters and managers of money, bank employees are quite used to facts. However, many products are not sold on the basis of facts, they are sold on the basis of the customer's perceptions of the advantages or benefits inherent in the service or product. The existing manuals primarily contained routine descriptions and facts. *Genuine sales arguments did not exist.*

A separate committee was established, consisting of the users, that is, customer service representatives and tellers, with the respective product managers as co-ordinators. The manual was to be updated regularly, partly because of product development, and partly because employees were to be encouraged to make suggestions for improvements, for example proposals for new, striking one-liners. An example may help to illustrate the method and structure.

Senior Citizen Account PIN

The Senior Citizen Account is a demand deposit account tailored for the customer in the 60 and above age group, and pays a higher rate of interest with no minimum deposit.

Related one-liners

- After you've reached a certain age, we can offer you an account which pays a high rate of interest. There is no charge for holding or using the account.
- If you need a current account which gives you certain advantages in the form of both travel opportunities and financial advisory services, open a Senior Citizen Account.
- With a high, fixed rate of interest, you earn a high yield with no minimum deposit.

PRODUCT FACTS	CUSTOMER BENEFITS
Capital is readily available and there is no charge for either having or using the account.	You save both time and money, since you have access to the account through your free bank card
The account pays a high, fixed interest rate	This gives you a very high yield with no minimum deposit
Each account-holder receives a monthly statement of the status of the account	You are provided with a means of checking the use of the account, as well as an updated overview of the balance
The account is a part of the Bank's senior citizen package	You may receive advice and guidance on all your financial questions, including your tax return

- The Senior Citizen Account is our reward for those of you who have worked hard throughout your life and now wish to enjoy life by travelling and cultivating your various interests.

Cross-Selling

The product manual served as the basis for product knowledge training at the weekly meetings. The mental transformation into thinking in terms of customer benefits was very difficult and time consuming. As illustrated above, it is not always easy to distinguish between product facts and customer benefits.

Furthermore, the orientation towards facts was deeply rooted. Employees tended to imagine that deposit products simply could not be sold if the interest rate was half a percent lower than that of the competitor's. The turn towards benefits had two additional advantages. First, employees became less focused on price. Thus the bank was able to sell more at the same price as the competitors, or the same volume as before at a higher price. This ability constituted a major part of the income potential represented by the investment in the SESAM project.

Secondly, awareness of the advantages of the products increased markedly. Employees suddenly discovered that qualities of the products which they had previously taken for granted (and which were thus 'tacit' or 'invisible') had considerable sales potential.[5] It soon became a popular sport to find new product advantages. Products which had earlier been negatively perceived by personnel in some cases became sources of a new-found pride.

In its first edition, the product manual described 28 products and encompassed approximately 80 pages. Employees were not expected to memorize all the product facts and customer benefits and be able to repeat them on a given signal from the customer, that is, a purely behaviourist logic. The objective was to stimulate and guide the employees in new ways of thinking and selling products, and to provide a foundation for learning and dialogue at the workplace.

Performance evaluation

The bank had virtually no experience in sales and performance evaluation. Measuring performance on the basis of the accounts was of course known, but such evaluations and appraisals were not carried out for each branch office or division. They were thus vague enough that less successful employees could avoid close monitoring and sanctions.

Sales measurement at the individual level, with the reward systems that this implies, was a central element in the American version of the programme. Early on, this part of the package was toned down on the basis of these arguments:

- American business is more individual oriented.
- American motivational theories are frequently based on a conception of the individual as an inherently egoistic and materially oriented being.
- Participation in the project would be motivating in itself. Higher sales would, for example, provide the necessary basis to ensure the survival of more of the existing jobs.
- Measuring individual sales could result in overly aggressive, short-term sales, leading to deterioration of good customer relations. The bank's goal was to develop stable long-term customer relationships.

Employee sentiments were mixed. Many wanted to demonstrate and visualize their own skills and capabilities in a specific way, for example as expressed in sales figures. Others, particularly the more labour union oriented, were sceptical. They partly expressed concern with the assumed 'weak' performers, and partly argued on the basis of their natural right to stick to the main provisions of the National Bank Agreement, in which it was stipulated that individual performance measurements would not occur. Evaluations at the group level were fine, the condition being that nothing could be traced back to the individual employee. This position was contested by the bank's management, however, since the point in question was included under the main section in the National Bank Agreement dealing with electronically based systems. Management therefore claimed that registration using an electronic medium was forbidden, while manual recordings and measurements were allowed.

Many possible avenues to compromises were attempted. One suggestion was that manual measurement of individual employee performance could be carried out at the workplace and that the results could then be collected by the closest line manager, in this context the sales manager. The condition was that the results were not to be accessible to the rest of the organization. Union representatives opposed this suggestion, even though the employees in many divisions found this solution desirable. However, the management was not interested in letting the issue evolve into an open conflict. A project which had otherwise been so positively received was not to be spoiled by an element that management did not consider vital to the success of the project.

Ultimately, the following agreement was reached: each individual employee should manually record his or her own sales figures every week. These were then recorded on a form without specifying who was responsible for each set of figures. The sales manager added the figures together and calculated the division's results plus an average individual result, which each individual staff member used as a measure of his or her own performance.

Each sub-unit's results (or in the new terminology, the results of the single sales office) were then collected centrally and published every month for the entire bank. These figures formed the basis for the selection of a 'Sales Office of the Month'. This recognition consisted of a symbolic sum of money and considerable positive PR in the bank newsletter. Similarly, each year the bank rewarded two prizes of 'Sales Office of the Year' and 'Sales Manager of the Year'. Furthermore, sales offices achieving their sales targets were eligible for membership of the 'Hundred Percent Club', which was restricted to those offices that reached their predetermined sales targets. Thus, virtually all performance measurement took place at the branch office or team level. The only individual reward, 'Sales Manager of the Year', was based on a number of qualitative criteria and was awarded by a committee.

An equally contentious issue was the question of *what* ought to be measured or evaluated. The bank's management ultimately decided the issue, on the advice of the project co-ordinator and the head of the Retail Market division. Ten representative products were chosen, on the basis partly of their measurability, partly of their importance to the bank. The product selection was also designed to grant all bank offices equal opportunities to reach the targets. (Too much priority on deposits, for example, would put the offices which primarily sold loans at a disadvantage.)

The development of sales targets and subsequent rewards undoubtedly had an effect on sales. This was not a function of the material goods accruing to the winners of competitions. The positive recognition, the chance to be the centre of the new rituals and the internal competition between similar offices were the essential elements. A sales office could, for example, aim to be better than other offices of the same size or others operating in the same market.

During the first year, the level of fixed sales targets was determined locally, without any particular influence or help from the bank's headquarters. This, naturally, led to certain instances of tactical budgeting. During the course of the year, however, this became a somewhat awkward and embarrassing matter, as a couple of offices were constantly being named sales office of the month even though their results were mediocre. In the subsequent year, this practice was changed. Each individual sales office presented its target figures to the regional administration, which co-ordinated the figures for that region. At the next step, the five regions were co-ordinated by the bank's headquarters. A number of key figures were set up as guidelines; for example, it was considered reasonable to expect that an equal percentage of a bank's salary account customers used a cash card. In several areas such 'objective' criteria were used.

It had thus taken the bank two years to establish a simple system for performance measurement that most employees and interest groups could accept. A crucial cultural barrier had been overcome, but in such a way that the new system could be integrated into the established culture without directly challenging it.

Removal of sales barriers

Removal of existing sales barriers was an essential step in the process of securing the project's position within the organization. Many such barriers had been identified through the establishment of special 'sales barrier teams'. These teams included personnel from different professional and geographical areas (the bank's five regions). Employees were asked to report sales barriers to their representative in the barrier team. The sales barrier teams reported directly to the manager in charge of the Retail Market division, who also at times participated in the team meetings. A number of problems could be solved relatively quickly, for example the preparation of new forms and sales materials, establishing direct access to key personnel, as well as minor adjustments of prices and fees.

Two problem areas became evident almost immediately. First, setting up a structure parallel to the established organization structure and authority system was immensely difficult. It turned out that the necessary flexibility was not present in the existing organizational structures. Certain staff managers, in particular, were concerned that a new element or level in the structure could alter the priorities of personnel. Part of this problem was a function of the SESAM project itself, since it had not included central staff administration. Consequently, these central managers did not participate in the work to develop new ways of thinking, or in the efforts to adopt the new tools and attitudes which were diffused among the sales managers and customer service personnel.

The second difficulty facing the sales barrier teams was the more or less permanent problems with the established computer systems. These were primarily administrative systems emphasizing accounting and control functions. They were, briefly expressed, useless as sales tools. The bank was dependent on Fellesdata, the Norwegian savings banks' common computer and information centre, for system changes. Gradually, positive attitudes developed at Fellesdata, but the systems used were hopelessly rigid and unchangeable. Changes of any magnitude in Fellesdata normally required agreement from several leading banks. Such consensus was in practice impossible to achieve, as SR-Bank was alone in its organizational development programme.

In some parts of the bank, a number of individual personal computers were deployed to compensate for some of the above problems. However, any large-scale use of such arrangements created new problems, as it could not in any case be integrated into existing systems. For example, communication with the bank's customer database was a serious obstacle to both retrieving, saving and updating of data. After two years the management had to admit, with considerable regret, that the uphill battle was too wearing, and the sales barrier teams were dissolved. Even though this decision caused a certain amount of regret, there were no real lasting negative effects. The process had been initiated, but the proposals for change had to be incorporated into the priorities in the regular way. It took longer to reach solutions, but the advantage was nevertheless that various proposals could be considered in a wider organizational context. The most eager employees worked through their managers to remove bottlenecks.

Summary

With our starting point in the problem areas identified in Tables 8.3 and 8.4, the SESAM project and the way in which it was implemented can be summarized as in Table 8.6.

Large projects aiming at profound organizational changes are time consuming. They require immense patience and drive, as well as consistent action. A number of employees in the bank probably believed that the SESAM project was just another training activity. They are likely to have based their behaviour on this belief as well, thinking, 'It's best to keep a low profile and wait until the storm blows over.' Lasting, visible support from the Managing Director was at times crucial for the project's continued progress. The most recalcitrant bank employees were the Managing Director's closest subordinates, the regional bank

Table 8.6 *Summary of problem areas and measures taken*

Problem	Solution	Measures
The employee does not know *what* is expected	Define the task	a) Winning plays b) Job descriptions c) Manager's expectations
The employee does not know *how* to meet expectations	Training	a) SESAM training b) Weekly meetings c) Follow-up seminars d) On-the-job training e) Product manual f) Product meetings
The employee does not *want* to meet expectations	Motivation	a) Performance evaluation b) Rewards c) Recognition d) Sales competitions e) Removal of sales barriers
The employee *cannot* meet expectations	Selection/placement	a) Job descriptions b) Hiring guidelines c) Recruitment d) Transfer
The employee doesn't understand *why* expectations should be met	Explanations	a) Strategic plan b) Commitment of Managing Director c) Financial results d) Securing job

managers. These managers were in charge of both corporate and retail market sections in their regional banks. Deep-seated beliefs that the retail market 'created itself' and that working with corporate customers provided higher status contributed to an attitude of ambivalence. On several occasions the Managing Director had to intervene and specify concretely the expectations *he* had for them.

The project was supported wholeheartedly by all of those who were directly involved. This was primarily the case because the employees were given practical tools to assist them in carrying out their everyday tasks. For the more reflective managers the project seemed in some ways trivial at the start. However, everyone was impressed by the way the project was able to address the problem as a whole, by using a multitude of different measures as summarized in Table 8.6.

What had originally started out as a typical behaviouristic programme was gradually transformed into active learning processes based on the participants' own experiences and co-operative potential.

Within a common framework a great deal of local creativity was unleashed. Precisely because local managers and their personnel now had a set of general tools, a large number of specific activities, aimed at local markets, could be initiated. A proposal, initially adopted at the central level, paved the way for a blossoming of decentralized decisions and actions.

Themes/issues to consider

The main organizational issues addressed in the SR-Bank case are the following:

1. Environmental change and the firm's strategic response.
2. Organizational changes resulting from strategic shifts and human resource realignment.
3. Organizational learning and the creation of pervasive learning.

Each of the three issues will now be briefly presented.

Environmental change and strategic response

Within the organizational behaviour literature applying the open system perspective, emphasis is put on the capability of organizations to adjust to altered conditions in their external environment. When external environments are transformed from being predominantly stable to being unstable and hence less predictable, the organizations affected have to be redesigned so as to fit better the demands posed by the changed environment. Similarly, according to the strategic management literature, the strategy has to be reformulated when major environmental changes occur. In the case it was demonstrated how the bank was forced to accomplish a radical strategic re-orientation caused by external developments. Yet a paramount problem concerning rapid environmental change concerns how to alter the human resources of the firm to fit the new situation better (see Lengnick-Hall and Lengnick-Hall, 1988 and 1990). This leads us to the second key issue.

Strategic shift and human resource realignment

Any organization that wants to stay competitive and survive must ensure some minimum alignment of its overall business strategy and the competencies held by its employees and teams.

In those instances where the business strategy remains virtually unaltered or is only marginally revised, the needs for competence resources will normally be incrementally adjusted and changes can be relatively easily brought about. The really serious challenge to human resource development and rapid learning in the organization emerges when the overall strategy is shifted or radically changed. It is then often necessary to alter substantially the firm's competence base as well as the configuration of competencies (see Nordhaug, 1994). Expressed differently, the problems of realigning the competence base and the organizational design with the new strategy are crucial during such transformation processes.

Creation of pervasive learning

The challenge of aligning the competence base with a profoundly altered strategy cannot be met without pervasive learning among the firm's employees and teams. Since incremental adjustments are in this context clearly insufficient, the organization is confronted with a need to carry out a comprehensive learning project which extends far beyond the traditional formal personnel training. The learning project has to include substantial informal elements and, not least, elements aimed at generating the necessary motivation for change among employees. In summary, one can say that both relevant technical competencies fit to cope with the new competitive situation and motivation to unlearn and learn are necessary to secure a successful turnaround.

Owing to the emphasis on informal elements, such learning projects are very difficult to plan and not in any case easy to carry out. In the case, it was shown how the management of the bank was forced to make adjustments along the way in order to try to make the project compatible with the realities as they emerged. Naturally, the actual development of realities could not be rationally calculated in advance, and consequently a hands-on approach involving a close scrutiny of the learning process was required.

At the same time, management had chosen to apply a formal training programme originally developed in the USA. Initially this proved to be problematic because of cultural differences regarding work life in two dissimilar countries. The issue of inter-cultural differences and their consequences for cross-cultural adaptation of human resource development programmes was thus highlighted. In a broader sense, this addresses the question of imports of foreign management practices and methods, which are necessarily coloured by the cultural norms and values in the country of origin (see Grønhaug and Nordhaug, 1993).

Assignments

1. Evaluation of the project As Personnel Director of the bank, you are asked by the top manager to propose a way of evaluating the effects of the SESAM project in a systematic manner. Although there is a common view in the bank that the project has been quite successful, the board has demanded a well-documented and thorough analysis of the project. Your assignment is then to suggest:

- a way of carrying out the evaluation, including a careful consideration of the information that is actually needed; and
- methods to be applied and the validity and reliability of the results of the evaluation.

2. Rewards and incentives

- Discuss whether the bank could have used economic incentives and rewards more actively in order to increase the sales of credits more effectively.
- Explain which types of incentives should have been used in your opinion as well as how a tailored reward system should have been designed.

3. Gaining top management commitment Discuss courses of action that can be taken by higher-level managers who want to obtain top management support and commitment to an organizational development programme, and what these managers consider vital for aligning the organization and its competence base with a radically changed strategy involving a shift from internal to external focus.

4. Cultural compatibility of the programme The SESAM programme was modified on the basis of a belief that it was not fully compatible with the culture of Norwegian work life. Discuss the degree to which the programme could be adapted to a selected bank in your own country and, if necessary, outline which adjustments should then be done to make the programme more compatible with local conditions.

5. Alternative options The bank chose to implement the SESAM programme in order to accomplish realignment of its competence base to the new strategy. However, an important question relates to what else the bank could have done to promote such a realignment. Suggest and discuss at least two alternative ways that could have been considered from the wide range of organizational and human resource management measures which can be applied to promote this type of realignment.

6. Future development: scenario A Two years after the completion of the SESAM project, the bank starts to incur heavy losses on its loans. Although this is at the time fairly commonplace among Norwegian banks, it is nevertheless quite serious for the future of the bank. An internal analysis of the problem concludes that the bank has been overselling credits and that much of the losses stems from poor financial judgement by employees, partly caused by the fact that lower-level employees were granted generous margins of freedom to make loans to customers owing to the considerable decentralization of lending authority.

You are an external consultant who has been hired by the bank's top manager, and the assignment you have to carry out is formulated in this manner:

- Suggest changes that will reduce the current overselling of credits and strengthen the average level of financial judgements made by employees, while concurrently not reducing the market sensitivity and responsiveness developed in the bank.
- Delineate how the changes are to be implemented, in what sequence they should be initiated, and what the timetable for the changes ought to look like.

7. Future development: scenario B Two years after the completion of the SESAM project, the bank is doing very well financially, and the top management and the Board are looking for new areas of business expansion. Ideally, they would prefer to diversify by entering the insurance industry. This is, however, not possible since Norwegian law prohibits the establishment of combined banking and insurance companies. Yet, one of the Board members proposes that the bank considers co-operating with a recently established retail insurance company which has just started to build a comprehensive branch network.

'We possess such a network in large parts of Southern Norway, and there must be some time slack among the employees', the Board member, Mr Brightidea, argues. 'Why not sell personal insurance in our branch offices? We could make a good profit and the insurance company does not have to create a costly sales network in this part of the country. If this is not an excellent win–win game, I'll eat my oldest hat.'

After checking out that merely selling insurance was within the legal limits, the bank and the insurance company agreed to go ahead with the co-operative project.

In the capacity of personnel director you are asked to do the following:

- Conduct an analysis of requirements for additional human resource development that emanate from the co-operative insurance sales venture.
- Suggest a programme that can fill these needs. In particular, you should take into consideration the knowledge and skills that have to be

developed in order for the bank's branch offices to be capable of handling the new sales challenge and plan how these competencies are to be generated.

- Consider possible organizational changes that can serve to facilitate the daily operations within the new business area without harming the ordinary business of the bank.

Suggested reading

Grønhaug, K. and Nordhaug, O. (1993) 'Strategy and competence in firms', *European Management Journal*, 4: 438–44. The article discusses the relationship between competencies and strategies in firms. It is argued that the competencies of firms are normally their most basic resource and, as the opportunities for winning on technological leadership are diminishing, a firm's capacity to develop and utilize its competencies are vital to its competitive position. Changes in strategy and competencies are highlighted and the concept of competence-propelled strategy is launched and delineated.

Lengnick-Hall, C.A. and Lengnick-Hall, M.L. (1988) 'Strategic human resources management: A review of the literature and a proposed typology', *Academy of Management Review*, 13: 454–70. The authors argue that past efforts to relate human resource management to the business strategies of firms have taken three approaches: matching managerial style or personnel activities with strategies, forecasting manpower requirements stemming from certain strategic objectives or environmental conditions, and presenting means for integrating human resource management into the overall efforts to match strategy and organizational structure. A typology is elaborated that posits a reciprocal dependency relationship between a firm's business strategy and its human resources strategy.

Lengnick-Hall, C.A. and Lengnick-Hall, M.L. (1990) *Interactive Human Resource Management and Strategic Planning*. New York: Quorum Books. The authors first explain the rationale for strategic human resource management and outline the potential benefits and costs of such management. Then they provide an overview of fundamental concepts in strategic management and highlight how strategies and human resource management practices can be integrated. A contingency approach is suggested based on the firm's growth expectations and readiness to achieve the chosen strategic objectives. Finally, a step-by-step process for strategic human resource management is presented.

Naugle, D.G. and Davies, G.A. (1987) 'Strategic-skill pools and competitive advantage', *Business Horizon*, 30: 35–42. In this article, it is contended that most corporate planning systems tend to view the firm as merely a collection of strategic business units, while the corporation's major strengths, the skills and abilities developed to support existing businesses, are often ignored. It is also argued that these strategic-skill pools may provide the resources necessary to reorganize competitive relationships within an existing business and can supply the foundations on which a new competitive business can be built.

Nordhaug, O. (1991) 'Human resource provision and transformation: The role of training and development', *Human Resource Management Journal*, 1: 17–27. It is argued in this article that the traditional individual-level evaluations of personnel training and development are clearly insufficient given the intentions to generate organizational effects. The author then goes on to discuss the role of training in solving the two fundamental problems of providing human resources in organizations and transforming these resources into work performance. As a part of this discussion, concrete effects are outlined.

Nordhaug, O. (1994) *Human Capital in Organisations*. New York: Oxford University Press.The book outlines and discusses conceptual, theoretical and empirical aspects of human capital and human capital formation in organizations. It emphasizes work-related competencies, personnel training and learning in firms. The presentation is multi-disciplinary, drawing on insights from economic theory, organization theory, and the literature on strategic management and human resource management.

Schuler, R.S. and Jackson, S.E. (1987) 'Linking competitive strategies with human resource management practices', *Academy of Management Executive*, 1: 207–19. The authors demonstrate how different strategies in business firms require different human resource management practices. First, the nature and importance of competitive strategy are reviewed. Second, the concept of necessary role behaviour, intended to bridge competitive strategies and human resource management practices, is delineated. The article builds on the distinction between innovation, quality-enhancement and cost-reduction strategies, and discusses the choice of related human resource management practices.

Notes

The authors are indebted to Professor Françoise Chevalier and Professor Michaël Segalla of Groupe HEC, and Professor Knut Ims of the Norwegian School of Economics and Business Administration for their constructive and invaluable comments on earlier drafts of the case study. However useful their comments, none of them bears any responsibility for shortcomings in the study.

1. In 1987, 3000 bank employees were asked why they did not cross-sell. An overwhelming majority of 85% reported that they were afraid of looking foolish through insufficient knowledge regarding the facts, advantages and sales arguments for the products and services. Preparing bank employees for selling by strengthening their actual competence in this field can hence be regarded as a necessary step in motivating them to want to sell.
2. PBM is the Norwegian acronym for *Problem, Behov og Muligheter*, 'problems, needs and opportunities'. The rationale is that the customer comes to the bank with a problem which may be transformed into a need, and this represents an opportunity for the bank.
3. PIN is an acronym for *Produkt I Et Nøtteskall*, 'the product in a nutshell', and signifies a simple definition of the product encompassing a maximum of 25 words. PINs should be written so that the average customer can understand them. 'One-liners' are short phrases which translate the facts about a product into an advantage for the customer. They thus respond to the question 'What can it do for me?'
4. Sales managers are the immediate superiors of customer service representatives and tellers, and were assigned their own winning plays.
5. This has been documented in several studies (for example Geert Hofstede (1983) 'The cultural relativity of organisational practices and theories', *Journal of International Business Studies*, pp. 75–89.

9

Rodeby School

The successful organization of professionals

Jan Löwstedt

In Sweden, as in many other countries, the school system employs more people than most other sectors in the economy. Until recently, however, school management has been a neglected area. Now a major reform has been introduced whereby the highly centralized public (state) school system has been decentralized into a system where the local governments of municipalities are given responsibility for how schools are to be organized. This creates both stress and considerable opportunities for those who are in charge of a school.

This case is the story of a school that has gone through dramatic changes: from a school with a bad reputation to national recognition as a good example for others to follow. Nevertheless, the future of the school is subject to a severe threat. The municipal administration is launching a new organization for the management of primary schools.

The focal point in the case is the management team of the school. They have to design a new organization in an ambiguous situation when both internal and external affairs are concerned. The case also introduces questions about how to manage and develop professionals, and how to analyse efficiency and effectiveness in organizations where the organizational goals are ambiguous. The case includes international comparative data from a study of successful schools in Sweden, Denmark and California, USA.

Cultural context

Mass education began in Sweden 150 years ago, when compulsory schooling for everyone was introduced. Individuals were obliged to obtain basic education by attending school for a certain number of years. The first task was to learn how to read and absorb a certain amount of religious instruction. At the time there were not the impetus, opportunities or resources for the majority of the population to obtain this knowledge on their own. The importance of education for a child's development under these circumstances can not be overestimated.

At that time, in the mid-nineteenth century, Sweden was a poor undeveloped country where more than 90% of the population lived in rural areas. More than 1 million people, approximately 20% of the population, had emigrated, mainly to the USA between 1865 and 1914. During the last 100 years, however, the country has industrialized and become one of the wealthier nations in the world. This partly can be explained by the fact that it has not been involved in any war during this time. Other often suggested explanations for this dramatic growth, second only to Japan in the first 70 years of the twentieth century, are the early development of institutions important for the development of a modern welfare state, such as a stable credit and banking system and an educational system serving all people, not only a few.

Consensus, participation, industrial democracy and a highly developed public sector. These, and similar characteristics, are often used to describe work life in Sweden. They are also central elements in what is often referred to as the Swedish model, a model which until only recently has been considered by many as a good example of a capitalist welfare state. A long period of stable socio-democratic government, strong unions and a highly centralized negotiation system where salaries and working conditions could be agreed, are also main ingredients of the model. The model originates from the 'historic compromise' which was reached between unions and the employers' federation in 1938, an agreement which ended worker–employer hostilities and paved the way for the economic growth of the construction of the welfare state.

Since the 1980s the Swedish model has been in transition, from a centralized to a more decentralized one. The policy of equal pay and lowered wage differentials, a cornerstone of the model, has been questioned as well. This can be explained by the deregulation of financial markets and the new policy of the employers' federation not to engage in central agreements, but to support its member companies in local negotiations. The trend towards decentralization and privatization has been strong in the public sector since the four conservative parties came to power in 1991. As a result of economic necessities this transformation of the public sector will continue after the comeback of the Social Democratic party to office in the autumn of 1994.

Schools are in many ways an essential part of society. The compulsory nine-year schools are a workplace for nearly 1 million of Sweden's 8.5 million residents. There were 881,523 students during the 1990–91 school year. These students were taught by 93,420 teachers, which accounts for just over 2% of Sweden's workforce (Ministry of Education and Science, 1992).

Schools take on a different role as society begins to change. Many new responsibilities have been incorporated into the Swedish school system. Societal goals and the students' smooth adjustment into social and work life have taken on a greater importance. Urbanization and the development of isolated housing areas where individuals must commute to jobs and family have created a situation in which schools adopt the role of surrogate parent by caring for neighbourhood children while their parents are working. This is the case not only literally where schools are integrated with after-school activities provided by the community, but also the increased responsibility taken by the school in providing the pupils with a school doctor, dentist, nourishing lunches etc. In addition, the schools are becoming a political instrument with the expressed goal of creating a 'better' society.

The educational system

School starts for the overwhelming majority of children in Sweden in the autumn of the year they are seven. Prior to that a majority have participated in daycare and pre-school activities organized by the municipality, none of them compulsory. After the nine years of comprehensive school pupils are entitled, at the age of 16 but dependent on grades, to a place in the Gymnasium, which holds more than 100 different three-year programmes, from vocational training to theoretical programmes preparing the student for university. Until recently all but a few per cent of comprehensive schools have been municipal schools. Therefore it could be said that more or less all Swedes have experienced the same type of schools during their first nine years of schooling.

This very homogeneous school system has given the government and the Department of Education a major role in forming educational policies and practices. Since 1991 when a conservative coalition came to power in Sweden, the public sector has been in a state of a major transformation. Privatization and decentralization has been the *leitmotif*. State-owned companies have been sold to the public and the healthcare system has been decentralized and partly privatized. The comprehensive school system is one of the areas on which the conservative government decided to set its seal before the next election. An increased freedom for students to choose schools has been introduced with a school-cheque system. Teachers are today employed and paid by the municipality, but were until the end of the 1980s paid by the government. Schools are given increased opportunities locally to form their curriculum and the school organization. They are also given more control of their budget. Correspondingly there is increased attention to leadership and the role of the principal in the school and traditional management tools are imported into the system. However, programmes for the improvement of quality and efficiency are generally connected to the management and organization of a business rather than an educational institution. School management has been generally discussed in terms of pedagogy, time allocation of various subjects, the grading system, the educators' competence and working methods. Schools are now confronting requests to be run according to a business-like rationale.

Clearly the years that a child spends in school are of enormous importance with regard to that child's personal development, not only cognitive but emotional and social development as well. It is difficult in today's society, if not impossible, to discuss the specific meaning that school has for the individual child. Children absorb knowledge in a variety of ways, especially today when the mass media and society in general offer such a breadth of information. Many children are quite active socially and have already gained broad social and cultural experience from recreational clubs, music, theatre and travel, etc.

Education research does show ambiguous results regarding the importance of school in relation to students' level of knowledge and proficiency. Studies done during the 1970s (Coleman, 1966; Jencks, 1972) showed that students' social background and indigenous talent played the greatest part in their scholastic performance. Even when schools were compared, students' home environments were still seen as an explanation of individual variations in absorbing knowledge. Later research has shown that the individual's school situation also plays a significant role, although the home situation is still regarded as the most important single factor. These two principal approaches in education research are reflected in widely differing attitudes to school. There is tangible competition between the goals of knowledge and proficiency on one hand and those of socialization on the other hand.

A school's long-term goals are complex, if not confusing, and therefore difficult to evaluate when it's job is no longer simply to teach but also to be responsible for the socialization of its students. Therefore schools must be considered as operating under dual goals: social as well as cognitive goals for child development.

Evaluation of comprehensive schools has traditionally been aimed only at their goals for student knowledge and proficiency. Standardized tests have been developed in order to test students' level of knowledge fairly. The resulting marks or grades can also be regarded as a system for judging quality. It can, however, be stated that such conclusions are not an essential part of the financiers' plan for the organization. The established tradition of follow-up and evaluation is based on a quality control system of regularly testing students' knowledge at specific ages. The fact that the evaluations only reflect a portion of the educational goals implies that the importance of checking knowledge as a factor in the governing of the institution is reduced.

The organization of compulsory schools

In Swedish schools, classes are organized according to two different principles and pupils meet teachers in four categories. When students are aged 7 to 9, they are taught by a 'class teacher' in all subjects. After their first three years they move up to what is considered the middle school (*mellan stadium*), where they meet a new class teacher with somewhat different training. At the secondary level – from 13 to 16 – students are taught by teachers specialized in two or three particular subjects. The fourth category of teachers are handicraft instructors and teachers of art, music and athletics. During the first six years of study, however, athletics, music and art are mainly taught by the class teacher.

There are some major educational differences between teachers at primary and secondary level. They belong to different unions and have different kinds of education. Teachers at the primary level are trained for two and a half or three years at university colleges specialized in child development and didactics. Teachers working at the secondary level usually hold a university degree in their subjects, for example mathematics and chemistry, and have a one-year training in methodology. Over a 15-year period salaries for the two groups have been equalized. It is a widespread opinion among secondary-level teachers that their group was the loser during the second half of the 1980s. Both salaries and status are lower than they used to be, and at the same time the workload has increased. During this period there has also been a reform which aimed to bring education and the two categories of teachers closer to each other.

The social dimension has grown in importance, however. Until the beginning of the 1970s, students at secondary level were grouped into classes according to interests. There were classes for those preparing for continued theoretical education and other classes more directed towards vocational training. This is no longer the case, as even at secondary level students remain in the classes they have been in since they first started school.

The students' week is divided into blocks of time which correspond to particular subjects, such as language, technical, or practical and aesthetic subjects. The student is partly free to choose which subject he or she will study. There is no freedom of choice in the curriculum until the pupil reaches the secondary level. There are no different tracks where pupils can chose degrees of complexities in a subject until they reach secondary school. There they can chose between two tracks in mathematics, English and other languages if desired.

Professional teachers working in secondary schools are usually organized into two groupings, based on the type of subject and on students taught, for example class groups. This kind of organizational division can in organizational theory terms be said to facilitate a 'product organization' (the students and class groupings) and a 'functional organization' (the subject areas) respectively. Swedish national teaching plans have until recently stressed the second grouping and call such groups working units. Such a group is led by a co-ordinator (WUC) who has specific responsibilities for co-ordinating the course plan. Teachers are also grouped according to different subjects such as language, science, civic and practical-aesthetic areas. Within these groups one teacher is normally responsible for maintaining an overview of the development of each subject and subject area.

The priority given to the work units has been argued to be of importance to the opportunities to follow students' development, organize class instruction plans and co-ordinate the teaching of all the different subjects and encourage group organization. The creation of teaching teams is one part of overall decentralization, but it also helps to balance the work load for each individual instructor. Teachers within a 'team' are responsible for carrying out their fellow teachers' work if need be. Teamwork facilitates the possibility of local development of the organization and the need for outside control is reduced. This type of group organization makes it easier for each teacher's particular knowledge to be utilized and properly communicated to others. At the same time, less experienced teachers can absorb the knowledge and practical experience of other educators. The advantages of teamwork have been recognized in other industries for quite some time. However, the system has met with some resistance in Swedish schools.

Rodeby School

Rodeby is a small community with just over 3000 residents. It is located 20 km from Karlskrona, a town known for its harbour industry and military associations. The community is the administrative centre for the neighbouring inhabitants who are mainly occupied in forestry and agriculture. Rodeby School's district has a population of 10,000 residents; 90% live in small houses and 70% of the children live in neighbouring villages and therefore need to travel to school by school bus.

Rodeby School and its 900 students constitute one of Sweden's largest comprehensive schools. The school encompasses both primary and secondary levels. At the secondary level there are six parallel classes, 497 students, 89 teachers and 20 staff members.

The oldest section of the school was built in 1948, but most sections date from the early 1970s. The secondary level is located in some of the more recently built sections of the school. Overcrowding has resulted in classes being held in various nearby buildings, for example a building belonging to a local church. Not all of the neighbouring buildings are used specifically for classroom teaching, even though they are utilized mostly by students from the school. A community library, gym, recreation centre, indoor and outdoor swimming pools, ski slope and access to track and field activities are all available in the immediate environment of the school.

Rodeby School had significant problems during the early 1980s. The general atmosphere was uneasy and the student body's grade average was below the national average. The school had a bad reputation for student problems and widespread disorder. There were also difficulties with the physical environment. The buildings had been run down since the early 1970s; there was a problem with mould and damp and the entire building was in need of renovation. An overall renovation was financed and took place from 1985 to 1987, and was the signal for a broad overhaul of the complete organization.

The school's grade average has also risen from below the national average to slightly above it. The social climate of the school has been deemed exceptionally good by national experts, perhaps one of Sweden's best. The school has also enjoyed great success in athletic competitions. What has been done at the school to accomplish this successful development?

Every possible opportunity is taken at Rodeby to influence positively the public's image of the school. The school is in regular contact with the local papers and aims to have at least one positive article per month published about itself. This has been school policy for the last five or six years – since the school buildings were renovated. The majority of the articles report on sports events, student participation in contests, special activities and the like. Rodeby School's sister-school programme with schools in the Baltic area, including exchange of teachers and students, has also been of interest to the newspapers. The school has other imaginative projects such as its co-operative work project with companies from the region, within the context of work-experience activities. The project aims to improve students' attitude to industrial work. The school publishes an annual catalogue for students of various activities and opportunities available from the local community. Parents and students are kept actively informed regarding relevant information such as the teachers' weekly and yearly teaching schedule.

Rodeby School is known for its pleasant and courteous student atmosphere. The teachers seem to be able to spend the majority of their time in classroom teaching. The school took advantage of the physical renovation also to improve the general working environment both for teachers and students. For example, most of the interiors were painted white, which creates a much lighter environment but also allows graffiti to be visible and simpler to deal with immediately.

The students are involved, as a part of their art and workshop classes, in the interior design of the school. The design process is constantly changing as one class graduates and a new group takes over the classrooms.

There are a number of projects concerning increased student influence on their surroundings. One example was an exhibition outside the dining hall displaying the results of the latest evaluation of the school. Teaching was adjourned for half a day to allow for discussion and written documentation of students' opinions and suggestions. One much-mentioned suggestion was a desire to 'do more experiment-oriented work' in several subjects.

The school has a very active sports organization. The club provides the means for friends and family of students who participate in different events to follow along and form a 'cheering section'. The club arranges theatrical events and an annual Christmas party which is open to students' families.

The school's general policy is to create a positive working atmosphere for all concerned by having a specific routine for discussion of problems, questions or new ideas. A relatively simple matter, such as who is in charge of keeping the classroom environment well organized, is solved by assigning one teacher to every room. Problems or dissatisfaction that occur between parent/student and teacher are handled according to a specific plan. The situation is first discussed between student and teacher in the classroom. If a solution cannot be found at that stage then the form teacher is called in as a negotiator. The next stage is to involve the parents and the principal.

Organization

The school is managed by a Principal and two Vice-Principals. The Vice-Principals are responsible for the primary and secondary level respectively. They also have a smaller teaching load which is equivalent to 15–20% of a teacher's weekly load. Kerstin Mattsson, the Principal, and the two Vice-Principals, Anita Hjelm and Lars Johansson, constitute together the management team of the school. The two Vice-Principals are responsible for timetable planning and for the work in the work units, especially matters concerning the social functioning and health of pupils. The Principal is the representative at the school for the employer and is therefore involved in hiring, developing or firing teachers and other personnel and also represents the school in various situations. Since the Principal at Rodeby School, before being appointed to the post, led the renovation programme where both the physical and the psychological climate at the school was dramtically improved, she is heavily engaged and interested in contacts with pupils to maintain what has been accomplished.

Altogether there are 85 teachers employed at Rodeby School; 32 of them only work with pupils at the secondary level (grade 7 to 9/age 13 to 15). These teachers teach two to three subjects in three to five different classes. Normally there is a form master/mistress for one class of approxiomately 25 pupils. Practical or aesthetic subjects are taught by 24 teachers who work at both primary and secondary level (grade 2 to 9/age 8 to 15). The rest of the teachers are class teachers for the primary level (grade 1 to 6/age 7 to 12). The last group of 29 teachers is divided into three work units, one for grade 1 to 3 (Lågstadiet, age 7 to 9) and one for grade 4 to 6 (Mellenstadiet, age 10 to 12). A small school (Flymen) in the countryside some 10 km from Rodeby forms the third work unit. Because of the few pupils in the school the work unit consists of the teachers for pupils in grade 1 to 6 (age 7 to 12). Class teachers at the primary level teach most subjects to their class. The exception could be such subjects as art, woodcraft, music or athletics. Owing to the special needs of some pupils, class teachers at the primary level are to some degree assisted by teachers specialized in pedagogics for these children.

At the secondary level (age 13 to 15) the pupils are taught by teachers specializing in two or three subjects each. The teachers of six classes, two from each grade, form a work unit (Figure 9.1). This means that a pupil in the seventh grade typically has one teacher in mathematics and science, one in social science, one in Swedish, one in English, one in music and one in athletics. This amounts to six teachers in the compulsory programme. To give a complete picture, teachers in electives must be added (foreign languages, technology, etc). A pupil therefore has approximately seven or eight teachers during a week. Pupils from Rodeby town belong to one work unit, the other two consist of pupils from villages surrounding Rodeby. The organizing principle behind this is that adminstratively it is easier to keep commuting pupils together, but it is also in order to keep classes formed at the primary level intact at the secondary level.

The work units are co-ordinated by one of the teachers in the group. These co-ordinators meet regularly with the management team. Together they form what sometimes is referred to as the 'extended management group' of the school. These work unit co-ordinators (WUCs) do not, however, consider themselves to have a managerial role, but more as representatives for their fellow teachers than an integrated part of management function in the school. They describe their role as 'to co-ordinate and take some administrative responsibilities for the work unit'. A unit meets regularly once a week in 90-minute meetings. These co-

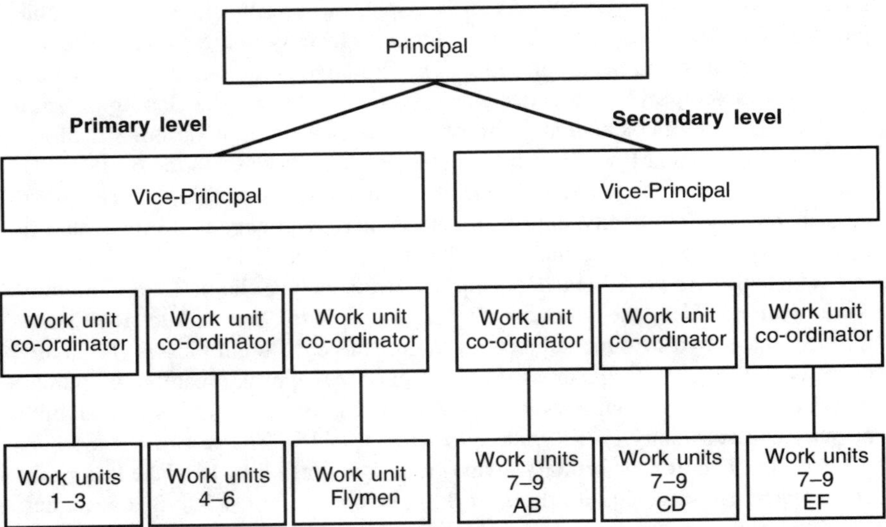

Figure 9.1 *Rodeby School organization*

ordinators have a four-hour per week reduced teaching load for this assignment. A teacher at the primary level and teachers in practical and aesthetic subjects teach 26 classroom hours per week full-time. The equivalent for subject area teachers at the secondary level is 24 hours. The latter group of teachers is also organized in subject area groups, which meet occasionally and also have co-ordinators. They have a one-hour per week reduction of their teaching load. There are 17 subject area co-ordinators (SACs) at the school because 17 subjects are taught at Rodeby. In reality subjects are co-ordinated in six subject areas; science, social science, languages, mathematics, technology and aesthetics.

A new management organization for schools in Karlskrona

As a response to decisions taken in the Swedish Parliament in 1989 and thereafter, the school board and the school administration in Karlskrona are planning for changes in the overall organization of schools in the community. These decisions have decentralized all the responsibilities for how schools are organized from central authorities to local governments and their school boards. One of the main problems with which this reform tries to deal is that Principals generally work as administrators and not the pedagogical leaders they are desired to be. The administrative role of the Principal is a result of the highly centralized national school system where their task was to administrate the school organization according to its intention. A new, more decentralized school organization requires management which is more independent of central authorities, but at the same time capable of and willing to integrate school operations with complementary local public sector activities, such as daycare centres and other social arrangements.

The explicit goal for the reform of the school management organization in Karlskrona was stated by the school board in an official report from the Central School Administration as:

> to create a more efficient school management with clarified and more downright assignments and managerial personnel at every school. This new organization should be formed under the influence of acting principals. (New Management Organization for the Primary and Secondary School in Karlskrona, March 1991)

This formulation was more or less literally taken from a Bill to Parliament presented by the Minister of Education.

Until 1992 there were eight major schools in Karlskrona, all including both primary and secondary levels (Figure 9.2). The organizing principle was that every secondary school was led by a Principal and that one or more primary schools belonged to the school. Only Rodeby School had both levels in the same buildings. These eight schools were governed by the Central School Administration (CSA), led by a school director and a school board. The board consisted of people appointed by the local government. The CSA could be considered to fulfil both administrative and personnel function for all the schools in the community: it hired and fired teachers and other personnel, administered salaries and negotiated with the unions, they were responsible for school

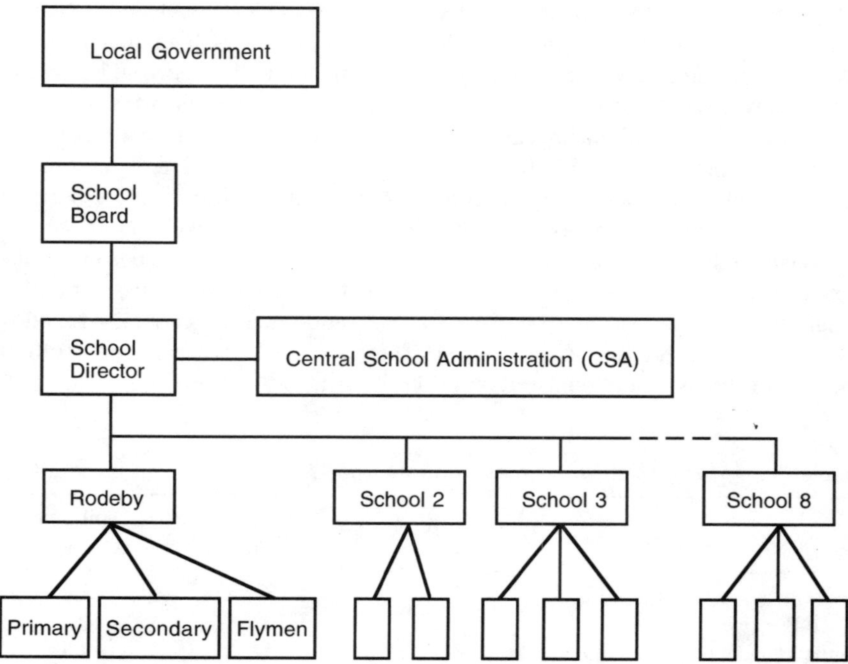

Figure 9.2 *School organization in Karlskrona before 1992*

buildings, carried out investigations and took initiatives for development activities for both schools, their Principals and personnel.

A new plan for the organization of schools and their management was to be implemented in the beginning of 1993. The CSA had during the first years of the 1990s devoted considerable resources to investigating different alternative management organizations for Karlskrona. To improve pedagogical leadership in schools' day-to-day affairs, the idea was to increase the number of Principals from 8 to somewhere between 18 and 25. The guiding principle was one Principal in every school, primary schools included. The planned reform also suggested decentralizing administrative and personnel functions from CSA to schools or school districts. This raised questions of how to organize management as a whole in Karlskrona. The restriction, however, was that the new management organization had to be launched within the existing budget. Resources for the existing management organization are presented in Table 9.1.

It was the opinion of the school board and the CSA that resources needed for the increase in the number of Principals should be taken from the Vice-Principals and Superintendent. Since every school was to have its own Principal there was no longer a need for these categories, whose job used to be to take care of the day-to-day supervision of the smaller schools.

Two competing models for the overall organization of school management in the municipality were suggested by the Central School Administration (Figure 9.3 and Figure 9.4). Model A introduced five school districts under the School Director and the CSA. In this model a new hierarchical level and a School District Principal are introduced. Administrative and personnel functions are decentralized from CSA to the district level. This model is argued to be able to adopt new activities from the municipal organization and is also favourable in the sense that school management will be concentrated to a small group of people. On the negative side this model will be more expensive.

In model B the idea is to decentralize the administrative and personnel function to a district organization but managed by an Administrator. This office is considered as a service function for three to five schools all reporting to the CSA. This model, it is argued, will create a 'flat organization' less expensive than the one described in model A. Administration and the caretaker function will be rationalized and decentralized. There is a risk, however, of conflicts between schools and administration at the local level.

Table 9.1 *Management resources in Karlskrona, 1992*

	Number of people	Full-time equivalents
Principals	8	8.0
Vice-Principals	10	9.0
Superintendents	35	4.8
Work unit and subject area co-ordinators	117	9.5

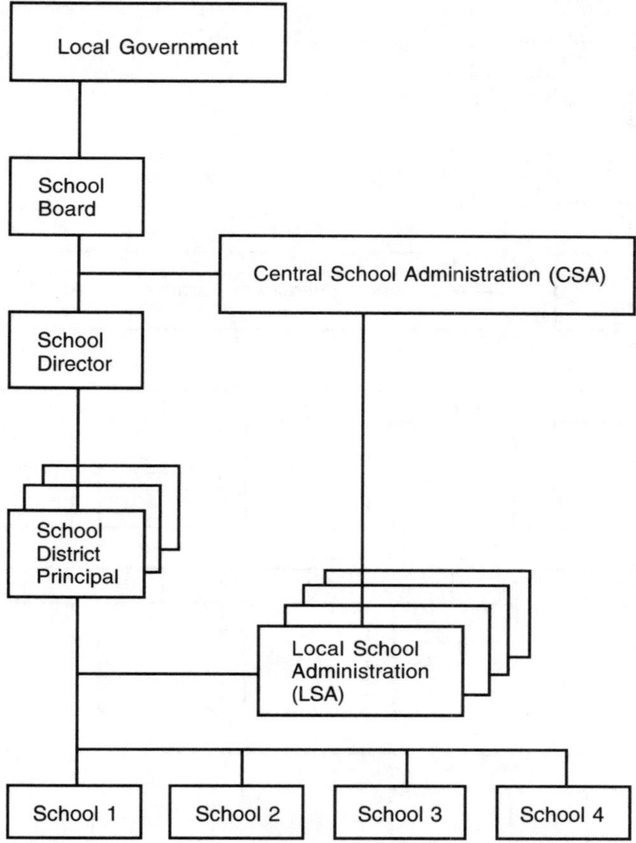

Figure 9.3 *School organization model A*

Changes at Rodeby

During the autumn of 1992 it became clear that Rodeby School should be divided into one primary school and one secondary school from the beginning of 1993. It also became clear that the management of the school(s) had to be redesigned. Instead of three people (2.5 full-time equivalent) in the management team and two part-time Superintendents, there were supposed to be two full-time Principals under the same roof forming their own organizations.

There was severe resistance to the division of Rodeby School into two schools. The teachers and their unions protested. The parents' association also tried its best to hinder the division of the school, both formally as a body referred to for consideration and more informally by trying to influence the members of the school board. Names were collected for protest letters at the supermarket and the post office in the village. Much of this resistance could possibly be explained by the successes of the school during the previous five

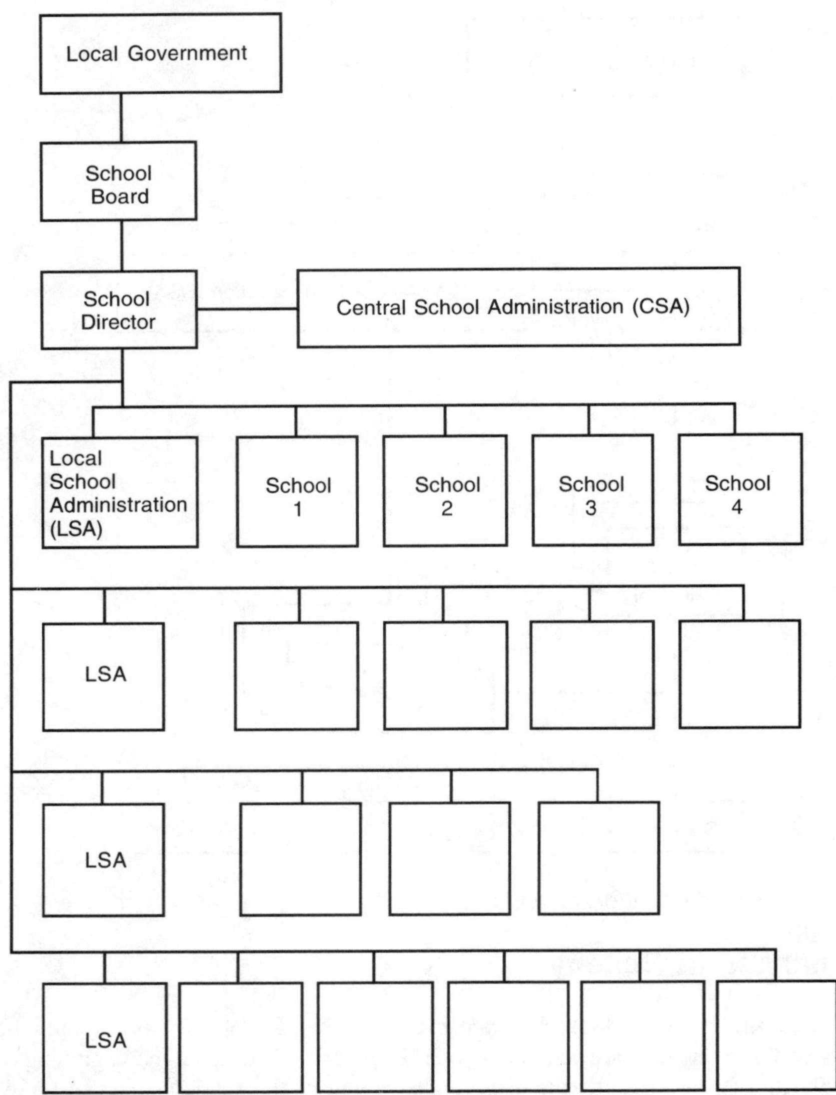

Figure 9.4 *School organization model B*

years. Considerable efforts had been put into making the school one of the best, especially for the children. Some of the resistance was also owing to a decision to reduce the successful and very respected Principal Kerstin Mattsson to only managing the secondary-level school and the fact that the Vice-Principal Anita Hjelm had to go back to her teacher's position at the school. Together they had a key role in turning the school from a problem school to a successful one during the previous five years. They had worked closely together since the renovation of the school started, some years before they attained their managerial positions.

Under the new reforms, the leadership function had to be reduced from 1.63 to 0.85 full-time equivalent at the secondary school which meant one Principal with a 3.5-hours weekly teaching load. The school could still count on budget resources corresponding to the existing 17 + 12 weekly hours of possible reduction for work unit and subject area co-ordinators. Kerstin Mattsson protested to the Central School Administration and the school board and argued for the need to keep Anita Hjelm, the Vice-Principal for the secondary level, in a managerial position. The reaction from the school board was that according to the new management organization in Karlskrona schools there should be no Vice-Principals. At the end of 1992 when it was clear that Kerstin Mattsson had taken major responsibilities for the administrative function not only for her own school, she managed to negotiate some more resources for the management function of her school. On top of the earlier resources for the reduction of teaching load to 29 weekly hours, she obtained 16 more hours of reduction.

The Christmas holidays and then . . . ?

Owing to internal politics in the school board and at CSA, no formal decision was taken about the new management organization before pupils and teachers left for the Christmas holidays on 18 December 1992. The final meeting of the school board was scheduled for the 21st of the same month. This meant that when Kerstin Mattsson talked to all the teachers at the traditional Christmas lunch, after the children had left the school on the last day of term, she could thank all the personnel for their hard work during the term and all the support she had received in her fight for keeping Rodeby together as one school, but she could not say much about the future. She was not even sure if they would still belong to the same school when they met again in the second week of January.

The only people left at the school late in the afternoon of the Friday before the Christmas holidays were the management team: Kerstin Mattsson together with Anita Hjelm and Lars Johansson, the two Vice-Principals. In an attempt to summarize the situation they all agreed that it was ‘close to 100%’ sure that the schools would be divided when the new term started in January. The only other possibility they could see was that the decision would be delayed for a month or two. They were convinced that Kerstin Mattsson and Lars Johansson would be appointed as the two Principals. They were more unsure in their evaluation of whether the board would introduce school districts according to model A, or stay closer to the existing overall organization of schools in Karlskrona as suggested in model B. They agreed to plan for the second alternative.

Excerpt from a research report (Löwstedt 1993) During the winter of 1992/93 Rodeby school was chosen by the National Agency for Education (Skolverket) to be one out of two Swedish schools in a comparative study of successful schools in Sweden, Denmark and California. To be selected as one of the Swedish schools to participate in this research study was a considerable recognition at the national level of what had recently been accomplished at the school.

Management and organization of public schools: a comparison of 'model schools' in Sweden, Denmark and California

This is a short summary of the report. Four model schools in Sweden, Denmark and California were studied. The investigation was a kind of benchmarking study which aimed at studying factors that contribute to making schools excellent. The study was conducted by a group of researchers from the three countries. The researchers asked Skolverket (the National Agency for Education) and its equivalents in Denmark and California to suggest some appropriate schools to study. These organizations presented us with information about a number of schools. After contacts with the suggested schools the following were chosen:

- Rodeby School in Karlskrona, Sweden
- Bräckeskolan in Bräcke, Sweden
- Skolan vid Rønnebaer Alle, Helsingør, Denmark
- William H. Crocker School, Hillsborough, California, USA

These schools have succeeded, better than others at developing excellent working conditions. They manage to create positive and supportive social conditions and therefore meet social goals to a greater degree than purely educational goals. The schools are interesting examples of successful work achieved through inspired and visionary management. Some of the issues in question are: the parents' role in the educational process; the development of a positive image of the school – for both the students and the general community; re-organization and development of staff; and reconciling opposing interests within an organization.

It is worth mentioning that the Swedish and Danish authorities chose schools whose students tested as average on a national scale. Owing to extra efforts on the part of the school administration these schools have enjoyed remarkable improvements during recent years. The Crocker School in California is one of the most highly rated schools, not only in California but the USA as a whole. The students at the school have very high marks and the school is located in a prosperous neighbourhood.

By choosing these schools we were able to explore an evaluation of the Scandinavian schools where the schools' social goals are prioritized and the American school where knowledge is more emphasized.

Productivity

Schools must be considered as operating under dual goals: social as well as cognitive goals for child development. It was therefore not surprising to find that productivity is not a commonly used concept in the evaluation of schools. In this paragraph we simplify this issue and relate the number of people employed in the school to the student body that they serve.

Teacher to student density in Swedish schools is comparatively high; 10 students per teacher on average. This is including the many teachers involved in native language training for immigrants, special education instructors and the relatively low student-per-teacher ratio in the numerous less populated areas of Sweden. Denmark has 11 students to one teacher. The number of students in compulsory school in Sweden dropped by 15% from 1980 to 1990. The number of teachers only decreased by 5% during the same period which is an expression of inertia in the face of changed expectations. The average number of students per class in Sweden today is 22.1 and in California 28.

Table 9.2 compares figures from the four schools. According to the table the Crocker School has a markedly higher productivity than the other schools. Rodeby School and Rønnebaer Alle School, however, both have a higher productivity than other schools in their respective countries.

Can one therefore state that the Crocker School is more productive? If the definition of productivity hinges on the number of students per teacher, then the answer is yes. However, further examination is required. It has previously been shown that there is a strong connection between a student's socio-economic background and his or her academic performance. A school which is located in a comfortable neighbourhood such as that of the Crocker School has less of a need for special education teachers than for regular teachers. Rønnebaer Alle School's students come from a problematic background. As a result, a quarter of the teaching staff are occupied with providing services for those students.

When making such comparisons it must be remembered that instructors have different teaching schedules and class times in different countries. The Crocker

Table 9.2 *Productivity measures*

	Rodeby	Bräcke	Rønnebær	Crocker
Students per teacher	13.1	7.8	12.5	15.8
National average	10	10	11	n.a.
Students per school leader	368	263	312	197
Students per non-teaching staff	51	19	30	39[1]
Students per total staff	8.8	5.6	8.6	10.6[2]
Number of students at secondary level	497	84	137	394
Total number of students in the school	925	263	625	394
Total number of school leaders	2.5	1	2	2

[1] If the total parent contribution were included the figure would be 21.
[2] If the total parent contribution were included the figure would be 8.8.

teacher's week consists of 23 sixty-minute lessons and a Swedish teacher's consists of 24 forty-minute lessons. The work year is approximately the same length, 180 days. The Crocker School enjoys a higher productivity rate partially because its teachers spend more time actually teaching in the classroom.

If we examine the non-teaching staff as a whole, including those who work in the library, cafeteria and housekeeping department, it is Rodeby School which is the most productive. Parents provide much of that type of service at the Crocker School; when their contribution is converted into the calculations the school's productivity is reduced to 21 students – approximately the same as Bräcke School's. Total productivity, taking into account the parents' contribution of time, becomes equal to Rodeby and Rønnebaer Schools – 8.8 students.

The number of people in the management team (school leaders) varies from 2.5 in Rodeby to 1 in Bräcke School. Productivity here is lowest at the Crocker School. One possible explanation for high productivity among the teachers at the Crocker School is the relatively larger amount of funding that is available for the school management and the extra support the school receives from parents. This allows the teachers to concentrate on teaching and therefore be more productive. Whether this method is superior or more effective can only be determined by examining the goals the school has set.

A simple productivity comparison is not the sole basis for local evaluation of the schools in question, although a cost account analysis which focuses on unit costs in the school is in line with the budget-linked system's evaluation of resource needs and distributes costs to the bearer. To increase productivity by focusing on unit costs is, analytically speaking, very simple. To increase productivity in schools is more a matter of increasing class size or the ratio between students and staff. Whether or not that type of action is desirable is a much more debatable question.

Success factors

Questions of productivity and effectiveness in the school system are both problematic and controversial. The immediate purpose of this report is not to determine how good the schools are or to explain differences in productivity. In the following paragraphs we compile some of the external and internal factors which contribute to explaining why these four schools are indeed 'good schools'.

Every organization is influenced by and dependent on its environment. Owing to the complexity of a school's goals and responsibilities, the daily evaluation of a school is decided by those who have the most at stake: parents, students, teachers and the administration. It is important that the school's personnel judge the institution in relation to its environment; an environment which can be influenced in many ways. What these four schools do have in common is just that – the interested parties are actively involved in influencing the environment. Some examples follow.

External factors The management of Rodeby School actively works to create a positive attitude towards the school from its local environment (parents, social clubs, politicians, local business). This is part of a strategy to use external demand, pressure but also resources to change the inner life of the school. The school's projects with the local press and business world are a further attempt at positively marketing the school. The broad range of contacts that the Crocker School possesses because of parents' activities is also another form of marketing and customer relations. Parents quickly discover both defects and improvements at the school as well as contributing constant feedback regarding the latest developments.

All four schools are capable and energetic when it comes to finding resources. This is partially owing to funding for special development projects. But it is also an awareness of the importance of securing resources in terms of qualified and motivated personnel and good physical conditions in terms of buildings, playgrounds, etc. This ability is closely related to changes and improvements; it is also an example of the close connection between activities and the interested parties.

After examining these four schools the following external factors are recognizable as necessary for a good school:

- The school works actively to raise funds from available sources. Fundraising should be undertaken not just for special projects or more teachers, but consciously to involve parents and the community in the school's organization.
- The school is an important 'member' of its surrounding society. A school cannot, as a company can, react strategically and choose its market. But a school can have an actively co-operative relationship with its community.
- Decentralization and decreased regulation increase the possibilities for schools which have the power and competence to change. A strong leadership gives the school freedom of action in a way that means regulations can be overcome sometimes without the influence of local politicians.
- Participation in a greater network of schools is a way of supporting developing ideas, projects and experimentation. That the school's management is active in a network is essential for continuous input of new thoughts and resources.
- A school's image is important. What opinion do the concerned students, parents, personnel, politicians and public have of the school? A positive image perpetuates success.

Internal factors As can be seen from the study, schools in rural areas as well as cities, schools in troubled areas as well as upper-class neighbourhoods can all function well. One common denominator for all four schools is a leadership that works hard to develop the school's relationship in the community and fosters networking with other professional systems. This differs from the management of schools which operate within a more traditional bureaucracy, where more energy is spent procuring and guarding resources from government or local authorities.

To summarize, three internal areas emerge as being most central to the success of the four schools.

Leadership The effect of the four Principals' ideas and values on the work of the schools is striking. Leadership is development oriented, but differs between the four schools. Examples can be found of leadership which is directed towards the outer characteristics of activities, towards finance and administration, towards the development of human resources and towards the development of competence. Leadership is action oriented. External change becomes a signal which leads to internal development.

Work organization The way in which teachers are organized in teams, working units, subject groups and a matrix organization is important. The matrix organization was used to equalize cognitive (subject area groupings) and social (student groupings) development in the formal organization. Organizing teachers administratively into units increases opportunities for development and efforts which are not solely focused on direct teaching, and at the same time discourages professional isolation. The organization represents a framework for co-ordination and co-operation, facilitates a decision-making process that is in touch with activities, and gives teachers duties other than direct teaching. Teachers are forced to take on responsibility for the school as a whole, and not just for their own teaching.

Evaluation Students in the Swedish schools work actively with evaluating teaching. They are also given information about, and some influence over, the content and form of education. The evaluations carried out at Rodeby School, and the systematic involvement of pupils in both planning and evaluation, can be compared with how other types of activity investigate customer attitudes. The Crocker School, on the other hand, is characterized by the fact that students are evaluated and that teachers are regularly evaluated by the management of the school. In other words, an evaluation that to a greater extent than in Sweden is used as a basis for development and modification of, in the first place, the school's work routines – that is, evaluation as a type of production control.

Recommendations: Rodeby School

In our report we describe the excellent social conditions of the school. There are good working conditions for the pupils, a very positive school climate and a social support structure which leave very little to be asked for. The recommendations of our group therefore are directed towards methodology and the cognitive development of the pupils. Major results have already been accomplished and grades have been raised from a very low level. Taking the very good social conditions into account, there is still possible potential for further development. Probably this leads to a demand for new arenas for methodology dialogue and development. How to organize such a development is, however, not within the scope of this report.

Themes/issues to consider

This case can be used to discuss questions related to notions of different types of organizations. It is only recently that schools have been thought of as specific organizations. In Sweden at least their existence has grown out of the educational system. This could be used for a discussion of what constitutes an organization. How can schools be characterized in organizational theory terms?

Other, possibly more obvious, topics in the case are organizational design, organizational change and management of professional groups. Here the special needs of organizations with ambiguous goals are of special interest. Is organizational design theory applicable to schools? If so, when and why? What types of theories of organizational change are suitable? Which are not? How can teachers be managed if they do not consider school managers but the society in general that constitutes their mission?

Assignments

The assignment in this case is to design a new organization for Rodeby Secondary School. In doing this you need to:

- analyse the strengths and weaknesses of the present organization;
- consider the special needs of this particular professional group of teachers, working with a complex goal structure and a tradition of a high degree of integrity, paying attention to the information provided in the case about numbers of teachers, students, work units, etc.
- consider the process of change and the best way of implementing or developing a new organization in relation to opinions and feelings within the school. Here the case does not contain any detailed data, so you have to use additional knowledge of the conditions required for successful organizational change.

Suggested reading

Daft, R. (1992) *Organizational Theory and Design*. Fourth edition. NY: West Publishing.

Mintzberg, H. (1973) *The Nature of Managerial Work*. New York: Harper and Row.

Morgan, G. (1986) *Images of Organization*. London: Sage.

Mortimore, P. (1993) 'School effectiveness and the management of effective learning and teaching', *School Effectiveness and School Improvement*, 4 (4).

Schon, D. (1983) *The Reflective Practitioner*. New York: Basic Books.

Thompson, J.D. (1967) *Organizations in Action*. New York: McGraw-Hill.

Notes

This case could not have be written without the help of the management team at Rodeby School, Kerstin Mattsson, Lars Johansson and Anita Hjelm. Their insights and interest are much appreciated.

The case uses a study of four case schools as a point of departure. Martin Rogberg, Birthe Ryberg, Rami Shani and Bengt Stymne made important contributions to the study presented in case reports by Rogberg and Löwstedt, Stymne and Ryberg and Shani and Rogberg. Their work is greatly acknowledged.

References

California Department of Education (1987) *Caught in the Middle: Educational Reform for Young Adolescents in California Public School*, Sacramento.

Coleman, J.S. (1966) *Equality of Educational Opportunity*. Washington, DC: Department of Health, Education and Welfare, Office of Education.

Cooper, R. and Kaplan, R. (1991) *The Design of Cost Management Systems*. Prentice-Hall, NJ: Englewood Cliffs.

Jencks, C. (1972) *Inequality: A Reassessment of the Effect of Family and Schooling in America*. New York: Basic Books.

Löwstedt, J. (1993) 'Secondary Schools', in Hornell, E. and Hjelm, P. *Achieving Service Productivity*. London: Pitman Ltd.

Ministry of Education and Science (1992) *The Swedish Way to a Learning Society*. Report to OECD. Stockholm.

Statskontoret (1991) *Grundskola i Norden*, del 1. Kronprojektet 1991:21.